Experiences of an Optimist
The Memoirs of John Redcliffe-Maud

Experiences of an Optimist

THE MEMOIRS of
JOHN REDCLIFFE-MAUD

Hamish Hamilton
London

First published in Great Britain in 1981
  by Hamish Hamilton Ltd
Garden House, 57–59 Long Acre
London WC2 9JZ

British Library Cataloguing in Publication Data

Redcliffe-Maud, John
    Experience of an optimist.
    1. Statesmen, British-Correspondence,
    reminiscences, etc.
    I. Title
    941.085′092′4   DA591.R/

    ISBN 0-241-10569-2

Text set in 11/12pt Linotron 202 Bembo, printed and bound in Great Britain at The Pitman
Press, Bath

Contents

FOR JEAN

List of Illustrations

Acknowledgements

Without my wife I could not have written this book nor would my experiences in the last fifty years have been what they were. Her music, her flair with a garden and her genius with the inside of a house, her style as hostess or matriarch, have set their creative stamp on the life we have shared in Oxford, London and South Africa. I want first to acknowledge my unique debt to her. But I must also thank friends and far-flung family (in Madrid, Little Rock Arkansas and nearer home) for patient help in the book's long and sometimes difficult gestation.

I am grateful to the photographers named in the list of illustrations for leave to use their work, to the publishers of the few lines of prose and verse that I have quoted here and there, and to Delia Twamley for her skill and speed in deciphering my manuscript.

Finally I must thank Jamie Hamilton for much personal kindness and endorse *The Times* description of him on his eightieth birthday as 'prince among publishers'.

CHAPTER 1

Introduction

I have never been a party politician but my working life for more than fifty years has been in politics of one kind or another. I taught and thought about the subject as an Oxford don from 1929 to 1939 and got my first taste of politics in practice as an Independent city councillor for six years and, in 1938, in support of an Independent candidate who stood, unsuccessfully, against the Chamberlain appeasement policy in the first Parliamentary by-election after Munich.

The war changed my profession. I found myself a temporary hack in a huge temporary part of Whitehall and worked in London for a great Minister of Food, Lord Woolton, at all levels of the Home Civil Service, from Acting Principal to Acting Permanent Secretary. Before the war ended Woolton was made Minister of Reconstruction in Churchill's War Cabinet and took me with him; I became deputy-head and then head of a minute new part of wartime Whitehall (whence came the famous White Paper on Employment Policy which all parties in the Coalition Government endorsed); and I stayed with him when Coalition gave place to Churchill's 'Caretaker' Government and he became Lord President of the Council.

At one moment in the summer of 1945 I was working for Lord Woolton and at the next for Mr Herbert Morrison: a General Election, for the first time in British history, had put a Labour Government in office with a House of Commons majority in its support. Morrison could not have differed more from Woolton, either in politics or personality, but he gave me his confidence as Woolton had done. He was now Leader of the Commons (as well as the Lord President), with a huge legislative programme to prepare; and during the few months that I was head of his office I began to learn a quite new kind of work – for a party politician who had chief responsibility for relations between Cabinet and Commons.

This experience whetted my appetite for a new peacetime profession. When I was asked to become the permanent head of the new Ministry of Education, it was unthinkable to say anything but yes. Here was the chance to pick up and knit together two of the main strands in my past working life. And there was a further coincidence. The part of politics that I had made my main concern for ten years as an Oxford don was local government, and local government was the chief instrument of public education under the great Act of 1944.

My new Minister, Ellen Wilkinson, was the one woman in the Attlee Cabinet. The Act provided for the compulsory school-leaving-age to be raised to fifteen by 1947. Could post-war Britain afford the resources to allow that to be done? If not, was the same fate in store for the Butler Act as for H. A. L. Fisher's Education Act after the First World War? Miss Wilkinson was a sick woman but she lived just long enough to persuade the Cabinet that the Act must not be amended or the crucial date postponed.

I enormously enjoyed seven years in Education (the last of them under a Tory, Florence Horsbrugh). And in 1952, when I became permanent head of the Ministry of Fuel and Power, though I continued to enjoy myself it was for quite different reasons. Now for the first time since the war I was near the margin of great political events. My Ministry shared with the Treasury and Foreign Office our government's relations with the oil industry. The oilfields of the Anglo-Iranian Oil Company (in which the British Government had a fifty-one per cent interest) had just been nationalized by the Iranian Government under Moussadeq. They were producing no oil; but by 1954 a new consortium of major international oil companies had been formed and had reached agreement with a new government in Iran. Then in 1956 the Suez Canal was nationalized by the Egyptian Government under Nasser. For the first time since the war the United States and Britain were in open conflict; the country and the Commonwealth were both divided – and Britain's attempt to go her own way did not succeed.

But my Minister was also responsible for coal, electricity and gas, which had been nationalized by the previous Government and now formed a substantial part of the public sector of industry. The Tories in Opposition had fought against these controversial changes but the new Churchill Government of 1951 was of course out to make them work. When Mr Macmillan became Prime Minister in 1957, he was determined to reduce our dependence on the Suez oil route and to increase our efforts to develop nuclear power. The consequence for me was to become permanent head of a new Ministry of Power, with two Cabinet Ministers to serve – Lord Mills, a close friend of the Prime Minister, in the

Lords (as my Minister) and Reginald Maudling in the Commons. It was a great moment for the Ministry and its permanent head.

This proved to be my last job in Whitehall. By 1958 I had had first-hand experience, over nineteen years, of several strongly contrasted parts of central government, each of them concerned with intensely interesting bits of British history; I had been the notionally permanent head of half a dozen departments, and I had served a variety of political masters (of both sexes) in Coalition, Caretaker, Labour and Tory Governments. Now I was asked to go abroad, as British High Commissioner to South Africa.

Some years before, I had been asked to go to New Delhi as British High Commissioner and had agreed to go, but with extreme reluctance because at the time my wife could not have come with me, and I was let off. Now she could come with me and I agreed to go. I think myself it was an experimental guinea-pig appointment: could someone be transferred from the Home Civil Service to an overseas post without disaster? However, when the news broke, *The Times* took a more generous view and headed its leading article 'An Imaginative Appointment'.*

We had spent a six-month honeymoon (at the expense of Cecil Rhodes) between Cape Town and Cairo in 1932; I had helped to celebrate the golden jubilee of Johannesburg a few years later, and my sister Dorothy was a pioneer of missionary work with urban Africans in what is now Soweto.† So before we set off for Cape Town on New Year's Day 1959 we had some idea of what we were in for.

Some idea, but not much. I knew there were two different jobs to do concurrently. One was diplomatic: to represent Her Majesty's Government in all relations with another Commonwealth government and be responsible to the Commonwealth Secretary; the other was to govern three High Commission Territories – Basutoland, Swaziland and the Bechuanaland Protectorate. I knew these three Territories were united to South Africa in a customs and monetary union and had for fifty years been destined for incorporation in the South African state; I had no inkling that by the time I left South Africa each of them would be well on the way to sovereign independence, indeed within a

---

* *The Times*, 20 May 1958. The style of that article reminds me of the man who was then the paper's expert on Colonial and Commonwealth affairs, Oliver Woods. His wisdom was the greatest help to me until 1972, when he died tragically young. What I then said about him at a memorial service in London is reprinted, in Appendix III (1), from a report in *The Times*.
† See *Peace-making in South Africa (The Life and Work of Dorothy Maud)* by Audrey Ashley, New Horizon, 1980.

few years of achieving it. I knew Dr Verwoerd had become the South African Prime Minister in 1958 and was committed to *apartheid* policy. I did not foresee that my Prime Minister would himself soon be telling the South African Parliament that Britain could not support *apartheid* 'without being false to our own deep convictions about the political destinies of free men'.* Nor did I foresee that South Africa would withdraw from the Commonwealth and become a republic, or that in consequence I would end up as an ambassador to a foreign country.

The war had made me an amateur member of the Home Civil Service, and that I had remained for twenty years. By 1963 South Africa had made me an amateur member of three other services – Colonial, Commonwealth and Foreign. Extraordinary good fortune now gave us the chance of a return to Oxford, and back we came – to the same college where I had been don and dean for ten pre-war years and where now (if I survived till I was seventy) I could be Master for thirteen. Our luck held, so that by 1976, when I retired, my working life had been almost equally divided between two professions, one academic and one in government.

Nor was that all. Besides comparing post-war with pre-war Oxford, I now had the chance of return to school in a new capacity: as a Fellow of Eton I could compare it, forty years after, with what I had known as a boy. And I was lured back by old friends in English local government and invited to take part in its reform. I took a new plunge back into familiar waters. How could a council improve its inner working and induce more councillors of high calibre to give their time to it? Before that enquiry finished I was chairing another, this time into the whole system of English local government (a Royal Commission, with no holds barred). And thirdly, in October 1973, Mr Edward Heath persuaded me to chair a Prime Minister's Committee which considered 'the adequacy of present rules governing the conduct of local authority members and officers', and made recommendations – which I think have had some practical effects.

Meanwhile, in 1967, I had accepted a life-peerage in the House of Lords. The Leader, Frank Longford, and Peter Carrington, then Leader of the Opposition, were my two sponsors when I was introduced and, as an Independent member, I have enjoyed experiences of a new kind for thirteen years – listening, speaking, voting and serving on Select Committees, with no commitment to either side of the House.

What follows is an account of some experiences in successive chapters of my life, and in an Epilogue I have tried to explain why the

---

* Harold Macmillan, *Pointing the Way,* Macmillan, 1972, p. 478.

4

book is called 'Experiences of an Optimist'. It is a volume of memoirs rather than autobiography, for I am only the peg on which are hung the few bits of contemporary history that I know at first hand and can remember. Except for a few quotations the whole book is written from memory, or it would never have been finished. I have tried to check facts but some mistakes may well remain and I regret them.

CHAPTER 2

Boyhood, 1906–1924

I was an afterthought. My four sisters and my only brother had been born in Leeds, while my father was Vicar of Chapel Allerton. When he became Vicar of St Mary Redcliffe, Bristol ('the fairest, the goodliest and most famous parish church in England', according to Queen Elizabeth the First) I suspect that he and my mother, neither of whom had money of their own, thought that their family was now complete. If so, they were mistaken. On 3 February 1906, my sister Dorothy's twelfth birthday, my luck began. I was born in the vicarage (where, it was thought, no male child had been born before) and given my Father's Christian names, John Primatt, with Redcliffe added for good measure. Only a hyphen between that and Maud was needed sixty years later, when I became a peer and was forbidden to use 'John' in formal correspondence but was reluctant to sign letters with a girl's name.

If my first stroke of luck was to be born, my second was to survive tuberculosis. This gradually put one of my lungs out of action, starting when I was three years old. I lived in a tent in all weathers on a neighbouring Somerset hill, in fresh air and the care of a small heroic Welsh lady. She had been part of my parents' home since they were first married and Nanna to each of the six children in turn. She now saved my life. By the age of seven I was told by the family doctor he could not tell which of my lungs had been defective, and this seems to have remained true ever since. No doubt in many ways it was bad for me to be the youngest member of the family by six years and to grow up an invalid with no friends of my own age, but there were great compensations.

Nanna, my one constant and often sole companion, was a genius: her passionately loving heart went with a strength of character which made her a sensitive, inflexible disciplinarian who never lost her self-control. I remember once asking her when I was five or six and our wills had clashed: 'Have you lost anything, Nanna?' and when she said 'No, John, I don't think so' replying

'Oh I thought perhaps you'd lost your temper'. I now think she never did.

Another consequence of sickly childhood was that I could not go to school till I was nine and meanwhile had my mother to teach me. I have had a number of wonderful teachers from childhood onwards but my mother was the best of the lot. She already had twenty years' experience as a teacher; for when she was nineteen her own mother had died, leaving her to look after nine brothers and sisters younger than herself; and she had later started my brother and four sisters on their education. But, besides experience, she must always have had special gifts as a teacher. I enjoyed all my lessons with her and was never bored. Reading, writing and arithmetic were all delightful, and when I was eight and began Latin (which she had never learnt before) that was no less exciting. A year or two later Father began teaching me Greek – and I enjoyed that still more. My pre-school education was very happy, for, besides lessons, it included much singing, reading aloud and learning by heart.

Nineteen-eleven, when my own health was still precarious, was the year of our first family disaster. In 1909 my brother Christopher had won a King's Scholarship at Eton (from Summerfields, Oxford) and for a year and a half had been triumphantly happy there. He was a good-looking boy, with an exceptional treble voice and an intelligence of great promise. One day he complained of a pain in the stomach but examinations were beginning and he was told by the matron to carry on. Before his appendix could be removed, it burst and he was dead.

From now on I was the only son, and as I grew up I became gradually aware that I should try to be a substitute for Christopher. That was of course impossible, and neither Father nor Mother wanted me to be anyone but myself; but for me that was by no means the whole story: I wanted to match Christopher's success. For example, thirteen was the normal age to go to Eton, but when I was twelve (as Christopher had been when he won his scholarship) I was entered for a preliminary shot. When I failed, my disappointment was appalling: I had failed to do what Christopher had done. In fact I was not ready for Eton and this failure was another stroke of luck. I went back to Summerfields for the best year I could remember.

L. A. G. Strong, the poet and novelist, was then teaching at Summerfields, and became my friend. As he lived near us in London it was with him that I heard my first opera, lunched for the first time in Soho, experienced the Old Vic, started to envy experts in the mimetic art and first heard of the Wild Swans at

7

Coole. During that year, too, I stopped thinking that games were not for me. By the low standards of schoolboy golf, I was a tolerable golfer and that year so-called champion of the school. Though utterly remote from the Harold Caccia★ class, I did scrape into the same first elevens. As I could sing in tune, I played the lead (it was a triumph) in a 'musical' that two masters had composed.

At the end of this happy year I was elected to an Eton scholarship and my next five years of schooling cost Father about £30 a year. All things considered, that earlier failure was the best thing that could have happened to me – and later experience suggests that this is often true. Nothing succeeds, in fact, like failure to achieve a job you are not ready for. Nothing fails like over-promotion (say, to the Cabinet) if you are not up to the job.

Anyone who goes to Eton as a Colleger is fortunate; but those (like me) who went in 1919 had special luck. The war was just over. Most of the boys who had left Eton during the last four years had gone straight into the army and most of them had been killed. Those who had not left but were still in College had lived on the assumption that their future would be much the same. Now peace had come and they could abandon that assumption. No wonder revolutionary ideas were in the air. Privilege of any kind was frowned upon. You could make friends with anyone, regardless of his age. Fagging continued, but your fag-master was distinguished by his desire to help you. Corporal punishment was so rarely used that I was never beaten (nor later did I ever beat). Order was kept and I for one was never bullied. But what was important was the friendliness engendered: authority, you felt, was on your side.

Jan Crace, the Master in College, had much to do with this. Ten years before he had been my brother Christopher's Eton tutor and had stayed with us each summer since his death. He had gradually become my own ideal – an artist and a scholar, kind, imaginative, humorous. He married my sister Eileen as soon as I left Eton but for ten years he had been part of the family. Having declared my interest, I can say one thing with total objectivity: College was a different place when he became a housemaster and H. K. Marsden succeeded him as Master in College.

King's Scholars can be the luckiest of all Etonians. They live in a close society of seventy boys of more than average intelligence

★ Then school captain of both football and cricket. Later our Ambassador in Washington, then Head of the Diplomatic Service, and now an Independent life-peer.

and get most of their education from one another. But they are part of the one school of twelve hundred Etonians. Collegers and Oppidans (as boys are called who live in Houses) work in the same forms, play games together, meet in whatever societies they choose to join for music, acting or debates. Some Oppidans despised us Collegers and some of us, especially if we preferred cricket to rowing, had more Oppidan friends than most Collegers had. But after the first year or two most of us thought we had the best of both worlds, in College and outside it. For example, six of the twenty members of the Eton Society (better Known as 'Pop') in my last year were Collegers.

I would not quarrel with a description of Pop as 'the most powerful self-perpetuating oligarchy of schoolboys in the world'.* But Pop served some useful purposes ingeniously. What clothes, for instance, should Etonians wear? The official answer (since the school first went into mourning on George III's death) was formal morning dress – tail-coat, dark waistcoat and trousers, white collar and tie. By letting you, when in Pop, dress up each morning (if you chose) in braided tail-coat, coloured waistcoat, sponge-bag trousers, the authorities made certain that those *not* in Pop were uniformly dressed. Pop had its own constitution; but wise provisions limited its size and ensured some sort of link with other parts of the establishment; so the Captain of School and the Captain of Oppidans were *ex officio* members of Pop. Otherwise its freedom to elect and disappoint was absolute, and the broad result was easy to predict. Gamesmanship of one kind or another was the chief thing that members had in common, and those who were good at games like cricket were better known than wet-bobs and therefore likelier to find themselves in Pop. In no election that I remember was there a hint of social snobbery, straight or inverted: titles and wealth (like scholarship) were beside the point. The only thing that made non-election certain was evidence that someone had taken steps to get himself in.

Pop had no rival, for there were no School prefects. If Pop was the Eton equivalent of an Order of Knighthood, there was one great difference: the fount of honour was neither Provost nor Headmaster but the existing membership of Pop. Like any Order, Pop had its own premises and officers; and like most Orders Pop had little to do. We had one debate (or perhaps two) during my year of membership. Occasionally we linked arms and shepherded a crowd, but we were not responsible for discipline and we had no collective power. However bad or good for individuals, Pop was in

* The *Guardian*, October 1979, in a review of Jo Grimond's *Memoirs*.

9

no sense a secret society: we were delighted to reveal that we were members and we had no hidden purpose to pursue.

Eton is less a school than a collegiate university. You have your own room to work and sleep in; and your House (or College) is your home base. But neither House nor College is 'an island entire of itself': from first to last it is 'a part of the main'. For certain periods of the day you must be in a classroom and prepared to answer questions; but the rest of your time is all your own. In your early days you must take some kind of exercise but, unless needed for a team game, you can choose what form the exercise shall take. From your first day, then, you take your own decisions, to prepare yourself for ends that are prescribed. As you go up the school you have increasing freedom, but at each stage you must complete your work on time.

Eton is also like a university in this respect: from your first day you are in personal touch with several masters – and with any luck you get on well with at least one. There is your housemaster. There is a 'division' master with whom you do most of your work each term. (I have never forgotten being taught, for my first thirteen weeks at Eton, Latin, Greek, French and English, history and divinity by one man, Cyril Butterwick, who made them all seem equally worthwhile.) You are 'up to' another master for mathematics, and you have a tutor with whom a complementary but closer relationship can be established.

In 1861 a book was published (now long out of print) entitled *Eton Reform*. The author, William Johnson Cory, was a distant relative of mine and a great Eton schoolmaster. In seeking to describe the purpose of education he wrote, among other words, the following: 'You go to school at 12 or 13, and for the next four or five years you are not engaged so much in acquiring knowledge as in making mental efforts under criticism. A certain amount of knowledge you can, with average faculties, acquire so as to retain. Nor need you regret the hours that you spent on much that is forgotten, for the shadow of lost knowledge at least saves you from many illusions. But you go to a great school not so much for knowledge as for arts and habits. For the habit of attention, for the art of expression; for the art of entering quickly into another person's thoughts; for the habit of submitting to censure and refutation; for the art of expressing assent or dissent in graduated terms; for the habit of regarding minute points of accuracy . . . for taste, for discrimination, for mental courage and mental soberness. Above all, you go to a great school for self-knowledge.'

My experience of Eton as a schoolboy convinces me that Eton was in those days a great school by Cory's standard, but I am also convinced that she is now a much better school than fifty years ago. (And let me at once declare my personal 'interests'. Our son was in the school some years ago and at the time of writing we have a grandson there; I was a Fellow of Eton for twelve years; Robert Birley, headmaster before I was a Fellow, and Michael McCrum, the only headmaster that I helped to appoint, are two men I very greatly admire.)

The acquisition of 'mental' courage and 'mental' soberness are no longer thought enough. Intellectual sweat and self-discipline are of course parts of any education: you must learn to think and memorize and number, and most of all when you are in your teens. But what you must also learn is to *make* things, and to do that you need more than your mind; you need all your faculties – of sight, ears, hand and heart. These you must learn to correlate unconsciously if you are to grow up as a whole person and make things – music, prose, poetry, pictures, artefacts of any kind. Eton today cares far more for these things than she did in my time as a boy.

In those days we acted an occasional play in College, because people like George Rylands happened to be there to act and a Master in College (who had a flair for 'direction') to direct. Members of sixth-form performed at 'Speeches' individual and collective acts of their own choice. (The Provost, M. R. James, was at work on his translation of Hans Andersen's Fairy Stories when I was searching for a Fourth of June speech in 1924. He gave me an advance copy of 'The Emperor's New Clothes' to learn by heart – and no-one has ever done me a better turn.) The Shakespeare Society read plays weekly in private and once a year in public (at eighteen I was as old a man as ever over-played King Lear). There was a school concert once a term (when the Musical Society sang Coleridge Taylor's 'Hiawatha', and as a treble I once sang 'Oh mistress mine'). Each year houses competed for a quartet cup (which singers in College invariably won so long as we had Victor Hely-Hutchinson to train us). But that was about all.

Nowadays there is a school theatre and most Houses act their own plays. Music is constantly performed, on instruments of all kinds and in all forms of composition. Music scholarships have been established, from funds previously spent on a choir school. Everyone now has the chance of learning to draw, paint, sculpt or turn a pot. The old School of Mechanics has been replaced by something altogether more sophisticated where boys can take the first step towards a life in productive industry. So the fine arts and their application have moved from the periphery towards the centre.

11

And this widening of Eton's educational purpose has not been at the expense of intellectual standards. Nowadays before you can start life at Eton you must achieve a much higher 'mental' standard than that of fifty years ago, and throughout your time there you have to work a great deal harder than in the old days. If this were not true, Eton could not have achieved the results it now achieves each year in General Certificate examinations, both at Ordinary and Advanced levels, or in the number of Etonians that go on to universities as commoners or scholars.

> 'We should be in less danger
> From the wiles of the stranger
> If our own kin and kith
> Were more fun to be with.'
> Ogden Nash

Both my grandfathers and one maternal aunt, each had ten children; so the clan I was born into was numerous and closely knit. But it was also talented in many different ways and I found most of my relations extraordinarily good company. So, however much I enjoyed life at Eton, I think I was still happier in the holidays.

I was never at all frightened of my father, and he never bored me; but what I specially enjoyed was being taught by him. Besides starting me on Greek, he tried to teach me fly-fishing and, with rather more success, he taught me golf (it was the only game I played for Eton – and only once, against the Masters at Stoke Poges, when for the first and last time in my life I did a hole in one). I was forty-six years younger than Father but by the time he died (when I was twenty-six) the difference of age was quite irrelevant. I always admired him: his intellectual power, his huge capacity for work and, most of all, the sense he gave me that life on earth could have eternal quality. But Father's goodness (it seemed to me) was always growing and my admiration for him steadily grew. When he was courting Mother, his sisters (I was told by one of them) were so fond of her that they implored her not to marry him because they thought he was a bully. That illustrates, I think, how much the sweetness of his character must have increased over the years under my mother's influence.

In 1911 he became Bishop of Kensington, and as I watched him happily at work there for more than twenty years (until he died in harness), I delighted more and more in his and Mother's total disregard of worldly wisdom. He gave unfashionable support to women's suffrage before the First World War, and that, I know, did not endear him to the Establishment. He spoke out for Maude

Royden and her courageous pioneering as a preacher. Though neither a party politician nor a pacifist, he loved people like Dick Sheppard, vicar of St Martin-in-the-Fields, and was always ready to defend them. He preached the Gospel with intelligence and fire and was beloved by his parish priests, whether high church or low, and by all kinds of laymen. But he was never asked to accept a diocese of his own – and if he had, he would not have thought himself 'promoted'.

Charles Wellington Furse, my mother's father, had married into Ireland, a Miss Monsell of County Dublin, whose father wrote the hymn 'Fight the good fight.' I have always been grateful for my drop of Irish blood. 'How like a Furse!' was an exclamation I often heard, especially from Mauds. Certainly most Furses have some things in common: ebullience (verging on effusiveness), the mimetic instinct, a sense of the dramatic, delight in letter-writing and conversation (face to face if possible but otherwise by telephone). All the same, my mother's family was a heterogeneous bunch. My uncle Mike was bound to become a bishop – first of Pretoria and later of St Albans. Tall, handsome and athletic, he stood out in any company: an Eton games-player, an Oxford actor and fellow of his college, then Prelate of St Michael and St George. He and I became great friends who disagreed on almost every subject (he was against all contraceptives and intolerant of divorce), but he was a marvellous host and I greatly enjoyed his company.

Joshua Reynolds was an ancestor (without direct descendants) and many of my family were artists in their time. Charles Furse, the portrait-painter, died of tuberculosis too young for me to know him, but his pictures ('Timber Haulers', 'Return from the Ride' and 'Diana of the Uplands') were the first I ever loved. His formidable widow (Founding Mother of the WRNS), Dame Katharine Furse, did not alarm me, and both sons of hers were artists, one of them (Paul Furse) an admiral and distinguished botanist as well.

My mother's eldest brother, Henry Furse (my Uncle Harry), was crippled as a child and lost his wife when Ralph, their only son, was born. But he persisted as a sculptor, inheriting the small Devonshire country house of Halsdon in the woods above the valley of the Torridge. Here I stayed often, with indescribable excitement – finding my first bird's nest, catching my first fish, making my first landfall from a pony. Uncle Harry was the one tutor of my boyhood years who scared me, but I shall always be grateful to him for two feelings that I caught from him: devotion to the horse and envious admiration of the creative artist.

Halsdon was a home from home for me and by the time Ralph Furse became its owner, though he was much older than me, we were close friends. Ralph was a gunner in the First World War and just survived it, with the Distinguished Service Order but nearly deaf. Entering the Colonial Office as a temporary private secretary, he was the father of the inter-war Colonial Service, without which Britain could not have converted her colonies into sovereign states. He worked out and perfected a new method of recruitment which eschewed patronage but made no use of written examinations. It brought into the last phase of colonial government a generation of young graduates who worked themselves out of a job by training local administrators to take their place.★

Uncle Bill (another Furse) was a distinguished soldier and I had a special sense of kinship with him. In 1914 (when I was eight) this was for snobbish reasons: he wore red tabs and was a general. But, apart from that, he was the one Furse who married into Scotland and his entrancing wife was quite unlike a Furse. When I later dared to follow his example, the two Jeans (his wife and mine) found much in common. For example, my Aunt Jean was often silent (when sisters-in-law sought news about the war); but her Kemble blood made her a spell-binding story-teller. The general (known in the mess as Windy Bill) was a great talker and shared his children's passion for the arts. His younger daughter Judith was a talented actress, and his son Roger a distinguished stage-designer.

There are some things about my boyhood that I now deeply deplore. The first, and much the most serious, is the fact that all my friends went like me to independent schools, so that I grew up for eighteen years knowing none of the great majority of my contemporaries – who went to 'maintained' schools (and in most cases left at fourteen). Secondly, though I could translate Shelley's 'Music when soft voices die vibrates in the memory' into fine Greek Sapphics, I left school with no language but English that I could use in easy conversation, nor had I learnt the habit (in H. A. L. Fisher's words) of 'wide, voracious, desultory reading' even in English. Thirdly, though I had begun to enjoy singing, acting and reading poetry, I could play no instrument and had never drawn or painted, written a poem or made anything with my own hands since making a wooden piperack for my father at the age of nine.

On the other hand, I had played games just well enough to enjoy them greatly for the rest of my life; I had fallen happily in love; I had

★ Ralph later described what he had tried to do for the Colonial Service in a book of Memoirs with the apt but mysterious title *Aucuparius* – a Latin word for bird-catcher, OUP, 1962.

learnt how to work with intense enjoyment; I had lived happily at home in the company of people who tried to practise their Christianity seven days in the week; I had begun to learn from them the art of worship, and to have a faith of my own.

CHAPTER 3

Pre-war Oxford, 1924–1939

I always knew that Oxford was not for me unless some college gave me a scholarship, but this knowledge at no stage blighted my happiness at school. When I was sixteen Balliol offered a newly-endowed scholarship 'with preference for an Etonian' and, as it happened that my promise as a classical scholar was then brighter than at any later time, I was entered for the scholarship – and rightly passed over, Balliol awarding it to Roger Mynors, an Old Etonian who had already won an exhibition and was in residence. Next year I tried for Trinity and failed again. In those days groups of colleges examined applicants for a scholarship at three successive dates, not simultaneously as they do now, and I had one more chance. This time I put New College as my first choice. The standard was apparently so low that they gave only one open scholarship in classics. But my luck had turned: it was to me they gave it. Even so, my father could not have found my fees and maintenance at Oxford unless I also won a leaving scholarship from Eton. But all was well and in October 1924 I went up to New College.

During the summer holidays between Eton and Oxford I was a guest of F. F. Urquhart ('Sligger' to all his undergraduate friends), the ascetic bachelor dean of Balliol, at his Chalet des Mélèzes in Haute Savoie, high on the Prarion slope of Mont Blanc above St Gervais-les-Bains. This was a terrifying experience. I had met Sligger at lunch with Cyril Connolly during my first abortive shot at a scholarship. Now at the Chalet I found myself in one of the reading parties which Sligger organized each year for Balliol undergraduates and other friends of his. It was the most beautiful place that I had ever stayed in. The sun shone almost every day. For a schoolboy like me (though not for epicures) the plain food was sumptuous and the hard beds incapable of keeping one awake. There was no sense of compulsion, inside the Chalet or in the mountain air outside, but a great deal of reading was done each day and as much walking as you liked. Then what was terrifying in my first Chalet experience? Certainly not Sligger, as gentle, kind and affectionate a man as you could meet. (When I was later assured by one of his detractors that he was kind to me because my father was an Anglican bishop and Sligger saw me as a future convert to his Roman Catholicism, I was disgusted by what still seems to me a ludicrous misjudgment.) No; it was the other formidable members of the company that made me quail. Roger Mynors and Richard Pares, both of them three years my senior, did what they could to treat me as an equal but I knew well that I was nothing of the kind. They were two of the best men I have known. Both of them were outstanding scholars of their generation, Roger in classics (a Balliol don in 1926 and a professor, first in Cambridge then in Oxford) and Richard in history (fellow of All Souls and then Edinburgh professor). Both were brilliant wartime civil servants. Each was an extraordinary character, enigmatic and lovable, but the word 'good' describes them both. Richard died tragically young, from a ghastly disease which deprived him of one faculty after another but never defeated him.

At the end of the reading party, Sligger took us to Annecy, Chartres and Paris on our way home. So by the time I started undergraduate life at New College the schoolboy had already been thrown into Oxford at the deep end. The schoolboy, I should add, had been thrown into another deep end two years before. My heterosexual life had dawned several years earlier, but when I was seventeen I fell deeply in love with someone of twenty-four and she with me. We were still friends when she died in her eightieth year but for the first two years of our friendship she was the most important person in my life.

At Oxford my undergraduate life was somewhat disjointed. I never settled in one island but lived in a kind of social archipelago. There was the OUDS (the Oxford University Dramatic Society), the SCM (the Student Christian Movement), Sligger, Maurice Bowra (then dean of Wadham), Tom Boase (then dean of Hertford College); and inside New College there was the old tithe barn (now part of the Warden's Lodgings), where two undergraduates then lived in splendid isolation, with oil lamps and kettle-boiled hot water; there were the soccer players, the cricketers, the Wykehamists and the musicians (led by Sir Hugh Allen, conductor of the Bach Choir in which I sang).

Undergraduates migrated constantly between these islands and some were equally welcome wherever they turned up. John Sparrow, for example, was a distinguished soccer player (in my last year we only just failed to win the cup after a replay) as well as a close friend of Bowra's. John Betjeman played Starveling ('this lanthorn doth the horned moon present') in an OUDS production of *The Dream*, wrote enviable ironic verse

(There's something about a Varsity man that distinguishes him from a cad;
You can tell from his tie and his blazer he's a Varsity undergrad . . .)

and was welcome in Bowra's or any other company. But unlike Sparrow and Betjeman, who were unmistakably the same in any context, I took more of my colour from the company – and remained several slightly disjointed Mauds.

I certainly enjoyed myself in several ways – in fact, whenever their incompatibilities were not too glaring. I worked hard at my books. Though nothing could have made me a real classical scholar, I regret none of the hours I spent in conscientious efforts to become one. (The shadow of lost knowledge has at least saved me from many illusions.) My New College tutor Henderson was not much help to me but Bowra with characteristic generosity sacrificed hours of his time in private tutorials on Propertius and Catullus. Greats (philosophy and ancient history) were much more to my taste than Classical Moderations, and here New College dons could not have helped me more. But again it was Bowra whose advice (to read Dostoievsky) gave me the first clue when I set out on work for Greats.

Sligger deplored my joining the OUDS. I still thank heaven I did. Here was a new world for me where I made friends of many kinds unknown to me before. I blush to remember the poor Bottom that I played one summer in Magdalen deer-park, but to work under J. B. Fagan's direction in company with Jean Forbes-Robertson (Titania), Denys Buckley (Oberon) and Alan Ker (Puck) was a new and wonderful experience. I do not regret any of the hours spent understudying Harman Grisewood's Lear, still less my own performance in OUDS Smoking Concerts. These Smokers were for men only, in the OUDS private dining-room, with no holds barred. Richard Addinsell and Temple Abbady composed and played the music. Wilson Wiley sang the lyrics – written (by Roland Leigh), like the rest of the script, in the satyric modes of Aristophanes or Shakespeare.

Emlyn Williams had reached Christ Church from Wales with a scholarship in English at the same time as I reached New College. We joined the OUDS together, and quickly became friends. He was a born actor and his undergraduate hopes were as clearcut as his achievements proved to be: 'I want to have three of my plays running in the West End simultaneously and to be starring in one of them.' Meanwhile he was convinced that he could make himself up as a girl and perform a song-and-dance number in the next OUDS Smoker – and he asked me to partner him. We were also successful hosts at a candlelit dinner in New College, when our one guest was the actress Lilian Oldland (her husband Reggie Denham was producing *Peer Gynt* for the OUDS, with Robert Speaight as Peer and Emlyn as the Button-moulder). Not all my Christian colleagues in the SCM can have thought acting in Smokers something their President should do, but only one told me that he had lost his faith as a direct result of seeing my performance. I still feel shame when I remember what he said, but I still think it would have been going too far to resign either from the OUDS or the SCM in consequence.

Sir Hugh Allen was at this time Heather Professor of Music in Oxford (and a professorial fellow of New College) as well as Director of the Royal College of Music, and, as 1926 would mark the tercentary of Heather's creation of the Chair, he had long planned a musical festival in Oxford for that year. Part of the festival was to be a week's performance in the Playhouse of Purcell's *Gentleman Dancing Master,* for which the Royal College and Oxford would combine forces. The name-part was to be danced by Richard Austin (then a student at the College, where he later became conductor of the orchestra) under Penelope Spencer's professional direction, and I was to recruit New College under-graduates for the chorus (it was to be my first appearance as a ballet-dancer). We rehearsed in London and were all set for the opening night when the General Strike was called. Sir Hugh and the Oxford authorities saw no reason to cancel the festival; so it went forward, without let or hindrance.

Like most of my friends, I was quite ignorant of contemporary politics and unaware of the real issues at stake. Once the festival was over, I joined the strike-breakers without a qualm and, after a spell as black-leg porter at Paddington, I was posted to Acton as a shunter, making my first successful coupling of two coal-trucks just as the strike collapsed.

At no time in my four years of undergraduate life was my mind seriously worried about the purpose of being at Oxford or about what I should do to earn a living when the four years were up. At the time of the General Strike, when I was twenty, I decided whom I wished to marry – Jean Hamilton, a Somerville College undergraduate reading music who had been the pianist in the fourth Brandenburg Concerto at a Festival concert in the Sheldo-nian, and who fifty years later is still my wife; and that decision effectively narrowed the choice of jobs to those which could fairly soon offer a livelihood that would support a professional pianist and myself. Neither industry nor commerce ever occurred to me. The Diplomatic Service at that time required success in a highly competitive examination in which modern languages were so essential that you must spend at least a year abroad before competing. The Home Civil Service? Perhaps, but what chance of success in the exam? Schoolmastering was a more likely starter, but later on, when I asked advice from my old headmaster, Cyril Alington, he strongly advised (as few public school headmasters of that period would have been wise enough to do) that I should first put in a year of post-graduate teacher-training – and that would mean longer postponement of marriage. At various times I longed to be a barrister, but that would be too expensive, in terms of time as well as money. For a variety of reasons I never came near the point of trying to become a parson and, though I know that is what would have pleased my father and mother most of all, both of them were at pains never to say so. The one profession that neither I nor any of my friends thought of as a possibility for me was that of Oxford don.

During my last undergraduate year the Warden of New College (H. A. L. Fisher had succeeded Dr Spooner as Warden after my freshman year) suggested putting my name forward to the authorities of a Methodist college at Oberlin, Ohio, who wanted someone to stand in for a year as their Professor of Classics. This improbable suggestion struck me (and the professional pianist) as irresistible. It would mean that I got the hell out of England, Eton, Oxford and all familiar things. I was appointed, and each day that passed I found myself the more anxious to become acquainted with the United States. So it was sickening when Oberlin wrote to say that after all their classical Professor was not taking his sabbatical year and they had no need of me.

However, there was still time to enter for a scholarship recently founded by the widow of a distinguished American banker and philanthropist, Henry P. Davison, which took one graduate from Oxford and one from Cambridge to Harvard, Yale and Princeton for a year. Selection lay with a group of Oxford and Cambridge dons who had to make their choice before most of the candidates had sat their finals. This year they gave the 1928/9 Princeton scholarship from Oxford to Jack Wolfenden and the Harvard one to me. Mrs Davison was in due course a fairy godmother to both Jack and me, as she was to all her scholars. But when reports on the 1928/9 scholars became available, the Davison trustees decided that the experiment must end. I do not know how much this had to do with the behaviour of the 1928/9 scholars, how much with the Wall Street crash, how much with Mrs Davison's recognition that her initiative in bringing British graduates to American universities had been followed by the Harkness Trustees on a still grander scale. I am profoundly grateful for my year at Harvard, and sad that I was one of the last to benefit from such imaginative American goodwill.

As soon as my year at Harvard was over, I hurried back to England (with an A. B. degree *magna cum laude* and a *phi beta kappa* key) and put myself in the hands of a London institution long dedicated to coaching civil service candidates. My new tutors shared my own pessimism about the outcome of our efforts – until those efforts could miraculously cease. The last week-end before the date when I must pay my entrance fee for the Civil Service competition, I was summoned to Oxford. There I was interviewed by the Master of University College, Sir Michael Sadler, and the few fellows still available in Oxford (it was July). One of the dons responsible for offering me the Davison scholarship a year before was David Lindsay Keir (later the Vice-Chancellor of Queen's University, Belfast and then Master of Balliol). He was the one unmarried fellow of Univ, living in College and therefore happy to be dean. Returning recently from a sabbatical spell in North America, he had appalled the other fellows by announcing his engagement to be married and his intention in consequence to resign the deanship. 'But you can't,' they said; 'we're all married.' 'Then,' David answered, 'you must elect someone who's not.' So started the search for a junior research fellow prepared to live in college and start learning the dean's job forthwith. One of my Greats tutors had mentioned my name to David Keir and, before the week ended, I had accepted a three-year appointment as junior dean and research fellow in 'politics', with teaching responsibilities.

But why politics? This was the Oxford name for an undefined subject which was one part of a recently established undergraduate honours school embracing three aspects of the modern state – philosophy, politics and economics (PPE). It was then known hopefully as Modern Greats, in the belief that it would offer undergraduates who were inexpert in Greek and Latin some kind of equivalent to Greats (*Literae Humaniores*), the honours school which called for first-hand knowledge of Greek and Latin texts. In those days politics was taught, often with some reluctance, by dons whose primary interest was in modern history or constitutional law. Those reading the school were all examined in modern political institutions and British constitutional history since 1760; but they had also to choose two special subjects from a wide range of options, one of which was called public administration.

Reading Greats as an undergraduate I had become deeply enough involved in both philosophy and ancient history to end up (with five New College friends) in the first class, but I would never have been considered for a College fellowship in either part of Greats. Before my Univ fellowship had been announced H. W. B. Joseph, the philosopher who had been one of my New College tutors, hopped off his bicycle to say with ill-concealed delight: 'I hear they've elected you a fellow of Univ. But in what subject? Not in philosophy I presume.' At Harvard I had done economics and won praise from Sir Ralph Hawtrey (who was there, luckily for me, on leave from Whitehall) and from the local veteran, Professor Taussig. But it was ludicrously improbable that the first politics don to be appointed by any Oxford college should be someone as ill-equipped as me.

Nor did it turn out, I dare to say, a bad appointment. I had been marvellously well taught by dons of strongly contrasting styles at New College. Horace Joseph, Alec Smith and Christopher Cox had little in common as tutors but each of them was a superb model of a teaching don. And I loved teaching from the start. My first two pupils were Tommy Gubb, a South African Rhodes Scholar and that year's captain of the Oxford rugby football club, and Roger Low, a rowing blue and later no less successful as a banker, both of whom had already acquired an honours degree. Neither was still in residence for purely academic reasons, and that made them the more tolerant of my tutorial immaturity. Their courtesy gave me the beginnings of self-confidence. I worked hard over the next ten years to mend my general ignorance of politics since 1760 (the gap between the death of Trajan and that date remains unbridged) and, in particular, to learn something about local government.

And why local government? At the time of my election at Univ. G. D. H. Cole was the college fellow chiefly concerned with Modern Greats and it was arranged that I should come back to Oxford a week later to discuss with him what part of politics I should research into. In those days the correspondence column of *The Times* frequently gave hospitality to letters from Conservatives deploring the 'intrusion' of party politics into city government. The day I went to Oxford for my talk with Douglas Cole was no exception and I asked him whether 'party politics in local government' was a possible subject of research. 'No,' he said; 'impossible. But local government itself would be first-rate. It's most important and no academic knows anything about it.' So that was that.

Warden Fisher (whose kindness had already headed me towards America) was one of the three general editors of the Home

University Library which, before the days of paperbacks and Penguins, had pioneered the production of cheap books on serious subjects. This Library needed a book on English local government, he told me, and I must write it: Sir Arthur Robinson, permanent secretary of the Ministry of Health, would advise me where to go for my research and introduce me to the appropriate local government experts. Nothing could have been more fortunate for me.

Sir Arthur, in the Whitehall office which was to change its name from time to time but remain the central hub of local government over the next half century, started me on a round of visits – to Sheffield, Blackburn, Newcastle-on-Tyne and other key points of English local government. I remember my first interview with Robinson, the windows on Whitehall open, traffic roaring past, his lips as he spoke seeming to remain sealed. I heard enough to assure me of his good will towards me – and his help with introductions was of course invaluable.

I went off round England, searching for clues which might reveal how councils and their committees took decisions and where power in practice lay – with councillors or with their professional staffs; in town and county halls or in Whitehall departments? I got myself elected to the Oxford city council as one of the University representatives and sweated it out for six years on education and electricity committees. I tried out my ideas on pupils from my own and other colleges who had chosen public administration as one of their special subjects in Modern Greats. I gave University lectures to small groups of faithful students, and rather different ones to adult education groups in Burford, Watlington and other villages in Oxfordshire.

The final draft of *English Local Government* was largely written in Simla or on board ship during the monsoon. Thanks once again to Warden Fisher, I was the guest of Sir George Schuster for the three-month long vacation of 1931. He was then finance member in the Viceroy's council and his two sons were New College undergraduates. He wanted them to join their parents in Simla but thought it more likely that they would also work at their books if some young don with his own work to do came out with them. Fisher suggested my name and off we went, by P & O from Marseilles, paying my first visit to the Cairo museum one Sunday while the ship dawdled through Suez, sweating it out across the Indian Ocean, pausing in Bombay (the gardeners were still watering the grass though the monsoon had broken), then a luxurious train journey by day and night to the foot of the Himalayas, hilarious zig-zagging through mud, sacred cows and bullock-carts by motor-car up to the outskirts of Simla, and my first rickshaw ride (with bearers fore and aft) past Viceregal Lodge to Peterhof where the Schusters lived.

Before this Indian summer was over I went down to the plains alone, stayed with a young district officer in Agra and spent two days in Delhi. But most of my time was spent in Simla. As Willingdon had only recently succeeded Irwin as Viceroy, Gandhi and Nehru were both out of prison; and when they came to Simla they were both entertained by the Schusters. I was enormously impressed by both of them, especially by Nehru. When Gandhi was later that year in England for official discussions and came to Oxford, I asked him to a meeting of political science dons in Univ. He talked with unequivocal lucidity about constitutional reform and gave direct answers to our loaded questions (especially one from Quintin Hogg about the sterling value of the rupee). But what has stayed clearest in my memory is the tone of voice in which our old-world college butler, after enquiring whether our guest would take tea, replied to Mr Gandhi's 'No, thank you: salt and hot water, please' with precisely the same sense of the expected as when the senior fellow called for port.

The great value to me of this Indian visit was that it convinced me not only that I knew nothing about India but that I would still know little however many blue books on India I might eventually digest. In much the same way my year at Harvard had warned me against supposing that I knew anything about the United States – or would ever know much, however often I went there.

In 1932, the night before my marriage to the professional pianist and three years after my election to the research fellowship, I finished *English Local Government*. Three weeks later the publisher returned the proofs, in time for us to take to South Africa on our honeymoon and send back from the Cape. I heard no more until five months later, when I found waiting for me in the palace at Khartoum a letter, many times forwarded, from Harold Laski. He had just read and reviewed my book and, with his characteristic kindness to beginners, wrote me this letter of congratulation.

My college had elected me, after my three-year stint as a bachelor research fellow, to a tutorial fellowship in politics for seven years – and with permission to marry. I was also given leave to be away from Oxford for six months, including the Michaelmas term of 1932, so that I could accept a travelling fellowship to Africa from the Rhodes trustees. This, like the Davison scholarship to Harvard, proved to be the last of such awards to be made. It was certainly the first time that anyone could thank Rhodes for giving him and his wife a six-month honeymoon. I was of course paid by the trustees as a bachelor, but thanks to the kindness of many hosts and the concerts that my wife gave on our journey, we arrived back at Victoria station one January night in 1933 with three shillings to spare. I became dean of the College as David Keir's successor, and that I remained until the end of the 1939 summer term when we left Oxford.

I enjoyed my deanship. The College was then small enough for the dean to know a little about every undergraduate and graduate in residence. When any of them wanted leave to be away from Oxford during the eight weeks of full term he was supposed to ask me for permission, and in practice he probably did so whenever he wanted to be away for a night. The College gate was locked at nine pm and the head-porter kept a record of everyone who knocked in before midnight and of all guests who went out. No one (except dons) had a college key; so if you wanted to get into college after midnight, you had to wake up the porter, if you could (and later be fined by the dean), or else climb over the spikes (with which the college was fortified), risking impalement if you were clumsy and a quite heavy fine if you were caught in the act. I hated these primitive arrangements (which were abolished after the war) but they helped to concentrate the undergraduate mind on life inside college during the eight weeks of each term. The disciplinary duties of the dean were certainly not heavy, but besides involving me in personal contact with occasional malefactors they opened my door to anyone who cared to knock.

The person who did most to help me as dean was the college butler, Frank Collett. When I first came to Univ, Frank was the deputy head porter, with some knowledge of pretty well every junior and senior member of the college, including all college servants and their wives, and he was the obvious choice when we needed a new college butler. The butler's job centred on the college hall but spread out into all parts of college life, especially relations between college servants and the rest of us. Frank had an uncanny touch with awkward customers of any kind – seniors or juniors, sober or drunk, male or female. This meant that, with Frank as butler, the dean need have no fears that undergraduate behaviour during dinner in hall would embarrass his senior colleagues or their guests, whatever success the college oarsmen or rugger players might have had that afternoon. But it was Frank's advice on more important problems that was invaluable. Each of us trusted the other without reservation and knew that breach of confidence was unthinkable. When later I had experience of the Civil Service, I recognized that the relations of Frank as college butler with me as dean had something in common with those of the permanent secretary of a department with his minister. I certainly owed a large debt of gratitude to Frank for my enjoyment of the deanship. Alas, he was dead before I became Master.

Compared with New College, Univ. undergraduates struck me as a close-knit community. But in those pre-war days there was a potential split between the few aesthetes that we had and a predominant majority of hearties. A dean whose friends included men of both kinds could do something about this. Barbaric outrage (which was extremely rare) could be requited with intolerant severity. But fortunately the leading protagonists on both sides tended to like each other. My pupil Stephen Spender (as well as writing essays on politics for me, he was publishing his first book of poems and foolishly I bought only six copies of it) had good friends in the boat club; Noel Hutton (rowing blue, first-class scholar and in due course chief parliamentary draftsman) was the friend of all civilized men; and when years later both of them were elected honorary fellows on the same day, it confirmed memories of happy pre-war undergraduate life. Univ. had begun to lose its reputation as 'The Pub in the High' and, as I shall describe later, its blues had already helped to found the Univ. Musical Society.

The pianist at that Society's inaugural concert in 1930 had by now become my wife and our first house was a sometime Tudor pub behind the college. It was called Kybald Twychen and retained a faint savour of its earlier life. None of its floors or stairs were even, and you did well to bow the head on moving from one room to the next. Here Jean, despite a hawthorn bush (which the next tenants of this Corpus property quickly cut down), made her first garden for us and exploited every small-scale possibility of a house where you heard nothing from outside but birds and chiming bells. Here our first guest was William Temple, then Archbishop of York, when he returned in 1933 to preach in Oxford, following his week's Mission to the University two years earlier when he had filled St Mary's church night after night. (The book he had brought with him for bedside reading, we were delighted to discover, was Dorothy Sayers' recently published *Murder Must Advertise*.) I still regard him as the most courageous and articulate of all the Christians of my lifetime, and I owe him a great personal debt of gratitude.* He was almost too spherical to get up the stairs in Kybald Twychen but he was an ideal guest once he had reached a chair.

Next year another important person appeared in Kybald Twychen – our son Humphrey. But by 1936, when Pamela, our first

---

* See Appendix II for a talk I broadcast on the BBC about William Temple after his death.

daughter, was born we had moved to a Univ. house (now part of the college) at the Merton Street end of Logic Lane. A second daughter, Caroline, arrived there in 1939.

Nine Merton Street was another beautiful house, in what must be one of the loveliest streets in Europe. The drawing-room bow window looked south over Merton garden, and as the street was cobbled there was no offence from passing traffic. Merton and Magdalen bells tolled the time – and there was never enough of it.

During full term few of the twenty-four hours were free from tutorials, lecturing or decanal duties; so the one serious snag was that I saw far too little of Jean or the children. As soon as term was over, there was always a book to get on with. And for two years I was a politics examiner in Modern Greats, with colleagues like Humphrey Sumner or Richard Pares, papers to set and hundreds of scripts to mark (each paper was read by two examiners). Much of this I enjoyed, and I learnt something from every first-class candidate – Barbara Ward, for instance. For six years, too, there was the time-exhausting, often dull work of a city councillor from which to learn.

We had no car of our own for our first twenty-five years of marriage. Jean had taught me to drive six years before we married, in a car borrowed from a don when we were both undergraduates, and we continued to be shameless borrowers until 1957 when I gave her our first car (a Mini-Traveller) to celebrate our silver jubilee. But carlessness was characteristic of the pre-war don, and no great hardship if one had grown up in a carless family. Fortunately we were both of us bicyclists and sometimes, when it was feasible to desert the children for a week or so, we would put bicycles in a train, get out at Leeds or thereabouts and move on by side roads to the Roman Wall and Scotland. But holidays like that were untypical. More usual places of retreat were the Cotswolds (where I feel almost a native since playing cricket for Northleach as a schoolboy) and the Berkshire downs, and marvellous walks we had in both of them. But we took too few holidays, and I saw far too little of our children. All the same, as a married don I was becoming a less disjointed and a much happier person than I had been in earlier Oxford days.

Each year throughout the 'thirties, what Yeats before his death in 1939 prophesied in 'The Second Coming' became more nearly true – of Britain and the world:

> Things fall apart; the centre cannot hold;
> Mere anarchy is loosed upon the world,
> The blood-dimmed tide is loosed, and everywhere

The ceremony of innocence is drowned;
The best lack all conviction, while the worst
Are full of passionate intensity.

My mind had always been hopelessly muddled about war and peace. Someone who had been killed in action in 1916 had left me in his will a silver wristwatch which I had worn daily at school (till it was stolen), and the First World War left me with a hatred of killing. Schoolboy ambition drove me till I became Company Sergeant-Major in the Officers Training Corps at Eton. But at Oxford the thought of joining the Territorials never occurred to me. I shared the enthusiasm of my father (and other people I admired) for what the League of Nations stood for; but for years I failed ignominiously to spot the need for national rearmament if Hitler and Mussolini were to be stopped. It was only when Eden resigned as Foreign Secretary in February 1938 that the truth dawned, and it was not till Munich in September that I felt personally committed against Chamberlain. A few weeks later I was taking an obscure but active part, for the first and (so far) the last time in my life, in an election – and one that challenged the Government.

It so happened that Oxford City was the first constituency to have a by-election after Chamberlain's 'peace with honour' return from Munich. In 1935, at the last General Election, the Tory candidate had had a majority near seven thousand, and now his very able successor, Quintin Hogg, seemed almost certain to retain the seat. The Master of Balliol, Sandy Lindsay, was a lifelong member of the Labour party but was induced to stand against Hogg as a Progressive Independent anti-Munich candidate. The Liberals withdrew their candidate and officially supported Lindsay, but Labour was split, with Patrick Gordon-Walker, the official party candidate, reluctant to stand down or support Lindsay. Hogg and Lindsay were in the end the only candidates, and there was only one issue: did Oxford support or condemn Chamberlain and Munich?

Lindsay, whom I had always liked and admired, was a poor candidate, often inaudible and not always lucid. His supporters were a passionate but motley band of rebels, with no professional organization to match the Tory regulars. Frank Pakenham (who, like Gordon-Walker, was then a Christ Church don and later replaced him as official Labour candidate for Oxford) and Elizabeth, his gorgeous wife, were socialist 'rebels' who supported Lindsay. Another Christ Church don, Roy Harrod (not a rebel but a committed Liberal) supported him too. But how many local

Tories would rebel? That was the crucial question. Harold Macmillan, risking his future as an official Tory MP, told them they must. 'I feel myself,' he wrote in a well-publicised letter to Lindsay, 'in honour bound to say that if I were a voter in the Oxford constituency, I should unhesitatingly vote and work for your return to Parliament. The times are too grave and the issue is too vital for progressive Conservative opinion to allow itself to be influenced by Party loyalties or to tolerate the present uncertainty regarding the principles governing our foreign policy.' At a packed meeting in the Town Hall which Violet Bonham Carter (later Lady Asquith) movingly addressed, he assured us that the Government's foreign policy had so far been one of retreating before superior forces and that you could not always appease lions by throwing them Christians.*

Lord Cecil was another of Lindsay's senior supporters, and among his junior supporters was an ex-President of the Oxford University Conservative Association (next year's President of the Union), Edward Heath. But Oxford landladies were for the Peace of Munich and it was no surprise to me when Hogg won. Even so, the Tory majority was only half what it had been before – and far from satisfactory for the Government (the next by-election, in the Tory stronghold of Bridgwater in November, was an outright defeat for the Government by Vernon Bartlett, standing like Lindsay as an Independent).

I have never belonged to a political party. The reason, till I became a politics don in 1929, was simply lack of interest. From then onwards, as I researched, tutored and examined in politics, there was advantage in not having a party label round my neck; but that in itself was no conclusive reason for 'independence'. My Univ. colleague G. D. H. Cole scrupulously (and I think successfully) combined notorious personal partisanship with a complete neutrality towards his academic pupils, none of whom ever alleged that he was subject to propaganda from his tutor. No; for me there was no question of abstinence from party politics for the sake of professional integrity. I think the main reason was simply negative: I was a mugwump and found no compulsion in the appeal of either Tory or Labour party in pre-war Britain. It was only in 1938, when both parties were split, that I felt bound to take sides and had no hesitation about which side I was on.

So I toured Oxford suburbs every day in a loudspeaker van, snatching the mike from various Liberal and Labour colleagues when my turn came; canvassed the Dean of Christ Church (Dr

* Harold Macmillan *Winds of Change 1914–1939*, p. 583, Macmillan, 1966.

Williams, later Bishop of Durham) and was firmly shown the door; rang landladies' bells in North Oxford, with the same result; and drafted a one-page statement, for stuffing in letter-boxes, headed 'Appeal to Conservatives to vote for Mr Lindsay'. This last did not appeal to Arthur Goodhart (then law professor and Univ. colleague of mine), who rightly doubted whether those who signed it were all lifelong Tories. But it had at least one partial success. Professor Lindemann summoned me to his rooms in Christ Church, congratulated me on a brilliant piece of drafting and, when I asked him to repeat his praise in public, explained why his support must be 'behind the scenes'.

I regret none of the hours spent in that by-election, but at the time I hated almost all of them. It was humiliating to find how distasteful that kind of confrontation was. From my experiences as college dean I already knew that sometimes, when confronted with an alleged criminal, I had to be careful or excitement would take physical form (and my diaphragm would quiver); but though such confrontations left me exhausted, there was no offence in them. Flat disapproval, on the other hand, whether from deans or landladies, I did find offensive. It ran counter to my compromising temperament and proved the absurdity of trying to be 'all things to all men'. In short, the by-election was for me personally a new and invaluable experience – but far from comfortable.

Birkbeck College had been founded in 1823, as the London Mechanics' Institution, by George Birkbeck, an English physician and the pioneer of classes for working men. But since 1920 it had been recognized as a constituent college of London University for evening and part-time students who worked for internal university degrees as well as earning their livelihood by day as teachers, civil servants, or in industry or commerce. The college staff held whole-time appointments as University professors or lecturers, covering a wide range of science and the humanities.

In 1938 the chairman of Birkbeck governors was Lionel Hichens. He had been one of the original 'Milner kindergarten' in South Africa and was still a member of the group which edited the Commonwealth quarterly magazine *The Round Table*. In 1933 this group had recruited some younger men into membership, including myself on my return from our honeymoon in Africa. Hichens now told me that Birkbeck was in search of a new Master and asked me whether I would like to be a candidate. The more that Jean and I pondered this idea, the more we liked it. London had powerful attractions to us both, especially to Jean as a musician. The Birkbeck job would not start till September 1939

30

and by then I would have had ten years at Univ. Birkbeck was about to move from Fetter Lane to Bloomsbury, build itself a new home beside the Senate House and embark on a new life. We decided I should put in for the job (though almost all our friends thought we were crazy). I was short-listed with three other candidates and after our interviews we were all entertained at an uproarious lunch in Birkbeck by the selection committee. We were wholly delighted when the College pre-elected me as Master, to take office on 1 September 1939. Our second daughter Caroline was born, as a good omen, on Oakapple Day (29 May), and her christening in college chapel was the excuse for our farewell party to the scouts and other Univ. friends. At the end of the summer term we had what some of us thought would be the last of all Univ. Commems (it was later remembered as the Armageddon Ball) and the Mauds said goodbye to Oxford – for the last time, they thought.

CHAPTER 4

Wartime Whitehall, 1939–1945

In 1938 it was generally assumed that as soon as Hitler reached the conclusion that war with Britain was inevitable he would order the bombardment of London from the air. Communications would be disrupted and Britain would cease to be governable from Whitehall. Plans were therefore made for the conversion of our national government into a regional system. England was sub-divided into regions and a regional commissioner designated for each of them, as outposts of a new department of Home Security. Harold Butler was to be the regional commissioner for the south, with headquarters in Reading. He had recently been appointed the first Warden of Nuffield College, Oxford, and I was to be one of the first Fellows of the College. As I was supposed to know something about local government, he had asked me to join his staff as an intelligence officer if regional government were established. So in August 1939, a month before I was due to become Master of Birkbeck College London, I was summoned to Reading Gaol as one of a mixed bag of civil servants, retired soldiers and other recruits. We set rather feverishly to work and by the outbreak of war in September some kind of makeshift organization had been established. Fortunately the bombs did not fall and for a year the effectiveness of our improvisations was not tested. For the same reason my first action as Master of Birkbeck was to take counsel with my new colleagues there and cancel the decision taken earlier by the authorities of London University that if war broke out the College must close down. Instead we found ourselves to be the one College of the University still functioning in London. The other Colleges were all evacuated to places outside London, according to plans made before the war. As most of the Birkbeck students were part-timers who came to the College after earning their livelihood during the day, no evacuation plan would have been feasible. So now we had the chance to adapt our timetable and beat the blackout. We concentrated our normal courses on the week-end and set about organizing public lectures and concerts at lunchtime during the week. Myra Hess, Jelly d'Aranyi and Adila Fachiri gave recitals; Nikolaus Pevsner, Kingsley Martin, Cyril Joad and Leo Amery lectured; and so long as the phoney war lasted we had a marvellous opportunity to do something for Londoners as well as our own students. When real war began in 1940, we had to adapt our way of life rather more drastically – especially when the College was virtually destroyed by fire in the blitz. But my colleagues and our students persisted and the College never closed down.

Harold Butler agreed that it was absurd for me to combine this new Birkbeck life with work in Reading Gaol, and the new wartime departments in London were still feverishly in search of staff. The first Minister of Food was 'Shakespeare' Morrison. He was later to prove his considerable abilities as Speaker of the House of Commons and then as Governor-General of Australia. But meanwhile he had become a sitting rabbit for members of Parliament anxious to show marksmanship as critics of the Chamberlain government. I think it was William Beveridge, then Master of University College, Oxford, but with still vivid memories of his success as a food controller in the First World War, who contrived my transfer to the Food Ministry in London as a full-time 'acting' Principal. This meant that the Master could be in Birkbeck only at week-ends, lunchtime and after office hours, but my colleagues, especially Professor Pete Jackson (whom we made Vice-Master) and the Clerk, Troup Horne, more than made up for my long absences. By 1943, when I became Second Secretary at the Food Ministry, I knew it was time for Pete Jackson to become Master of Birkbeck and I could happily resign. He saw the College through the rest of the war and into the new Bloomsbury buildings (which we had started during the phoney war in 1939), but his outstandingly successful Mastership was tragically cut short when he was killed in a road accident.

At Food I found myself in the delightful company of Herbert Broadley (back in the Civil Service after success in advertising and with years of international good works ahead of him), Maurice Hutton and John Wall (both from the City and both exceptionally bright) in the Ministry's 'economics division' under the leadership of Ted Lloyd, an eccentric and highly intelligent civil servant of strong liberal views and great warmth of heart. Most of the Ministry's work was organized in vertical compartments covering either the supply of cereals, meat, bacon, butter, fats and other foods, or separate subjects such as rationing, finance and 'establishments' (meaning men and women). Our small division, unlike the rest, covered no one specific food or subject but the whole Ministry. 'Economics' was an inadequate description of its job, and it was later rightly renamed the 'general' division, for its concerns were multifarious: statistics, planning, 'new ideas' and (most important of all) the import programme.

We serviced a committee which assembled round one table once a week all the tycoons responsible for acquiring various kinds of food – Jimmy Rank the wheat baron, Sir William Rook the sugar daddy, Herbert Davis and Jasper Knight (of Unilever) for oils and fats. Under the chairmanship of Sir Quintin Hill their heads had to be knocked together and a single import programme produced, sufficiently convincing to persuade the Treasury to find foreign exchange to buy it and the Ministry of Shipping space to bring it in. As the secretary of this Overseas Purchasing Board, I had everything to learn about minute-taking, and the Chairman could not have been a kindlier coach.

I was an ambitious, slow and clumsy pupil from the start; and before I had learnt to swim with any confidence I found myself floundering in waters deeper than the Food Ministry pond: I became joint secretary of the War Cabinet food policy committee. But all was well. My secretarial colleague, Denis Rickett, was the ideal supervisor – an unmistakable fellow of All Souls but devoid of arrogance, an expert draftsman but so tactful a tutor that no pupil could feel hurt by his corrections.

However late into the night a Cabinet committee might sit, the minutes had to be dictated, stencilled and circulated, without reference to the Chairman, in time for Ministers to read them next morning. It has been well recorded:

And now that the great ones go off to their dinner,
The Secretary stays, getting thinner and thinner,
Tearing his hair to recall and report
What *he* thinks that *they* think they *ought* to have thought.

When I left Food in 1944 for the Office of the Minister of Reconstruction I found myself in pupillage to Norman Brook, one of the Grand Masters of this art, during the months before he succeeded Edward Bridges as Secretary of the Cabinet. Despite my luck in having this succession of kind and patient tutors, I could never match their standards of either speed or lucidity. But I learnt enough to recognize the immeasurable debt that British ministers of all political parties owe to the succession of top civil servants who have established the tradition of our Cabinet secretariat, and I doubt whether any other democracy enjoys an asset of greater value. Dick Crossman's *Diaries* show clearly enough that their author never understood the purpose of Cabinet minutes nor began to appreciate their value. What he wanted was a record of

34

debate. What Cabinet minutes marvellously achieve is nothing of the kind but, instead, a clear instruction to Ministers and their departments about action to be taken in consequence of the Cabinet's decisions.

Pre-war planning of the Food Ministry made no provision for a scientific adviser on nutrition. But it did provide a scientist to advise on 'the decontamination of food after gas attack'. Fortunately the need for advice on decontamination was not urgent. What we desperately needed, in building the import programme, was advice on the comparative nutritional value of different foods. And here on the spot, disguised as a decontamination expert, was Professor Jack Drummond, professionally equipped to give it and precisely the sort of person, because of his accessibility and obvious common sense, to commend himself to all and sundry as an adviser.* He quickly became a friend, not only of the economists and merchant bankers in the economics division, but of business tycoons in the supply department. I remember one telephone conversation with him when I was making a first draft of the import programme. It went like this: 'Jack, what about bananas?. . . What! no nutritional value?. . . Over 90% water?. . . So what sort of cut could we make?. . . You don't mean it! Cut them out altogether? . . . Thank you so much.' So no more bananas were imported for five years and the precious refrigerated tonnage could be used for meat.

Meanwhile somewhere in the country outside London nutrition experts were beavering away under a specially constituted Food Research Board. Later, when I had become private secretary to the new Minister, Lord Woolton, we went to visit them. They laid on a special luncheon for us: grass soup, nettle cutlets and whale-meat steak. That was the nearest they came to influencing food policy throughout the war. Drummond's influence, on the other hand, became steadily more powerful.

His influence was particularly valuable when we came up against Professor Lindemann.† As head of the Prime Minister's

* He and his wife died tragically in 1952 when they were murdered while on a camping holiday in the South of France.
† A Professorial Student of Christ Church, Oxford, known generally as 'the Prof', he later became Lord Cherwell, celebrated in the following lines:
        Lord Cherwell when the war began
        Was plain Professor Lindemann,
        But now from his exalted perch
        Prays silence for Lord Christ of Church.
        The Church of Christ, that patient ass,
        Seeing such wonders come to pass,
        Marvelling at virtue's just reward
        Salutes her newly risen Lord.

Statistical Office, he was well placed to influence Mr Churchill with his own eccentric views about nutrition. His personal dislike of meat was not shared by Mr Churchill, who, when First Lord of the Admiralty in the early months of the war, had resolutely resisted the demand for meat rationing as an insult to the Royal Navy.

But the Prof's dislike of meat was less virulent than his dislike of the Minister and Ministry of Agriculture. He regarded them as obsessed by a vested interest in beef-cattle and post-war farming, in preference to immediate milk-production. We in the Food Ministry inclined to share this conviction of the Prof's, and we were at pains to consolidate an alliance with him and his officials. But he was an unreliable ally who might turn at any moment and bite the hand that fed him. He would write cruel and wounding minutes to the Prime Minister, for example about our failure to encourage backyard pigs and poultry. It was at such moments that Drummond's nutritional orthodoxy and common sense were indispensable.

Another alliance that needed cementing with some delicacy was between the Food Ministry and a group of economists working as part of the Cabinet Office for Sir John Anderson when he became Lord President of the Council and, effectively, War Cabinet head of the home front. Quite rightly, they had an interest in various parts of the Food Ministry's work. They were highly intelligent men, and their influence was always liable to be decisive on policy questions which were primarily our business but needed War Cabinet approval. So we and they had a strong interest in understanding each other, whether or not we reached the same conclusions.

When Lionel Robbins became director of the economic section of the War Cabinet office, with Norman Brook as the link with Anderson, we in the Ministry could not have had more tactful or congenial allies. But difficulties were bound sometimes to arise, especially when our colleagues in the Food Ministry were not in agreement with one another, for example about the practical possibilities of a new method of rationing called the 'points' system. Bread was not rationed until after the war, but eventually almost all the other main foodstuffs were; they were all included in a single ration-book with separate coupons for each type of food. But what about minor kinds of food – jam, Spam, dried fruit, and so on? Imagination boggled at the thought of fixing a weekly ration for each one of these and constantly changing its size to match changes in available supplies. But why not lump all these minor foods together, attach a number of 'points' to units of each food (two points, say, for a tin of Spam, four for a tin of sardines), allot the housewife a weekly clutch of 'points' and leave her free to spend them as she chose? When more supplies of sardines went into the shops, points value of each tin could be reduced; when Spam became scarcer, its points value must go up. Our experts in retail trade firmly said 'No, quite impracticable.' But the Germans were said to manage it. Could not we try? Lionel Robbins thought we should. So we brought him and our chief retail-trade expert into direct personal consultation. 'Professor,' asked the expert in his Scottish accent, 'what would the grocer *do* with the wee bits of paper presented by the customer out of her book of points?' 'Well,' said Lionel, 'he could impale them on that sort of spike you often see on the counter in a grocer's shop.' 'O *no*, Professor,' was the horrified reply; 'there would be blood on the butter.' Lord Woolton eventually preferred his own experience as a shopkeeper to the advice of his experts in rationing. Points rationing was introduced, and no blood flowed. Housewives were delighted (at last they had some choice instead of merely 'collecting rations'), and the Ministry got much credit for inventiveness.

In April 1940 the Ministry had had a change of Minister: Chamberlain, on Horace Wilson's advice, appointed Lord Woolton in place of Mr Morrison. This turned out to be an inspired move. As Frederick Marquis, Woolton had proved himself an organizer of genius in procuring boots for the army in the First World War and clothing the new recruits before the Second. Between the wars he had made his reputation as a businessman by work for Lewis's, the highly successful multiple-store company in Liverpool, Manchester and Leeds. Without identifying himself with a political party, he had also done public work of various kinds with some success. A peerage was conferred on him early in 1939, to make him available for ministerial office if war broke out.

He was exactly what the Food Ministry needed. The pre-war foundations had been well and truly laid by an able and experienced civil servant of no great imagination, Sir Henry French. He had been head of the Food Defence Plans Department since its establishment and was now the new Ministry's permanent secretary. We were a gigantic United Kingdom wholesale food store, with responsibility for keeping the nation fed and in good heart for an indefinite period. We could succeed only if people believed us to be just, competent and on their side, and if the Treasury and Shipping Ministry trusted us to be claiming the smallest possible share of precious foreign exchange and shipping space. To help us we already had the most experienced businessmen from all the food industries. What we lacked was a ministerial chief unidentified by public opinion with any particular party, unafraid of his colleagues in the Cabinet, experienced enough to win the trust of businessmen inside the Ministry, tough enough to frustrate internal revolt, and above all a personality that the public could come to trust. Woolton almost perfectly filled the bill. When Churchill replaced Chamberlain as Prime Minister, we nearly lost him, but not quite. He was always a bit scared of Churchill and never became a crony, but Churchill came to have great respect for him. He let him leave food only at the end of 1943, when persuaded that public demand for post-war government planning could best be met by bringing into the War Cabinet well-trusted 'Uncle Fred' Woolton as Minister of Reconstruction.

I first met Woolton early in 1940 when Alan Lennox-Boyd, while still his House of Commons representative, one morning introduced me (as Master of Birkbeck College and a temporary hack in his department). Soon afterwards French sent for me. Lord Woolton, he said, wanted me to become his Principal Private Secretary. This, French admitted, was a strange choice, for I knew as little as Lord Woolton about how a government department worked: what the new Minister really needed was a professional civil servant. But, French said, he thought a Minister must have his own way in a matter as personal as this and we must make the best of it. The arrangement might work quite well if he and I became close enough allies. French was right: I was a queer choice for the crucial post of Minister's private secretary, but it worked out better than it deserved. The personalities of Woolton and French were poles apart, and the eventual dazzling success of the Ministry was due to their coming to terms with each other. It was my job to give both of them help in the early stages of that process, and this both of them encouraged me to do. My successors as Private Secretary, Rupert Metcalf (later British High Commissioner in Southern Rhodesia) and Robin Harrison (later Warden of Merton College, Oxford), were outstandingly successful in the later stages.

My first day with Woolton included an excursion to Manchester where he was to address a packed meeting in the Town Hall. Lady Woolton came in the train with us and, as her name was Maud, each time he addressed her I sprang to attention. Inevitably, by the time we reached our destination he was calling me John. This accident – indeed the whole expedition – was an encouraging start.

One of the Treasury mandarins with whom we in the Ministry had much to do was a bearded, endearing character called Edward

Twentyman. When it became clear that French needed additional help at the top of the Ministry (and Woolton was confident that Horace Wilson, then head of the Civil Service, would arrange a transfer), Twentyman seemed to us a strong candidate for a new post of Second Secretary. But would he and Woolton get on together? Troup Horne was not only my chief administrative colleague at Birkbeck College but also a distinguished chef who was delighted to lay on meals for me. So we arranged that, before any official approaches were made to the Treasury, Woolton and Twentyman should both be my guests at Birkbeck. The luncheon was a success. Horace Wilson did the rest and Twentyman moved over from the Treasury. Alas, he was later killed in an aircrash somewhere between London and Washington, but not before he had become a legendary figure in the Ministry of Food, much loved by all of us who knew him intimately.

In 1940, when Churchill succeeded Chamberlain and Woolton was confirmed as Minister of Food, Bob Boothby took Lennox-Boyd's place as spokesman for the Ministry in the House of Commons. He and Woolton were personalities as different from each other as French and Woolton, but all three of them gradually came to terms with one another. I always thought of Bob as an Elizabethan buccaneer – generous, warm-hearted, articulate, the greatest fun in any company but also an intelligent politician to his fingertips, with a voice in which these qualities were splendidly compounded. Neither Woolton nor French trusted his judgment but both of them recognized his value to them in expounding our policy to the House of Commons. It was he who first saw the importance of convincing the Treasury that if the level of wages was to be stabilized, retail food prices must be subsidized enough to keep the food element in the cost of living stable.

But to keep the Commons relatively happy was not enough. Direct steps must also be taken to explain to the public what we were doing and to listen and respond to their reactions. So weekly press conferences became an integral part of our work, taken usually by French, but by Woolton when something had gone wrong (such as our first effort to control eggs) or when there was something new (such as tea rationing) to talk about.

Our public relations department was headed by Howard Marshall, with A. D. Peters, the distinguished literary agent, as his deputy. Marshall's conviction was that the secret of good public relations was 'good conduct for which you take the credit'. He therefore insisted that his own ideas of 'good government' were not irrelevant: he must have his say before decisions on policy were taken. Woolton agreed with him and overbore French's reluctance. So Marshall had direct access to his Minister and was present at almost all policy discussions. Of course his views were often disregarded, but only after argument, and in the end they often won.

What should be done about meals in restaurants, for example? To control them would involve complicated arrangements, difficult to police and unpopular with restaurants and customers; and the total quantities of food that could be saved were only marginal. On the other hand, to leave people free to spend as much as they could afford on meals in restaurants was difficult to justify when fair shares were the order of the day. Besides, at a time when we were making special efforts to persuade the United States to send us food under lend-lease arrangements, it was dangerous to let Americans in London eat as much as they could buy at Claridges or the Ritz. After prolonged struggles Marshall had his way, and limits were imposed on the number of courses you could order at a meal and on the total sum you could be charged for food.

Marshall had made his national reputation before the war as a BBC commentator on test matches and royal occasions. Woolton had no experience of broadcasting but he needed no persuading that this was an art that he must learn and practise. He put himself without reserve in Marshall's hands and, after a shaky start, achieved such outstanding success that Robert Hudson, the Minister of Agriculture, asked Woolton's leave (readily granted) to become another pupil of the same master.

But the close partnership between Woolton and Marshall had more important effects than ministerial broadcasts or policy decisions: Woolton came to be regarded by scores of housewives and their children as a man who cared about them personally – and whose department shared his personal concern. It also helped Woolton to establish an extraordinary position for himself inside the Ministry. Here was a huge heterogeneous mix of people drawn from many walks of life; most of them (once the blitz on London began in the autumn of 1940) were working in North Wales at Colwyn Bay but others were in Oxford (the fruit and vegetable experts), London (with the Minister) and elsewhere; and local authorities everywhere were our agents for rationing purposes. Woolton was determined to convert this diverse mass of people into a team, so that each member felt himself a colleague of Lord Woolton, with Lord Woolton's reputation in his hands. He came astonishingly close to success. I remember one of the first things he asked me to arrange was a visit to the telephone switchboard at our headquarters. He had years ago learnt the art of shop-walking at Lewis's and now he practised it again. Perambulating the rows of telephonists, he left none of them in doubt of their importance: it was their voices that gave callers a first impression of the Ministry. The same message was personally (and constantly) conveyed to the wounded ex-warriors who now manned lifts and reception desk at the Ministry's front door. One morning after the 1940 blitz had started I found our London headquarters in Westminster had just missed a direct hit (the Minister's office was a shambles, with the wall-clock embedded in my chair). Woolton at once saw his opportunity: every letter reaching us that morning got some sort of answer before nightfall, explaining why the full reply must be delayed.

The Minister was of course 'responsible' for every decision taken by any member of his staff; but only a tiny fraction of the decisions taken day by day could be brought to his personal attention, and a still smaller proportion could await his decision. So there had to be an elaborate system of devolved authority. The Minister's 'mind' must be shared with the Permanent Secretary and passed down the line of command. However high or low your place in the hierarchy, you must take every decision you could without reference to your superior, but watch out for the sensitive points you *must* 'refer'. Trained civil servants tended to be over-cautious, experienced businessmen to decide things for themselves. One example that illustrates this constantly recurring problem came my way early in 1944. (Woolton had just been succeeded by Jay Llewellin and I was the Acting Permanent Secretary.)

One day at lunch the director of the fruit and vegetables division mentioned to me that a cargo of Spanish oranges had arrived from Seville. There were far too few to be distributed fairly and the director had decided to sell them to the jammers in Ireland who would pay a good price for them and help to improve the division's profit and loss account. I suggested caution. Next day the *Daily Telegraph* carried a story that oranges, brought to this country in British bottoms at the risk of British seamen's lives, had been sold to neutrals in Eire instead of comforting British housewives. Later in the day a minute sheet from 10 Downing Street was on the Minister's table, with the *Telegraph* story pasted on and beneath it a minute in the Prime Minister's red ink: 'Minister of Food. Pray report. WSC.' Meanwhile the director concerned had had second thoughts, and I was able to draft a reply to the PM's minute which Jay Llewellin quickly signed and despatched: 'The *Daily Telegraph* was misinformed. It had been suggested that the oranges should be sold to Eire, but I have arranged for them to go to the Women's Institutes in Scotland where they will be made into marmalade and much enjoyed.' Later that evening the minute sheet came back from number ten, with a further red ink addition: 'Minister of Food. Good. De Valera deserves no oranges. Lemons or raspberries would be more appropriate. WSC.' Considering the war problems besetting Mr Churchill in 1944 it was perhaps surprising that he found time for such minute-writing, but this was the way to keep ministerial colleagues on their toes.

In 1943 I had my first experiences of international diplomacy, at two conferences in the United States. The first was held at Hot Springs, Virginia and resulted in the establishment, after the war, of the first specialized agency of the United Nations, the Food and Agriculture Organisation (FAO). The second was at Atlantic City, where the first council meeting was held of the United Nations Relief and Rehabilitation Administration (UNRRA), which was established to feed and reconstruct allied and enemy countries once the war was won.

The Hot Springs conference was a brain-child of Eleanor Roosevelt, inspired by Henry Wallace, a wayward American politician of radical views and no small influence at that time. The whole idea was most distasteful to Mr Churchill: no time should be spared in 1943 from winning the war. But President Roosevelt was not to be deterred: now was the time to assemble experts from all the allied countries who would re-think, without benefit of politicians, the desirable pattern of post-war food and agriculture, and make recommendations to break the vicious pre-war cycle of famine and food surpluses. Churchill was somehow persuaded that the allied war effort would be prejudiced if Britain refused to take part. A powerful team of economists and experts in food and agriculture was therefore assembled, under the leadership of a Foreign Office Minister, Richard Law, MP (later Lord Coleraine), and despatched across the Atlantic, by sea or, in the case of Lionel Robbins and myself, on mattresses in the belly of a bomber.

The original idea of insulating the conference from politicians and the press, so that experts might concentrate their efforts on long-term world problems of food and agriculture, was at first interpreted by our American hosts as requiring physical isolation. When we reached the splendid hotel which had been taken over by the US Government for the conference, we found it ringed with National Guardsmen in shiny white helmets: no admission except for conference delegates who could produce an official pass.

Nothing, of course, could have attracted the press in greater numbers or made the media more determined to break in. The State Department yielded quickly and we proceeded to work in a blaze of publicity. The change of tactics did us no harm. Once admitted, the media soon discovered they were wasting their time and lost interest, especially when it became apparent that, far from breaking up in controversy, the conference was in danger of reaching general agreement. Before the final session, when the conclusions of the various commissions (into which the conference had been divided at the outset) were to be presented for general approval, there was at least a moment of intense excitement when the news broke that the powerful Soviet delegation were still awaiting instructions from Moscow on how they were to vote. Just, but only just, in time their instructions arrived – approving all our proposals.

Since then, I have attended a good many such gatherings, but Hot Springs remains easily the best I can remember. Its pre-natal stages, and in particular the abortive attempt to exclude the press, nearly proved disastrous. Its success was due partly to the high quality of many national delegations, partly to the evident advantage of devising ways in which the post-war world could avoid destroying food stocks while two-thirds of the human race stayed undernourished. But I think the main reason for success was the mere fact that we were meeting. For four years most of the countries represented at the conference had been exclusively occupied in fighting for their lives. Here we were at Hot Springs assuming that after all we *would* survive, confidently planning something in the nature of a new world, and finding that agreement between Russians, Americans, the Commonwealth and a Europe still occupied by Nazis was not beyond the range of possibility.

On our way back through Washington I was one of the guests at a luncheon in the Department of Commerce attended by our ambassador, Lord Halifax, and various members of the United States Government. I showed my old friend Felix Frankfurter, the Supreme Court judge, a telegram that had just reached me from my wife announcing the birth of our third daughter. We had earlier been considering names for a second son and had not thought about a girl; so the company were invited to name the new child. 'Hot Springs' was confidently suggested but I myself settled for 'Virginia', and this provisional decree was made absolute when a second telegram, already despatched by my wife, reached me next day: 'Baby exactly like Hore-Belisha [creator of street-beacons in his own image]. What about Virginia?'

A few months later I was on my way back to America for the first Council meeting of UNRRA in Atlantic City. Just before I left England Lord Woolton had told me, in deadly confidence, that Mr Churchill had invited him to join the War Cabinet as Minister of Reconstruction. There was to be no great Ministry of Reconstruction of the kind established after the First World War. On the contrary, Woolton was instructed to appoint a staff of no more than half a dozen, which would service a new War Cabinet reconstruction committee consisting of leading members of all three political parties. This committee and its Chairman would animate and supervise planning by individual departments for the transition from war to peace. Having confided this news, Woolton added that I too must leave the Food Ministry and head his new Office.

Jay Llewellin, the Minister of State in Washington, was the political head of the UK delegation to the UNRRA conference. Oliver Franks, the official delegate specially concerned with raw materials, and I myself, concerned with food, came out from England and, after consultations in Washington, drove with Llewellin to Atlantic City. As we left, Jay pressed a button, the glass partition rose between the front and back seats of the Rolls and I knew that something confidential was on its way. 'I had an interesting phone call from England this morning,' he said. 'It was from a Mr Martin' (and I knew from his pronunciation of the Prime Minister's private secretary's name that he meant Mr Churchill). ' "I want you," he said, "to be Minister of Food. Is that all right?" "Minister of Fuel?" I said, mishearing him. "No, Minister of Food – in place of Woolton." "Yes, Martin, delighted." "Say nothing about it for the present." '

Jay, who was immensely pleased with this news, went on to say what fun we should have working together in his new Ministry. I could not tell him of Woolton's move to Reconstruction, still less of his intention to take me with him; but I could tell him a lot about Henry French and other Ministry characters. The UNRRA conference seemed to be off to a good start. It ended well enough too, but not without several bad moments in the course of the ensuing fortnight.

One of these moments was a good example of the difference between times when you *can* speak ironically at an international gathering and times when you must not. The Russians once more sent a powerful delegation, with supplies of powerful vodka, and before the conference was over they invited the UK delegation to dinner in their hotel suite. Before we attempted to rise from the table a number of speeches were made. Our delegation was the

44

usual mixed bag of experts and temporary civil servants, but it included one professional diplomat and he began his speech as follows: 'Gentlemen, I wish to propose what may seem to you an unusual toast: Hitler's attack on the Soviet Union.' Our hosts froze visibly – and the frost gradually turned to growls. On went our diplomat, explaining that had it not been for that admittedly deplorable attack, we should not now be aimiably assembled round this hospitable board. Soon the room was in uproar. Jay Llewellin rose: 'No,' he shouted, 'let us drink rather to the success of our great leaders, Stalin and Churchill.' And he let loose our only Russian expert, John Russell, to perform a Russian dance down the dinner table, scattering wine glasses to right and left. Eventually, when we had taken leave of our hosts, Jay and I repaired downstairs to the bar for some reflection. There we were joined by Dean Acheson (leader of the US delegation but not yet Secretary of State) and Jan Masaryk, the Czech leader. Jay told the story of our recent dinner party. When the next round of drinks was brought, Dean begged leave to propose a toast and raised his glass: 'Gentlemen,' he said, 'the toast is Pearl Harbor.' When the next round was brought, Jan Masaryk made the same request and raised his glass: 'Gentlemen,' he said, 'the toast is Munich.' And all was well.

By the time the UNRRA conference finished, Llewellin's appointment as Food Minister in place of Woolton had been announced, and a major bacon crisis had arisen in Britain. The ration was already down to two ounces a week. The only chance of continuing to honour it was to get extra supplies from Canada. To Canada therefore he and I flew from Atlantic City. By good luck all the provincial ministers of agriculture happened at that moment to be in conference at Ottawa. We gave them a poignant picture of what the British breakfast had become. Mercifully they were impressed – and saved our bacon.

When I got home from Atlantic City I found a message from Norman Brook asking me to ring him urgently. He knew, he said, that Woolton had asked me to head the new Reconstruction Office. John Anderson, however, had pointed out that that office must work in close touch with the Cabinet Secretariat; its head, indeed, would be Secretary of the Reconstruction Committee of the Cabinet and also Chairman of the Committee of top departmental officials which would work under the Cabinet Committee and make recommendations to it. What Woolton needed therefore in his chief officer was Cabinet Secretariat experience and first-hand knowledge of all Whitehall departments. The man whom Woolton needed, in other words, was the deputy secretary of the

Cabinet, Norman Brook, and it had now been agreed that Woolton should have him as head of his Office. Norman went on to say that he (and Woolton) wanted me as deputy head and, until he knew that I agreed to this, he could make no move towards filling other posts in the Office. I told him that of course I agreed but Jay Llewellin would need squaring. Jay was duly squared, but on condition that I stayed at the Food Ministry some months longer, in order to act as Permanent Secretary while Henry French was on secondment to the Government of India. So later in 1944 I joined Brook in the Reconstruction Office as his deputy and some months later, when he became Secretary of the Cabinet, succeeded him as head.

Woolton the Minister of Reconstruction was not in the same class as Woolton the Minister of Food, but he was as good as his colleagues in the Reconstruction Committee allowed him to be, and that meant very good for certain purposes – of which much the most important was to get agreement from leaders of all political parties that in post-war Britain there should be no return to pre-war mass unemployment. Woolton's 1944 White Paper on 'a high and stable level of employment' was his major achievement as Reconstruction Minister and it was a considerable one by any reckoning. I do not think Woolton himself wrote a word of it, and that in itself is a tribute to his common sense. What he wanted was a well argued statement of current Keynesian wisdom about the conditions on which, without incurring the penalties of run-away inflation, the country could avoid the deflationary evils we had failed to avoid in the 1930s. Since 1940 these conditions had been satisfied in a country at war. The White Paper was to set out how they could be satisfied in time of peace – that is to say, without such things as the direction of labour or rationing or rigid import and price controls. Woolton knew that such a paper could not be written by himself but only by collaboration between the best economists and the most experienced administrators available; and he believed there was at least a chance that, if it were convincing enough, the leading Tory and Socialist politicians in the War Cabinet could be persuaded to endorse it before Mr Churchill's coalition government came to an end. And Woolton was right.

When the draft had been approved by the Reconstruction Committee, it had to go to the War Cabinet, and there it could not succeed without the Prime Minister's approval. It seemed most unlikely that Mr Churchill would find time to read it for himself. Neither Woolton's advocacy nor the unanimity of the Reconstruction Committee was likely to make much impression on him. What might make all the difference, for better or worse, was the advice given him by two of his cronies, Lord Beaverbrook and Lord Cherwell. We were therefore at pains to ensure that the officials closest to each of their Lordships understood the White Paper and were as convinced as we could make them of its soundness.

Eventually, when the paper came to the War Cabinet and had been presented by Woolton, Mr Churchill invited discussion, with a word or two from himself by way of introduction. He always attached special importance, he said, in matters such as this to the views of two of his colleagues, the Minister of Aircraft Production (Lord Beaverbrook) and the Paymaster General (Lord Cherwell), and he had noticed that more often than not their opinions differed, sometimes sharply. However, about this paper from the Minister of Reconstruction on a high and stable level of employment their opinions, to judge from the minutes each of them had addressed to him, seemed to be identical: 'Gentlemen, something must be very wrong.' There was virtually no discussion. The paper was approved without amendment and in due course presented to Parliament.*

Another question with which we wrestled long and hopefully, but ultimately with no success, was about planning the use of land. Could owners of land which *increased* in value because its development was judged to be in the public interest be made to pay back part of that increase, as a 'betterment' tax, in order to compensate owners of land of which the value was *reduced* because its development was not thought to be in the public interest? There would clearly be great public advantage if the war-time coalition government could agree on a new Town and Country Planning Act incorporating some method of balancing 'betterment' and 'compensation', in preparation for the burst of rebuilding and redevelopment that would follow the end of the war. Malcolm Trustram Eve, who was then chairman of the War Damage Commission and the leading expert on problems of land value, generously gave us all the help he could, and for some time there was just a chance of our getting ministers to agree. But time ran out. The nearer the war seemed to ending, the harder ministers found it to settle any question with party-political overtones, and in May 1945 the Coalition Government gave place to a short-lived caretaker one without reaching agreement about land.

During the two months of the caretaker government Woolton was Lord President of the Council. There was no longer a Minister

* Cmnd No. 6527 of 1944.

of Reconstruction and the Reconstruction Office became the Lord President's, with myself still at its head. After the 1945 general election Herbert Morrison became Lord President and inherited me with his Office. As he was also leader of the new House of Commons, the first job that I and my colleagues had to do for him was to make a first draft of the King's Speech, in which the legislative programme of the first socialist government to have a majority of seats in the House of Commons would be announced to Parliament. Clearly the speech must include the nationalization of coal, electricity, gas, the railways and the Bank of England. And iron and steel? 'No', said Mr Morrison, pretty firmly.

I had met him in Oxford before the war but only once or twice. On the Saturday after the General Election I paid my first visit to the dentist for six years and several teeth came out. As consciousness returned it occurred to me that I had better telephone the Office and see whether the new Lord President was expected to make his first visit that afternoon. Yes, the answer came, he was. So back I went to our beautiful Great George Street office with its windows looking over the park, wiped the blood from my lips and awaited the new master. Would he want me to stay as head of his Office, or go? I knew he had no high opinion of Woolton. (At the start of one meeting of the Reconstruction Committee, when Woolton began, as he often did, to introduce the subject for discussion with some personal reflections of his own, Morrison had whispered audibly to Oliver Lyttelton 'Call me when prayers are over' and relapsed visibly into private meditation.)

At our first meeting that afternoon Morrison was courteous but no more. Harold Laski had argued forcibly before the war that, when a Labour Government with a proper majority in the House of Commons took office, it would be mad to continue the tradition that heads of Whitehall departments could be trusted to serve Labour as effectively as they had served their previous masters. Would Mr Attlee's Government now follow Laski's advice and appoint to the top civil service jobs people known to be of their party political persuasion? The answer soon became clear. Edward Bridges and Norman Brook continued in office on the commanding heights. Donald Ferguson, temperamentally as conservative a permanent secretary as you could find, was switched from Agriculture to Fuel and Power, where he brilliantly master-minded the nationalization of three fuel industries. Fortunately for all concerned, Laski's advice was totally ignored by Mr Attlee. And for the next three months I stayed as Mr Morrison's chief civil servant.

I never got to know him very well. Once he had dismissed the doubt about me which he must have had that first Saturday afternoon, he treated me as he used to treat his chief officers when leader of the London County Council. He trusted me. He expected me to tell him exactly what I thought about everything we discussed, especially when he disagreed with me, and he knew that I would make the best of whatever he decided, especially when I had originally disagreed with him. It was a highly professional relationship. He never went further than that, and there were barriers that neither of us ever crossed. We never gossiped. We never discussed his colleagues. Still less did he ever talk about himself or his private life. One morning I remember his saying, when I asked whether he was feeling well: 'Never ask a politician that question. A politician is always well, whatever he's feeling.' As a matter of principle, Morrison thought ministers should not become *intimate* with civil servants. He knew there must be mutual understanding and trust between them, but there was a clear distinction between professional business, which they must discuss with complete frankness, and everything outside that area.

Nor did this mean that Morrison was not fun to work with. On ministerial titles, for example, he once said to me: 'I can't think why Rab Butler allowed that splendid title "President of the Board of Education" to be abolished. Lord Privy Seal is another good one. And Lord President of the Council. Yes, we'll keep the titles – but we'll make the buggers *work*.' And that summed up Morrison's determination over a wider field than titles.

Some time before the war ended I had been asked by the head of the Civil Service (Sir Richard Hopkins) whether I would stay on after the war and become an established civil servant. Later, Edward Bridges had suggested that I might become Permanent Secretary of the new Education Ministry established under the 1944 Act, perhaps after a spell as Deputy Secretary. I told him that was a job I could not imagine myself refusing, for education was my first love as a profession and the Civil Service my second.

Maurice Holmes, who had been Butler's Permanent Secretary at Education while the new Act was in gestation, was to retire in 1945. Butler had let Robert Wood, the Deputy Secretary, believe that he would succeed Holmes, and this was common knowledge inside the Ministry. After the general election Ellen Wilkinson became Minister and inherited Holmes as Permanent Secretary. Try as she might, she could not persuade him to postpone retirement. So who should succeed him? What happened next I have never tried to find out. All I know is that Bridges sent for me and asked me to be Holmes's successor; Morrison told me that Miss Wilkinson wanted someone from outside the Ministry to head her department; and when I walked into the Ministry in Belgrave Square it was Robert Wood, the Deputy Secretary, who assured me that I was welcome. None of his colleagues, I believe, would have agreed with him. All of them without exception behaved as if they did. In fact it was a perfect example of the Civil Service behaving as it is supposed to behave. But it was not an easy moment for me or Robert Wood. A year or two later, having done everything he could to teach me my job, he was appointed the first Vice-Chancellor when Southampton achieved full University status, and he proved an unqualified success.

CHAPTER 5

Education, 1945–1952

In 1945, when Ellen Wilkinson became Minister of Education and the only woman in the Cabinet, she knew she was not well but no-one else was allowed to know it. She had been a junior minister in Mr Churchill's Coalition Government but the whole of her pre-war political career 'Red Ellen' had spent fighting on the other side of the barricades. Marching in protest with unemployed workers from Jarrow to London was eminently characteristic of her, but to find herself part of the Government and sharing in collective Cabinet responsibility was a totally new experience. She set herself, with guts that were equally characteristic, to learn a quite new role, and she had made great progress towards learning it by the time, eighteen months later, when she died. But it was an uphill job. Her instinct was always to say what she thought, whether in Cabinet or in public and whether or not the question (say about India) was primarily her business. About the details of her own business as Education Minister she (like her new Permanent Secretary) had everything to learn; but from the start she was passionately determined that all children should have a far better chance of secondary education than she and her generation had had. It was not only, or chiefly, her red hair that made me think apposite what the psalmist had in mind when he wrote: 'He maketh his angels spirits and his ministers a flame of fire.' Nor was it only about children that she passionately cared. She wanted people of all ages to have the opportunity of growing to their full stature as individuals; and that was what she meant when she later declared, to the consternation of those who already thought élitism a dirty word, that she wanted Britain to become a 'Third Programme' nation.

She knew nothing about me when I became Permanent Secretary of her department, except what Herbert Morrison and Maurice Holmes had told her. Her Private Secretary, Antony Part, was a regular civil servant of quite exceptional ability who had joined the Service and the old Board of Education before the war, after a successful Harrow and Cambridge education, and had been recently demobilized after a meteoric army career. He was already a firm and trusted friend both of the Minister and of Robert Wood, and his acquiescence, however reluctant, in the appointment of the new Permanent Secretary played a major part in helping me to settle into the Ministry. As I had found when I became Woolton's Private Secretary five years earlier, a Minister's Private Secretary can do what no-one else can to help Minister and Permanent Secretary to get on valid terms with each other. That is what Antony Part did for Ellen Wilkinson and me; but he also helped both of us to get on terms with the department.

It was an exciting time. Rab Butler and his Labour colleague, Chuter Ede, had got the 1944 Education Act on to the statute book as a measure agreed between all political parties and all religious denominations except the Roman Catholics – and even the Romans had acquiesced in it. So well had the work been done that for the next twenty years or so no party in opposition ever found it necessary to tell the government of the day that on return to power they would reverse an educational decision. Indeed, consensus survived longer still. Although the Labour Governments of 1964 to 1970 did their best to persuade local education authorities to convert the pattern of secondary education from the selective system to the all-ability comprehensive (and abolish the examination of children at 11+ which gave the cleverer ones a chance of grammar school education), it was not until 1976 that an Act was passed (to be repealed in 1979) which deprived local authorities of their freedom and made comprehensive schools compulsory. Except in that one respect the 1944 Act remained virtually intact for thirty-four years. And neither Ellen Wilkinson nor her successor, George Tomlinson, had to bother much about the Opposition.

Where Miss Wilkinson's fighting qualities were needed was inside the Cabinet. Could the country afford to implement the provision in the 1944 Act which required the age at which children could leave school to be raised from fourteen to fifteen not later than in 1947? The bombers had destroyed a large number of schools. No schools had been built since the war began. If the school-leaving age was to be raised in 1947 a substantial slice of building resources would have to go into school-building at the expense of new houses and new factories. The number of teachers would have to be correspondingly increased and scarce resources found for training and paying them.

Ellen realized this was a fight that she must win. If she won it, the Cabinet would have to find for her the precious building resources and money which otherwise would go elsewhere. She would be able to offer training to all the young men and women who were anxious to join the teaching profession and rejuvenate it.

But she realized how much she was asking her colleagues to forego, for the birthrate was showing an unprecedented bulge and this was bound in any case to increase alarmingly the number of school places to be found in years ahead. Immensely to his credit, Nye Bevan came down on her side despite his own departmental interest. So did Mr Attlee – and Ellen Wilkinson had won.

That was the only Cabinet battle she had to fight. From then on, the battle for resources had to be won by daily combat between her officers and those of other departments. Just as the wartime Food Ministry succeeded in getting its share of shipping space by demonstrating to other departments that it asked only for the smallest possible share, so we now had to convince a Cabinet committee of top officials that we were asking for a minimum we really needed. To do this we made some major changes inside our own department and in our relations with local education authorities.

The old Board of Education had had an architects' department which prescribed minimum school building standards with which the local authorities had to conform. This was now not nearly good enough. So we created a new architects and building branch which itself could build a school – and which proved this could be done with a smaller use of building resources than ever before. In this new branch we brought together different kinds of expert: architects, experienced educators, finance officers and industrialists, with an administrative master-minder in the chair. Before the architect started his blueprint, he found out what educational conditions must be satisfied. The industrialist described what kind of school design would give him the best chance of mass producing parts of a school building. Each type of expert worked in partnership with others, and discovered by experiment how all the requirements could best be reconciled at the least cost in time and money.

The consequence was highly satisfactory. The schools were built in time for the compulsory school-leaving age to be raised to fifteen in 1947. And by 1952 the cost of a new school place was actually a smaller figure than it had been in 1945 – perhaps the only product, in the whole range of goods and services, of which this could be said. More important still, British schools built in this period, for all their imperfections, have proved to be *better* schools from an educational point of view than most of those built before the war. Our school building is as good as any school building abroad and compares well with other types of British building.

Chief credit for this achievement must go to local education authorities, and in particular to pioneering county councils such as Hertfordshire or London. But the new Ministry deserves some credit too. In 1948 we stole Stirrat Johnson-Marshall from the Hertfordshire council and made him our own chief architect. He was an artist and an architect of genius. After escaping from the Japanese to India, he there had the war-time experience of designing inflatable 'tanks' and getting them manufactured in large numbers for deception purposes. This in part foreshadowed the new 'Meccano' technique of school building: to design a school consisting of identical parts which the industrialist could mass produce and the builder fit together in ways appropriate to each site. Experience gained in this way enabled the Ministry to build a school for one local authority and lay down cost limits within which all local authorities had to work.

Antony Part left the Minister's Private Office on promotion and became the first administrator in charge of the Ministry's architects and building branch, handing over in due course to another exceptionally talented Civil Servant, David Nenk. When Harry Pilkington later undertook an independent government enquiry into school building, he endorsed enthusiastically the new technique and strongly recommended its use by local and central government for building houses.

Another bit of luck for the Ministry was the appointment in 1944 of Martin Roseveare as head of His Majesty's Inspectorate of Schools (the HMIs). After a brilliant Cambridge undergraduate career as a mathematician he had first become a schoolmaster and then a pre-war HMI. His war service had been in the Food Ministry, where he earned a great reputation as head of rationing. Now as Senior Chief Inspector (SCI) he proceeded to rebuild the Inspectorate. The pace of recruitment was probably too fast but the enthusiasm of Martin and his senior colleagues gave the Ministry a corps of fresh-minded educationists, and this was what we needed at a time when we were faced not only with administrative problems but with fundamental questions of education.

Now for the first time in our history we were committed to providing secondary education for every child. Only since 1870 had we accepted the belief that every child should have *some* education – the elements of reading, writing and arithmetic. In 1902 we had gone a bit further: secondary education should be available for some children – those academically clever enough to

54

profit from a grammar school education, and able to stay at school till they were older than the compulsory leaving age. So in 1945, when the war ended, broadly speaking the only schools in England and Wales were either 'elementary' or 'grammar', the grammar schools consisting either of independent fee-paying schools (most of which were for boarders only) or of day schools maintained by local authorities. Now that the 1944 Act was operative, what kind of secondary education must every child be offered? One kind or more than one?

If the answer were 'one kind', that would mean grammar schools for all. But the Act said that local authorities must make provision for all children according to their 'age, ability and aptitude', and no-one could pretend that academic grammar schools would suit the ability and aptitude of every child.

In 1926 the report of a committee under the chairmanship of Sir Henry Hadow* had recommended a break in every child's school life about the age of eleven, and this had been accepted by the framers of the 1944 Act. School education was therefore to be divided into two stages, primary (in place of elementary) and secondary. The vital question left open by the Act was this: what type or types of secondary education *other* than the grammar school should be provided if children whose ability and aptitude did not fit them for a grammar school were to have the best chance possible of profiting from secondary education?

The Inspectorate's answer to this question was that each local authority should aim at offering a *variety* of secondary schools which would include three types of education: grammar schools for the minority of children (say, ten to fifteen per cent of each age group) best suited to a traditional academic schooling; technical grammar schools for those bright enough for a grammar school but with talent for one of the applied sciences (such as engineering); and secondary modern schools for the rest. Schools of these different types might be grouped together on a single site so that they could share in certain activities. The 'comprehensive' school which could cater for all kinds of children was not ruled out, but the Inspectorate thought that such a school would have to be large enough to take some two thousand pupils if it was to meet the needs of children of both the highest and the lowest intellectual ability without an unjustifiably high ratio of staff to pupils.†

---

* 'Education of the Adolescent', report of the Board of Education's Consultative Committee.

† This was in line with another Report of the Board's Consultative Committee (the Spens Report) published in 1938, 'Secondary Education with special reference to Grammar Schools and Technical High Schools'.

The Act made local authorities, not the Minister, responsible for providing schools, but local authorities were to act 'under the direction and control' of the Minister; in particular, they were to draw up 'development plans' (requiring the Minister's approval) showing how they intended to provide primary and secondary education. The Act, in other words, left open the question of how far educational policy was in practice to be decided on a national basis by the Minister or left for decision by each local education authority. In any case the Minister could not escape a share of ultimate responsibility. Still more important was the obvious fact that under 1945 conditions (an acute shortage of school building capacity, money and manpower) the last word about all local plans must lie with the Minister.

So before local authorities could get to work on either long-term or immediate programmes, the Minister must declare her hand. She did – and approved the circular drafted by the Inspectorate. Local authorities could propose what they liked but they were given a broad hint of what would and what would not get her approval.

In practice every local authority concentrated on its short term problem. How could it contrive to get approval for a building programme that would enable it to cope with a bulging birthrate and a minimum school-leaving age of fifteen? Expand existing primary and grammar schools? Yes, certainly. Convert other existing schools into 'secondary moderns'? Only with great reluctance, for would parents of children who were not offered places in a grammar school (because they did not do well enough in the 11+ examination) believe that their children were being offered a genuine secondary education when the secondary modern school offered to their child occupied an old building that previously housed an elementary school?

The Minister and all of us were committed to securing equality of *status* for all kinds of secondary school. We did everything possible to ensure that local authorities treated their secondary modern and their grammar schools with equal consideration in terms of staffing, buildings and equipment. But 'status' depended inevitably on past history and the subjective judgment of the parents. Until new kinds of school had had time to establish themselves and prove their quality, parents were bound to think them inferior to the grammar school, if only because grammar schools had hitherto been the ne form of secondary education.

Looking back with hindsight, I think the Inspectorate gave the right advice and Ellen Wilkinson was right to accept it. Grammar school education had proved itself. It would have been mad as well as impractical to scrap it in favour of any one alternative. It was right to expand it on a grand scale and make it available to *all* children who had the ability and aptitude to profit from it. But it would have been mad as well as impractical to regard it as the only type of genuine secondary education. There was no sensible alternative to variety. The Minister was right to give the advice she did to local authorities and let each of them work out for themselves the best way forward from the *status quo*.

Their response was of course uneven. But I think it justified the faith placed in local government by the Minister and her successor, George Tomlinson. Still more certainly it justified their refusal to impose one national pattern on primary or secondary education. We simply did not know enough, during the seven years from 1945 to 1952 while I was Permanent Secretary, to justify a Minister's plumping for one single type of secondary education throughout England and Wales. Our Ministers were therefore wise to encourage local experiment, including experiment with various kinds of comprehensive school,* and to go on learning from results. I doubt very much whether even by 1976 we had learnt enough to justify imposing a national plan, and I am convinced that Ellen Wilkinson and George Tomlinson were sensible to do nothing of the kind. Both of them really believed in local self-government and were most reluctant to over-rule the decision of a local authority, whether the majority of its councillors were Socialist or Tory.

The merciful fact was that at this time differences of educational opinion very seldom corresponded to those of party politics and so had a chance of resolution on their merits. Some parents, for example, wished to send their sons to boarding schools; some local councils were prepared to meet their wishes. Almost all the boarding schools were independent schools but many were prepared to offer places. Why should not the department do an 'honest broker' job and bring boarding school and councillors together? Miss Wilkinson said 'certainly', and we worked out a sample scheme. For thirty years or so, Hertfordshire and a few other councils sent boys to Eton, Winchester and other boarding schools – until the 'seventies, when the Labour Government stopped it.

A more important question that Miss Wilkinson had to decide was whether to continue a pre-war practice of making direct grants from the Ministry to schools such as Manchester Grammar

* By 1958 some 50 schools of comprehensive type had been established, in London and other counties.

School. These 'direct grant' schools charged fees to the parents of half their pupils but offered free places, paid for by the local authority, to the other half. Some of them were among the most distinguished in the country and had the great advantage of including in the one school boys and girls from very different kinds of social and economic background. Miss Wilkinson approved the continuance of this system with a revised list of direct grant schools – and here again the practice continued until the 'seventies, when it was abolished by the Labour Government.

But far more important than these questions of educational framework is what happens inside each school; and that of course depends on the teachers and their pupils. Teachers in English and Welsh schools are left remarkably free to teach what they like and how they like. Certainly no syllabus is prescribed by the Ministry. I remember George Tomlinson trying to persuade an official deputation from the Soviet Union who visited the Ministry that this was so. They asked to see the syllabus we prescribed and assumed that we were lying when we said we prescribed none. 'No,' said George, 'we believe in making teachers earn their pay. What they teach is *their* business, not mine.'

But that is not quite the whole story. The examinations for which many pupils sit (and all who wish to go on to further formal education) are organized on a national scale with Ministerial approval. The status of qualified teacher depends also on Ministerial decision. But, at least in my time at the Ministry, it was chiefly through His Majesty's Inspectorate that our influence on what happened in the schools was exercised.

The word 'inspector' always struck me as misleading. It is true that formal inspections of a school were periodically carried out, by a team of HMIs who might spend several days attending classes, talking to staff and then presenting a detailed confidential report to the school governors; and these reports were generally regarded as particularly valuable, both by local authorities and by governors of the independent schools which voluntarily asked for inspection. But more important than these occasional full-scale reports was the informal relationship established between the Inspectorate and the schools whereby the personal experience gained by HMIs since they became inspectors (and normally they had all taught in schools before joining the Inspectorate) was shared with heads and other teachers in the course of frequent casual visits.

Music in schools was one striking example of this influence. After the war Bernard Shore, a distinguished professional player (who had been leader of the violas in the BBC orchestra) was appointed a member of the Inspectorate with chief responsibility for music (alongside other 'staff inspectors' for English, Mathematics and the other main subjects of the curriculum). He and his colleagues were convinced that music ought to be a central part of primary and secondary school life. They became missionaries and spread this gospel up and down the country. They organized short courses for teachers of music and one local authority after another came to share their conviction. Instrumental teaching started to spread from school to school. Saturday morning music classes were organized. County orchestras came into being. Thanks to the genius of Ruth Railton the National Youth Orchestra was founded – and quite soon won international recognition. Indeed, a great many pioneers have been responsible for the development of music-making by young people since the war -- Robert Mayer, Ernest Read, Mary Ibberson of the Rural Music Schools, to mention three of them. But it would not have happened without the gradual spread of instrumental teaching in schools – and that would not have happened without Bernard Shore and his colleagues in the Inspectorate. Their colleagues who had special responsibility for art, drama and the crafts had the same kind of influence on teachers and local authorities.

On the face of it the 1944 Act made no change in the relationship of the State to universities. Since the establishment by H. A. L. Fisher after the First World War of the University Grants Committee (the UGC), it was the Chancellor of the Exchequer not the Education Minister who decided how much of the taxpayers' money should be handed over each year to the universities, and the convention had been established that the Chancellor decided only the total sum and left its distribution to the UGC. This admirable system was untouched by the Act. I think Miss Wilkinson would have liked to take over the Chancellor's function, but Hugh Dalton, then Chancellor, would have stoutly resisted if she had made a serious pass in that direction. As it was, some minor changes were made. As permanent head of the department, I joined the UGC as an assessor, and its pre-war purity was further sullied by the inclusion of some members who were not university dons – a trade unionist, for example, or a businessman or the chief education officer of a local authority.

But one by-product of the 1944 Act transformed the state's relationship to universities. Local authorities were first encouraged, and later compelled, to pay the fees and maintenance (subject to a means test) of all men and women accepted as undergraduates. So higher education became no longer available only to scholarship-winners and the well-to-do, while each university remained free to choose its members.

There was one odd exception to the general rule that the Ministry did not itself provide a single school or college and did not itself appoint or disappoint a single teacher. The Royal College of Art (the RCA) had been founded by royal patronage in Victorian times and had come under the old Board of Education on its establishment in 1899. It was now an integral part of the Ministry, and it was to the Permanent Secretary's room in Belgrave Square that Robin Darwin had come for interview before his appointment in 1946 as the new head of the College.

After a distinguished pre-war period under the leadership of Sir William Rothenstein the College had languished and now seemed in need of a new start. If it was to become a proper college in its own right, the apron-strings attaching it to the Ministry needed to be cut. Thanks to the zest of its new head, the diplomacy of his Chairman of Governors, Colin Anderson, and the near-unanimity of all concerned (including the Treasury), the College received a quite new constitution. The umbilical cord through which public finance had always fed it remained intact. Almost all other strings were cut and the College came into its own. Some years later, when I was no longer a public servant and the College seemed ripe for university status, I was made chairman of a committee to examine its future. Our unanimous report was accepted by the Government and since 1964 the College has been indistinguishable from a university, except that it continues to receive substantial capital and revenue grants, not through the University Grants Committee but direct from the Department of Education.

Unlike the Royal College of Art, the Victoria and Albert Museum (the V and A) is still formally part of the Ministry. When I was Permanent Secretary I would have liked to treat it in much the same way as we had treated the RCA and give it independent status under its own board of trustees. However, its director, Leigh Ashton, was well content with things as they were: an advisory council appointed by the Minister under a sympathetic chairman with whom Ashton got on well, and a Ministry which got on well with him; so we agreed there was no case for sudden change. During my annual appearance before the Public Accounts Committee of the House of Commons, when any MP was free to ask me any question about the billions of pounds spent by the Ministry the previous year, I was more than once asked whether postcards on sale at the V and A could not make larger profits than they did. Such questioning did no-one any harm; but I am now more sure than ever that the V and A should have its own board of trustees (like the National Gallery or the Tate) and no longer be treated as a part of Whitehall bureaucracy.

Other activities which lay outside the main stream of our work enhanced the gaiety of life. One was the Arts Council of Great Britain (ACGB), which received its royal charter in 1946 with Maynard Keynes as its first chairman.

In 1940, for the first time in British history, some taxpayers' money had been spent on a Council for the Encouragement of Music and the Arts (CEMA) when the old Board of Education first made that body a small grant to match one from the Pilgrim Trust. The Council's work throughout the war gave professional artists the chance to show how valuable a contribution they could make to the life of a nation fighting for survival. Concerts were given in air-raid shelters, factories, village halls and gun-sites. Pictures were taken round the country in touring exhibitions. A wide public was delighted, and it was generally agreed, even by the Treasury, that this work must continue after the war and become one of the normal activities of society. A remarkable member of His Majesty's Inspectorate, Mary Glasgow, had been seconded by the Education Ministry as the first secretary of CEMA, and she became the first secretary-general of the new Arts Council. She was an astonishing success in both capacities, but the founding father of the Arts Council was Keynes.

His need to pay visits to the United States on government business (he was up to his eyes negotiating a new economic structure for the post-war world) led him to make me his deputy while he was Chairman of CEMA (and I the head of Woolton's Reconstruction Office). So I was already much involved in the gestation of the Arts Council when I became Permanent Secretary at Education. Keynes was rightly determined that Arts Council funding should not come from the Ministry but direct from the Treasury, and this was generally agreed. Ellen Wilkinson's personal interest was met by agreement that the new Council should have an assessor from her Ministry as well as one from the Treasury. So when CEMA gave place to the Arts Council, I became the Ministry's assessor and was still closely involved in its affairs. (It was not till 1967 that formal responsibility for the government grant to the Arts Council and the appointment of its members passed from the Treasury to Education, with a special Minister responsible for the Arts in charge.)

Some of my colleagues in the Ministry disapproved of my engagement in this extraneous work. But I still think they were wrong. The original Arts Council charter defined its purposes as to develop 'a greater knowledge, understanding and practice of the fine arts exclusively, and in particular to increase the accessibility of the fine arts to the public . . . and to improve the standard of execution of the fine arts, and to advise and co-operate with Our Government Departments, local authorities and other bodies . . ..' So from the start the Council was not concerned with support for the arts as an activity quite separate from education, just as the Act of 1944 was not exclusively concerned with formal education in schools and colleges but embraced the education of adults throughout life. So I think my Minister was right to regard her educational responsibilities as intimately involved with those of the Arts Council, and it was quite logical that when the charter was revised in 1967 it should no longer refer to 'fine arts exclusively' but simply to 'the arts'. Indeed, Keynes had himself written, just before his tragic death in 1946:

"We look forward to a time when the theatre and the concert hall and the gallery will be a living element in everyone's up-bringing, and regular attendance at the theatre and at concerts a part of organized education . . . How satisfactory it would be if different parts of this country would again walk their several ways as they once did and learn to develop something different from their neighbours and characteristic of themselves. Nothing can be more damaging than the excessive prestige of metropolitan standards and fashions."

Thirty years later the Gulbenkian Foundation gave me the chance to review what progress had been made towards fulfilling these Keynesian hopes and to make proposals for joint action by the Arts Council, Regional Arts Associations, local government and the broadcasting authorities.★ But during the ten years from 1942 (when our friendship with Benjamin Britten, Peter Pears and Joan Cross began) my wife and I became closely involved in various ways with artists and the arts. *Peter Grimes* was first produced (at Sadler's Wells) before the war ended; *The Rape of Lucretia* was written for Kathleen Ferrier and produced soon afterwards at Glyndebourne thanks to the generosity of John Christie (who had taught me chemistry at Eton but could not get on with Keynes). Quite apart from his musicianship, Ben Britten was a widely-read man of sparkling personality who had a genius for friendship, especially with children. He would turn up at our house in

★ *Support for the Arts in England and Wales*, Gulbenkian Foundation, 1976.

62

Regent's Park in his open touring car, hair flying in the wind, sweep up our family (then aged twelve, seven and three), sit them down on the folded hood at the back and go scorching round the Outer Circle – to their delight and their mother's consternation. (Later he dedicated to our children *The Young Person's Guide to the Orchestra*.)

The idea of holding an Edinburgh Festival in 1947 was ill received by doubters, both in the Arts Council and in the city of Edinburgh. Though the doubters included Keynes (but no assessor to the Arts Council) they were converted just in time and the result was a triumph. There were flags on the trams and great tubs of flowers in Princes Street; Schnabel, Szigeti, Primrose and Fournier played in the Usher Hall; Kathleen Ferrier and Peter Pears sang Mahler with the Vienna Philharmonic; Bruno Walter and Lotte Lehmann gave a Schubert recital; Glyndebourne Opera, the Old Vic Theatre Company and Sadler's Wells Ballet all performed. The Christies, Rudolf Bing and the Lord Provost of Edinburgh were proved right after all. We shall never forget it.

If some colleagues thought the Arts Council took too much of my time, almost all of them thought Unesco (the United Nations Educational, Scientific and Cultural Organization) took far too much. After the fall of France in 1940, exiled European politicians had found their way to London; and those who had previously been ministers of education had come together, at Rab Butler's invitation, to discuss what should be done after the war. They agreed that some parts of education called for action on an international scale. An international body must be set up by national governments, with a much broader scope and purpose than the Committee of the League of Nations for Intellectual Co-operation had ever had. Alfred Zimmern had in due course been made secretary-general of a preparatory commission charged with the bringing of such an organization into existence.

By the end of the war Zimmern was too sick a man to get this job completed in time for a Paris conference which was to convene in 1946, and a substitute had to be found. Julian Huxley seemed the likeliest candidate, and he has well described an uproarious occasion when Ellen Wilkinson entertained him and me to dinner in the House of Commons. We persuaded him to succeed Zimmern, and there was soon a momentous consequence: 'science' was added to 'education' in the title of the proposed body. By the time the Paris conference assembled, 'culture' had been added too, embracing all the media of communication, and a constitution had been drafted for UNESCO – a specialized agency of the United Nations Organization, alongside the Food

63

and Agriculture Organization (FAO) to which by now the Hot Springs conference of 1943 had given birth.

Considering that Rab Butler had taken the initiative in the pre-natal stages, it was not surprising that the Minister of Education rather than the Foreign Secretary should become the member of the Cabinet responsible in Britain for Unesco. And I think it was right. What was wrong was the light-hearted indifference of the Foreign Office to the fortunes of Unesco and the other specialized agencies (FAO, the International Labour Organization and the World Health Organization), which were all in turn farmed out to home departments. Thanks to the personal intervention of Miss Wilkinson, we secured the outright transfer to the Ministry of Richard Cowell, an uncharacteristic but admirable member of the Foreign Office who had started official life in the Stationery Office, worked during the war with General de Gaulle and from now onwards did more than anyone in Britain for Unesco. But this transfer was almost the only help the Foreign Office gave us. Their representative came to the inter-departmental meetings at which the brief for the United Kingdom delegation to each Unesco conference was settled; but each time it was the Treasury that managed to insist that our one goal should be reduction of the budget.

France and the United States, on the other hand, took Unesco seriously. France, for example, at the first full conference made a successful bid for Paris as Unesco headquarters, but on the clear understanding that this made it unlikely that France would ever provide the director-general. In 1962, however, René Maheu, one of the ablest Frenchmen in the secretariat, became Director-General and retained the office for more than ten years.

I could not understand this attitude of Foreign Office indifference at the time, but the explanation now seems fairly simple. From July 1945 till March 1951 Bevin was Foreign Secretary – with Potsdam, nuclear warfare, the ending of lend-lease, devastated Europe, Palestine, Malaya and the cold war on his plate. No wonder he had no time to bother much about Unesco. But one of his chief Foreign Office advisers might have made time to bother – about the general question of whether our post-war foreign policy should take some account of the new post-war international agencies (of which Unesco was of course only one). Was it in Britain's interest to make some use of them as instruments of a coherent British foreign policy? If so, how could this best be done?

During the six years from 1945 to 1952 I spent much time and tissue on Unesco business – in Paris, Mexico City, Beirut, Cairo,

Cleveland (Ohio), Florence and London. But at no time did I see evidence of leadership, or even guidance, from the Foreign Office. Each UK delegation was left to do what it could with a brief totally lacking positive direction. The British Council, through Ronald Adam its chairman and Nancy Parkinson, did a great deal to make up for this. So did the Colonial Office, especially through Christopher Cox (my Greats tutor at New College, who has done more than any other living Englishman for education in the new Commonwealth countries). So did the Royal Society, through Patrick Blackett, Robert Robinson and Lord Adrian. The Foreign and Commonwealth Office will, I hope, one day 'purge its contempt'.

As for the attitude of the United States, Francis Biddle, a lawyer who had deserved well of his country at the post-war trial of war criminals at Nuremberg, on his return to Washington was asked by President Truman what post he would next like to have. He suggested the US Embassy in Paris. The President gladly accepted the suggestion and passed it to Dean Acheson, the Secretary of State. When Dean reminded Truman that the present Ambassador in Paris had just been confirmed in office for another term, it was suggested that Mr Biddle might care to go to Paris as the first Director-General of Unesco – an appointment that was shortly to be made. Mr Biddle gladly fell in with this idea, and the US delegation left for the first Unesco conference in Paris with appropriate instructions in their brief. When their leader, William Benton, urged me to back Biddle, I had to tell him we could not.

Huxley was not only a distinguished scientist and man of letters but for the last year, as head of the preparatory commission, he had worked with total dedication to the Unesco idea. My government thought him the best man to launch the ship he had done much to design and had told us to propose him as Unesco's first Director-General.

This question took more of my time than any other at the Paris conference. (At one point Benton offered to drop Biddle, but only if he could propose me as the US candidate.) A compromise was finally agreed by all concerned. Huxley became the first Director-General – but for two years only, not for the five years mentioned in the first Constitution.

I shall have more to say about Unesco in Chapter 10.

CHAPTER 6

Power, 1952–1958

By 1952 it was high time I left the Education Ministry. I had immensely enjoyed my seven years as Permanent Secretary. We had made a smooth transition from Labour to Conservative political control, with no serious loss in continuity. Whatever cutbacks the Treasury might ask for, with Rab Butler as Chancellor of the Exchequer it seemed unlikely that the strategy of the 1944 Act would be scrapped. In any case it was time for the Department to have a different kind of Civil Service head (who made fewer speeches and was less often outside his office). Gilbert Flemming (my deputy) was just the man they needed, and that was precisely what he proved to be. But I had made some close friends since 1945, inside and outside the Department, and I hated leaving them. No parting present was more unexpected and delightful than that which the National Union of Teachers asked me to accept from the hand (and perhaps at the suggestion) of Ronald Gould, their General Secretary: fifteen volumes of Proust's *A la Recherche du Temps Perdu* and Scott Moncrieff's magical translation.

My move was to the Ministry of Fuel and Power. Years later I discovered that it might have been to Housing and Local Government – a near-miss that was most fortunate for English local government as it paved the way, one stage later, for that permanent secretaryship to pass into the hands of Evelyn Sharp. The near-miss was also fortunate for me, and I enjoyed my six years in Fuel and Power as much as any six years of my life.

This change of departments was just what my friend Lord Balogh would find, in terms of the public interest, most deplorable. Here was a 'generalist', innocent of all knowledge of science or technology, made head of a department which was the focus of the state's interest in coal, electricity, gas and oil. The timing of the appointment made it, if possible, still more laughable: it took effect just after the British Petroleum company's Iranian assets had been nationalized by the Iranian government. Within a week of starting my new job I therefore found myself giving lunch at the Savile to Paul Nitze, an able and most attractive American, sent by his government to persuade us that the Chairman of Anglo-Iranian (Willie Fraser, later Lord Strathalmond) must be made to co-operate with the major American oil companies in forming a new consortium through which Iranian oil could again start to flow.

My prospects of proving anything but a flop in Fuel and Power were certainly poor, but the appointment was not as crazy as it seemed. My Minister, Geoffrey Lloyd, was an able and experienced politician who had spent the war as Chairman of the Oil Control Board and in charge of the Petroleum Warfare Department and he needed no permanent secretary to advise him on oil. But he was now the first Tory minister to be responsible for making the best of three nationalized industries, and there were two facts which made this formidable task no easier. First, he had to work under an overlord. In 1951 Churchill had put his old wartime colleague Lord Leathers in general charge of all nationalized industries – and no-one knew what that was intended to mean. And, secondly, the Tory backbench then included more than one MP who thought himself more expert than the Minister. Gerald Nabarro and Colonel Lancaster headed a group of well-informed Fuel Furies who unmercifully harassed Geoffrey Lloyd. For four years of the preceding Labour government Alf Robens had been the Department's Parliamentary Secretary and he was later to chair the Coal Board for ten years. Meanwhile, as the Opposition's leader on fuel, he was well placed to put the Government on the spot.

So the political context of my new work was in startling contrast to that of my seven years in education. The substance of it was complex and fascinating. What should be Britain's short- and long-term fuel policy in 1952 and what were the best ways to make it effective? This was the first time that a Tory government had had anything like this question to answer. Nationalization of three fuel industries, with oil still in the private sector and nuclear energy in the offing, had given the Government responsibilities that no pre-war government had had. It was Geoffrey Lloyd's job to find the answer to quite new questions and my job to help him get the answers right. We had to do our best to predict the future growth of demand and ensure supplies to meet it as it grew. As for demand, Reggie Maudling's comment on its unpredictability well sums up our problem. In 1957 he made a great speech in the Commons about the future pattern of our energy consumption, based on the best estimates we could obtain for him from public and private sources. 'It created a considerable impression,' he writes in his *Memoirs*, 'as I was able to go into very detailed estimates of future consumption trends in a fairly lengthy speech, made, as was my custom then, without any use of notes. The only trouble was that all the figures I gave turned out in the event to be wrong. It was a salutary lesson on the dangers of economic forecasting, but it was also a lesson that private enterprise, in the shape of the great oil companies, could be just as far out in their predictions as Government Departments. We had been warned that there was a threat of a severe shortage of tankers in a few years' time . . . but when the plans came to fruition, the whole market position had changed and we virtually had tankers running out of our ears.'★

So, granted that estimates of future fuel demand were quite unreliable, we had to concentrate our efforts on supply, and here momentous choices had to be made.

Coal was our one traditional indigenous source of power and, until other reliable sources could be found, the Coal Board (and effectively the miners) had a powerful monopoly position to exploit. The productivity of miners could be greatly increased by mechanization, and for this purpose the Coal Board must borrow on a big scale. So interest charges, as well as wages, would go on growing. To pay them, should the price of coal be allowed to rise or should the Coal Board's annual deficit increase?

Another day in my first week at the Ministry was spent with Lord Leathers and the chairman of the Coal Board. The agenda was the industry's draft investment programme for the next five years. Would the Government back it? Would it ask Parliament to increase the borrowing powers that in consequence the Board would have to use? Lord Leathers wanted all the coal the miners could win for us and only the Board could say how that was to be done. So the programme was approved, the price of coal went up and the Board's account sank deeper in the red.

What I learnt from experience during my first week at the Ministry was strongly confirmed over the next six years. Government must stand at arm's length from nationalized industries and trust the Boards to do the best they can. The appointment and disappointment of Board members was therefore central to the Minister's success. This depended on ministerial judgment, but the Minister must have disinterested advice. So I must find time to know a lot of people and let them learn to trust in my good faith. Above all, I must know my Minister and he must have some

★ Reginald Maudling's *Memoirs*, p. 66. Sidgwick & Jackson, 1978.

68

confidence in me. Here I was lucky. I became close friends with each successive master – Geoffrey Lloyd till December 1955, Aubrey Jones till January 1957, then Percy Mills and Reggie Maudling till the end of 1958 – and their friendship lasted longer than their reign. Each of them was very different from the others and we disagreed in many different ways. But they all shared with me what they were really thinking; they all assumed I would stand up to them and fight – and then make the best of what they decided.

What could we do when we thought change was needed, in a Board's membership or policy or shape? How could we, consistently with the principle that we must stay at arm's length from a nationalized industry, check that we were right to want a change? Our answer was an enquiry by outsiders. In 1953 Geoffrey Lloyd appointed a powerful small group of businessmen, with Lord Fleck as Chairman, to study the Coal Board and make recommendations, and next year a similar body, with Edwin Herbert as Chairman, to study the electricity industry. As neither industry had been so examined since nationalization, neither could reasonably complain and in both cases major changes ensued. The Fleck Committee confirmed our view that the Coal Board was top-heavy and should devolve central powers to regional coalfield authorities. It also confirmed our fear that it was time for a new Chairman of the Board, and this followed a year after the Fleck report. The Herbert Report of 1955, like the Fleck Committee, recommended that the functions of the monolithic Central Electricity Authority should be divided between a new Generating Board and a new Electricity Council, and new legislation was passed for this purpose.

But how could our sources of energy supply be multiplied and the grip of the coal monopoly relaxed? In 1952 our electricity came exclusively from coal-fired generating stations, save for the Scottish hydro-electricity supply. We did our best to bring oil companies and the industry together but except for Esso they were not prepared to play. Nuclear power was the one exciting possibility. Christopher Hinton, as Managing Director of the Atomic Energy Authority's industrial group, was convinced that production costs would shortly be reduced. He saw relevance in the history of early steam engines, and we were all eager to believe that he was right. Accordingly in 1957 he became Chairman of the new Central Electricity Generating Board. Here seemed to be a marvellous pioneering chance for Britain, not only for our benefit but for the world's. But in his new office Hinton was naturally more cautious. The analogy with Stephenson's steam engine was now dropped. Private enterprise found tendering expensive.

Mergers were formed. Contracts for some nuclear power stations were signed by the Generating Board. But problems of engineering, cost and safety still persisted and competition for foreign contracts was intense.

Before my time at the Ministry was over, I had been bold enough to lecture in Rome and Milan about the reasons why Britain was feeding into the grid from nuclear stations a substantial part of its electricity supplies (and why Italians would be wise to buy stations from us – they did buy one). Before that escapade I had been to Harwell. There John Cockcroft had lucidly expounded how near we were to using *fusion*, instead of *fission*, for peaceful purposes, and yet how far from a final breakthrough we might be. I never mentioned fusion in my lectures. More than twenty years have passed – and no breakthrough. But the scale of the research is now European and the Community has chosen Culham as its home. There German, French and British scientists are in joint action (with their children in a new European school). If they succeed in the controlled release of energy on the scale of that released by an H bomb, we and the world will still have energy problems but they will not be what we ever had before.

In 1952 we did not foresee that four years later Nasser would nationalize the Suez Canal. Still less did we (or the oil companies) foresee that the oil-producing countries would, twenty-one years later, concert action and quadruple the price we had to pay for oil. But though the oil companies and geologists assured us that no oil or natural gas was within reach, we and the Gas Council declined to believe them and prospecting was vigorously pursued. Gas remained the Cinderella fuel but persisted, in total dependence on supplies of coking coal. However, she was excellently managed; the previous government, after gas nationalization, had recruited to the new Boards most of the ablest private enterprisers. All the Gas Boards competed with electricity for industrial and domestic customers, but each of them also rivalled the others for success (in terms of lower prices, cost efficiency and growth). For most purposes each board was its own master, and all chairmen were members of the Gas Council; but this Council had its own chairman and deputy-chairman. The Minister was bound to rely on their advice and it was with them that I was constantly in touch.

The future of the gas industry was still precarious when in 1958 my time was up. But its leaders were courageously determined to experiment. In particular, they found that Americans were freezing liquid methane and floating it in balsa-wood barges down the Mississippi to Chicago. Why not do the same from North Africa to London? The North Thames Gas Board, under Michael Milne-Watson's chairmanship, was anxious to try; the gas industry was determined that he should.

The Department was now the Ministry of Power, for in 1957 Mr Macmillan had done us very proud. He had made his old friend Lord Mills our minister, put Maudling in the Cabinet as well, made us responsible for developing nuclear power, and rechristened us to underline the change.* Alas, Lord Mills was far from keen on frozen methane and his scepticism yielded only to prolonged concerted pressure from his permanent secretary and the gas industry. The experiment was a success, but it was soon overtaken by one of a quite different order of importance. No sooner was the Ministry quit of me than the prospects of the gas and oil industries began to be transformed by discoveries of North Sea gas and oil under the ocean round our coast.

No such possibility had ever been mentioned to me during my six years at the Department, either by oil companies, my chief scientific advisers or any other Whitehall colleague. The urgent need to lessen our dependence on coal and imported oil was never in doubt, especially after the closure of the Suez Canal in 1956. Serious attention was therefore rightly given to the Athabasca shale-oil deposits in Canada, the underground gasification of coal and the South African experiments in converting coal to oil. If anyone had suggested that Britain could ever become a large-scale oil exporter, the idea would have been brushed aside as fantasy. Nuclear power seemed the only long-term hope.

Despite the North Sea miracle that followed (and the crop of quite new problems that it brought), in 1970 Mr Heath, the new Prime Minister, decided that the Ministry of Power should be scrapped. It was absorbed into an enormous new department which embraced all trade and industry. But not for long. Three years later, when the price of oil quadrupled, the Ministry of Power was resurrected, under the thin disguise of yet another name.

What nonsense. The new Trade and Industry Department (like the new Environment Department of the same conception date) was probably too ambitious a concept. But once it had been born (and given as great an administrator as Antony Part to make sense of it), it should have been given a longer innings than three years.

* 'Minfupo' was a telegraphic address which I was sad to lose. But our old name was associated with shortages and our old motto was no longer up to date: 'You can fuel all of the people some of the time and you can fuel some of the people all of the time; but you can't fuel all of the people all of the time.' Our new name suggested Cranmer rather than Abraham Lincoln: 'Lord of all power and might, who art the author and giver of all good things.'

Machinery of government was never given the attention it deserved during my time in Whitehall. The Treasury was then responsible but seemed to regard it as beyond their control and something bound to depend in practice on the Prime Minister of the day. Of course a Prime Minister must always have the last word about it. He or she appoints (and disappoints) all members of the Cabinet and in doing so must match the leading politicians in the party to work that reflects the ambition and status of each individual. But it has always seemed to me that a Prime Minister should have advice (whether he chooses to take or disregard it) based on a continuous study of the question of how far the existing pattern of departments matches (or mis-matches) the present and prospective work of Whitehall. I know that Mr Heath and his future colleagues had rightly given much thought to this problem while they were still in opposition and, for all I know, it may nowadays be true that a new government gets all the expert advice it needs about machinery. But I think that in my time that was not so. The advocates of a particular policy (say, planning of land use, or aid for developing countries, or help for the arts) will always press for a new minister, with his or her own department and a seat in the Cabinet. The consequence of such pressure in the past has seldom served its purpose, still less has it solved the general problem of machinery. Yet two post-war reform achievements point the way: one state department, instead of three, to control defence; one Foreign and Commonwealth Office for our relations with the outside world. Both involved overcoming powerful objections, especially from the services concerned. Neither would have occurred without planning and patience and strong personal leadership.

As for the future, let no-one kid himself. Until politicians and bureaucrats stop their mutual bitchiness, ask the right questions about openness and confidentiality in democratic government and together try to find realistic answers, Whitehall and Westminster will not adapt themselves to match the changing problems of home and European government. These problems are bound to become more serious as new efforts are made to recognize the compelling need of collaboration across national frontiers and the new part that governments must play. There is a lot to be said for the traditional British sport of baiting bureaucrats, especially when practised by the intelligent professionals of Fleet Street. But politicians cannot afford to be bloody-minded: they cannot do without the experience, goodwill and integrity of the professional civil service. Meanwhile there is everything to be said for the publication of 'green papers' and discussion documents before decisions are taken by Government, for the new use of Select Committees by Parliament, and for the development of the Royal Institute of Public Administration (whose membership includes not only central and local government but the nationalized industries) as a means of discussing the real problems of government.

CHAPTER 7

South Africa, 1959–1963

During our six-month honeymoon in Africa at the expense of Cecil Rhodes in 1932, Jean and I had travelled by ship, rail, road, river-steamer, donkey or seaplane from Cape Town to Alexandria, visiting on our way Rhodesia, the Belgian Congo, Tanganyika, Kenya, Uganda and the Sudan. I had twice been back to Johannesburg since then. I had lectured there in 1936 to celebrate the city's fiftieth birthday* and written a book about her municipal history.† I had also become marginally involved in the one-year pre-service training which the Colonial Office organized, with the Universities of Oxford, Cambridge and London, for young graduates chosen for service as Colonial administrators. But I had not set foot in Africa for twenty-three years when on 1 January 1959 Jean and I set sail from Southampton in the *Pendennis Castle* on her maiden voyage to Cape Town. The Commonwealth Office had not remembered either to buy our rail tickets from Waterloo or, as I discovered later, to give me the official document which a new High Commissioner had to present to the South African Prime Minister on taking up his post. Neither omission proved fatal. In the mail ship was waiting for us a sumptuous suite, overflowing with flowers and telegrams, and rather larger than the tourist-class cabin which had housed our honeymoon in 1932.

By the time we reached Cape Town we had taken our first faltering steps in learning Afrikaans (whenever Afrikaners were in a South African audience, I made myself speak a few sentences of Afrikaans), I had composed an Ode for presentation to the Captain (whose CBE had figured in the New Year Honours) and we had enormously enjoyed a fortnight's holiday. In Cape Town harbour we found waiting for us Ronnie Belcher, who had been

---

* Published, in English and Afrikaans, *Johannesburg and the Art of Self-Government*, 1937.
† *City Government: the Johannesburg Experiment*, OUP, 1938.

acting High Commissioner since Percivale Liesching left some months before; Peter Bridges, who had been Liesching's private secretary and, for a few days only, was now mine; the Lady Mayor of Cape Town, Joyce Newton Thompson, who was to become one of our dearest friends; the Anglican Archbishop of Cape Town, Joost de Blank, resplendent in a purple cassock; and a friendly crowd of reporters. Eventually we were driven to High Commission House in a Rolls flying the Union Jack, by a Zulu, Vincent Xabu, the first and last chauffeur I could call my own (and a friend for life).

Into a morning coat, built years ago for an ancestor, and down to a drawing-room full of my new colleagues. There I was sworn in as High Commissioner for Basutoland, the Bechuanaland Protectorate and Swaziland – one of the two posts that I was now to fill. The Resident Commissioners of the three Territories (who were my deputies and in effect the local Governors) had come to Cape Town for the ceremony. They and their wives, Tom Scrivenor (my chief 'Territories' colleague at headquarters), Belcher (my chief colleague on the ambassadorial side) and other senior staff from both sides of the establishment, now mingled indistinguishably over the food and drink. After the swearing-in I made a speech, prepared with some care beforehand, without use of notes (and swore secretly to follow the note-less precedent in future); the sun shone, and the impression left on us by almost all our guests was reassuring. When they left, late in the afternoon, we made the private secretary stay for a comprehensive gossip while we explored with delight the house and the large garden, blue with agapanthus and hydrangea.

As a completely inexperienced governor and diplomat, I was most fortunate in my two tutors, Tom Scrivenor and Ronnie Belcher. Tom had been Deputy High Commissioner for the Territories since 1953, after service in the Colonial Office as well as in Tanganyika, Palestine, Malta and Nigeria. He made the best of me from the start and we became friends. (The same was true of two other 'Territory' colleagues in my office: Robin Latimer, who succeeded Tom on his retirement in 1960, and John Steward, who was a tower of strength in any post.) Ronnie Belcher had had years of experience, first (like Robin Latimer) in the Indian Civil Service, then in the Commonwealth Relations Office before coming to South Africa in 1956 as Deputy High Commissioner on the diplomatic side. He was a marvellous tutor – in the same class as my Greats tutors at Oxford – and he coached me, with firmness and unfailing tact but no trace of condescension, through those first weeks in office when I had everything to learn. But his

75

time in South Africa was nearly finished and he was due back in London once I was installed. Who should succeed him had been agreed while I was still in England, but one morning soon after my arrival in Cape Town Belcher came in with a new job for me to learn: a 'DU' cable from London, which means 'Decipher Yourself'. Down to the cipher room we went and I was painfully instructed. But once de-coded, the message was all too plain: Belcher's successor was no longer available – would I have Jack Johnston instead? At first glance it seemed a ludicrous suggestion. This man was no more a diplomat than I was and had served most of his time in the Colonial Office. Surely he was not the man for me? Belcher was not so sure. Two Colonial Secretaries (Lyttelton and Lennox-Boyd) had each had Johnston as their Principal Private Secretary and had thought him outstanding. I most reluctantly decided to accept him and despatched a sulky telegram of thanks.

But soon afterwards my sulkiness was banished: Oliver Lyttelton wrote and told me what he thought. And by the time Jack Johnston had reached Cape Town and had lunched with us, I began to see what Lyttelton had meant. Jack was a bachelor and in his early forties, pleasantly plump and immaculately dressed – intelligent, warm-hearted, humorous, articulate. I knew at once that he would always be a friend, but I did not foresee that here was the new kind of diplomat that the new Commonwealth would desperately need.* Still less did I foresee that ten years later one of my favourite nieces would become his wife. Meanwhile I had him as my chief diplomatic colleague for two memorable years.

A few days later the diplomatic half of my job started: I had my first meeting with the Prime Minister, Dr Verwoerd. Belcher was horrified that I had no letter of credentials from the Secretary of State to take with me, but Verwoerd accepted my apologies without demur and I sat peacefully through an unembarrassing long lecture in his faultless English. There was nothing memorable in what he said but I was left with an impression of the man that was confirmed each time I met him later. There was an oleaginous tone in his voice which only disappeared when he was angry – and during this first interview he was uniformly smooth. When he spoke of the Bantu (as he always called black South Africans) his voice took on a slightly soapy tone, suggesting the avuncular concern of a trustee for these primitive children. On the

* Sir John Johnston was British High Commissioner in Sierra Leone 1961–3, the Federation of Rhodesia and Nyasaland 1963, Rhodesia 1964–5, Malaysia 1971–6 and Canada 1976–8.

other hand, he left me in no doubt that here was a formidable politician, with the mind of a highly intelligent and articulate don. Over the next four and a half years I got to know several members of his Cabinet, and some of them were men of what Whitehall would call 'Cabinet calibre', but Verwoerd towered head and shoulders over them all. He had not been Prime Minister more than a year but he already dominated the Cabinet and Parliament, and by the end of 1959 – the year when South Africa celebrated the Golden Jubilee of Union – Verwoerd was the unquestioned chieftain of the white tribe of Afrikanerdom.

He had worked out a cruelly clear blueprint of the future. There must be no concession to 'liberalist' ideas of a multi-racial society: the whole of South Africa was white man's country. The white man had arrived from the south at the same time as Bantu tribes were migrating from the north: it was historically erroneous, he believed, to think of blacks as the 'natives' of South Africa. Nor could anyone deny that the modern Union had been made the one highly developed, and the one 'civilized', part of Africa by the white man's initiative, capital, technology and political skill.

There could be no question of modern South Africa being *governed* by anyone but white men, and this must be made once and for all plain to the non-white. Any departure from this rule would be followed by the demand for further exceptions ('give him an inch, man, and he'll take an ell'). That was why all exceptions made in the past must be withdrawn: why, for example, the vote unfortunately given in the Cape Province in time past to coloured people (of mixed white and black descent) must be abolished in the next session of Parliament.

But white trustees must be just to these non-white children: they must ensure their separate development in certain parts of the Union. Hence the government plan for Bantu 'homelands'. Some thirteen per cent of the land surface of the Union (most of which for many years had been reserved by law for occupation by the blacks) was to be permanently set aside for various Bantu tribes. The Transkei, for example, containing some of the best agricultural land, would become the home of the Xosa, Kwazulu the home of the Zulus, and so on. In these homelands the Bantu would have political rights and, as soon as they wished, become 'self-governing'. Meanwhile they must be given their own universities: Parliament would this session be asked to pass legislation for this purpose – and all existing universities must of course in future be confined to whites.*

* Characteristically this law was entitled 'The Universities Extension Act'.

One asked (and I remember Harold Macmillan asking in 1960), what would be the position of the Bantu in that eighty-seven per cent of the Union which was reserved for the three million whites? A majority of the eleven million Bantu in the Union would presumably go on living in 'white' South Africa, and their labour would continue to be indispensable. Verwoerd's answer was firm and clear: 'Like Italians working as miners outside Italy, they will have no political rights outside the homelands; their position will be that of *honoured guests.*'

And would there be homelands for the Cape coloured and the Asiatics in Natal? 'No,' was the answer; 'that has still to be worked out.' But that was the only question to which Verwoerd had no answer. About all forms of sport, for example, he was emphatic that there could be no compromise: the simple principle must be applied that people of different colour should not mix but develop separately, and other countries must recognize South Africa's right to decide that question for herself. It was in the interest of all races that members of each race should keep themselves at all points to themselves. Hence the need for all South Africans to have their racial status fixed and defined by law. Hence too the need for separate entrances to the post offices and libraries for whites and non-whites, separate benches in the parks, separate lavatories and places of entertainment, separate parts of bus and train, separate beaches to bathe from and separate parts of the town in which to live. There must be no sleeping in one bed, and of course no inter-marriage.

Separation in economic life was admittedly more difficult: but here too the clearer the demarcation between whites and non-whites the better. Shops must be allowed to make money from all-comers, but non-whites must not compete with whites for jobs. And there was Old Testament authority for job-reservation: the dark-skinned sons of Ham had always been the hewers of wood and drawers of water. No doubt all were equal in God's sight but that was no reason why the work of all should be the same. In the homelands the Bantu should in due course have an exclusive right to decide who was to do what, and in the rest of South Africa white men should have the same exclusive freedom. Meanwhile, in 'white' South Africa the honoured Bantu guests should be free to do all domestic work (though Dr Verwoerd himself would have no-one but whites to black his shoes or those of his guests in the Prime Minister's house) and all work in mines, industries and shops that was not reserved for whites. But they must not be allowed to strike or to join the same trade union as the whites.

78

In 1909, fifty years before my arrival as High Commissioner, the British Parliament had created the Union of South Africa out of four parts: two British colonies (the Cape and Natal) and two Boer Republics (Transvaal and Orange Free State), which had been at war from 1899 to 1902. But German South West Africa* and three other parts of Southern Africa had remained outside the frontiers of the Union. Basutoland, the Bechuanaland Protectorate and Swaziland were still recognized as British High Commission Territories for which the British Government was responsible to the British Parliament.

But that was not the whole story. All three High Commission Territories formed part of a Customs Union with South Africa and shared with her a single currency. Bechuanaland, about the combined size of France and West Germany but largely consisting of Kalahari desert, with a population of some 600,000 and no exports but cattle, had no outlet but a single-track railway which ran down its eastern side between the Union and Rhodesia; and its capital, at Mafeking, was actually inside the Union. Swaziland, about the size of Wales, was land-locked between the Union and Portuguese East Africa and at that time had no railway. Basutoland, about the size of Belgium, mainly mountainous and with a population of nearly a million, was an island wholly surrounded by the Union, and its economy depended on the recruitment of its young men as wage-earners in the Transvaal mines.

No wonder, therefore, that the 1909 Act establishing the Union included a schedule which set out the procedure to be followed when the time came for the British Government to hand over the three High Commission Territories for incorporation in the Union. No wonder, either, that successive Union governments had assumed that the only question was *when* the transfer would take place, and had pressed, with varying degrees of urgency, for an early date. But for the Territories themselves the gravest consequence was that successive British governments did *not* regard them as a long-term British responsibility. So in 1959 it was not the Colonial Secretary but the Commonwealth Secretary

---

* After the First World War, what had been German South West had been accepted by the Union Government as a mandated territory under the League of Nations. It was treated for all administrative purposes as part of the Union, with white representatives (elected by white voters) sitting in the Union Parliament. The South African Government has always claimed that the mandate lapsed when the League was replaced by the United Nations Organization after the Second World War, but the International Court of Justice at the Hague has not accepted that claim. The status of Namibia (as the area is now generally called) continues in 1980 to be a subject of dispute between the South African Government and the United Nations.

to whom I was responsible as High Commissioner for the Territories; and for most of the previous fifty years the Colonial Office had not even been responsible for recruiting their administrative staff. No British government was anxious to spend taxpayers' money on territories that the Union would inherit; so they had consistently been governed on the cheap. We had promised them, in 1935, that they would not be transferred 'without consultation'; we had *not* promised 'no transfer without consent'.

In the general election of 1948 the South African Party under General Smuts (which in 1939 had brought the Union into the war on our side, against the wishes of the Nationalist Party) was narrowly defeated and the Nationalists (under Malan) became the Government. The Nationalists increased their majority at the next two general elections and, as Nationalist racial policy took clearer shape, it became increasingly doubtful whether British public opinion would ever stand for a transfer of the Territories against their will – and increasingly clear that the Territories would vigorously oppose it. However, no-one could deny that their economic future was largely dependent on the good will of South Africa.

In 1948, therefore, an acute crisis arose in Bechuanaland when Seretse Khama, heir apparent to the chieftainship of the Bamangwato, far the most powerful of the eight tribes in the Territory, married a white Englishwoman, Ruth Williams. Evelyn Baring, who was British High Commissioner at the time, and the Labour Government in London, were faced with an agonizing question. What Seretse had done was an outrage in South African eyes, and if the British Government nevertheless allowed him to succeed to the chieftainship, there might be most damaging consequences for Bechuanaland. Despite a long-delayed decision by the Bamangwato tribe that they wanted Seretse as their chief, the Labour Government eventually took Baring's advice and banished Seretse from Bechuanaland.* By 1959, when I arrived, the British Government had allowed Seretse and Ruth back three years before as private citizens, Seretse having meanwhile renounced the chieftainship. Refusing to waste time on resentment, he set himself to help forge a constitution which would be acceptable to the British Government and to the black and white citizens of the Protectorate. Most fortunately he found in Peter Fawcus, who became Resident Commissioner in 1959 (after five years as Government Secretary), a man of genius whom he could trust and who trusted him. The joint effort of the two men was irresistible

* See *Evelyn Baring* by Charles Douglas-Home, Collins, 1978.

and, when I left South Africa, Peter became Her Majesty's Commissioner, with responsibility to the Secretary of State.

In 1966, when Bechuanaland became Botswana as an independent sovereign member of the Commonwealth, the Democratic Party which Seretse had created, with the support of both Africans (of all tribes) and Europeans, was overwhelmingly successful in the first general election. Seretse became Botswana's first President and, after two re-elections, had been President for fourteen years when he died, much too young, in 1980.* By 1963, when I left South Africa, he and Ruth had become close friends of ours, and in 1972, when my wife and I stayed as their guests in the new capital of Gaberone, I saw for myself a multi-racial multi-tribal government at work in Southern Africa.

This success story is a good illustration of the changes happening in British Africa during the 'fifties and 'sixties of the century. Before the war there had been a Commonwealth of five sovereign states – Britain, Canada, Australia, New Zealand and South Africa – each ruled by white men, each relatively speaking 'rich', each calling itself Christian and each recognizing the British Sovereign as its head of state.† During the 'forties India, Pakistan and Ceylon became independent sovereign states. They freely chose to remain members of the Commonwealth and to accept the British Sovereign, not as head of their individual states but as Head of the Commonwealth. By the end of the 'fifties the transformation of the Commonwealth covered not only the Indian sub-continent but part of Africa (the Gold Coast had become the independent state of Ghana in 1957) and part of South East Asia (when the Federation of Malaya became independent, also in 1957). This process continued through the 'sixties, until only a small minority of Commonwealth members could still be described as white, rich, Christian monarchies.

In 1959, however, the idea that some day each of the South African High Commission Territories might achieve sovereign independence had never, so far as I know, occurred to anyone – and if it had, I think it would have been dismissed as moonshine. When I was preparing myself for South Africa in 1958, I found no hint in any document (or in anything said to me

* See Appendix III (4) for what I said about him in Westminster Abbey at his memorial service.
† Between the Anglo-Irish agreement of 1938 and legislation in 1948, Ireland was effectively partitioned. The six counties of Northern Ireland (or Ulster) remained part of the United Kingdom. The other twenty-six became a separate sovereign state, known as the Republic of Eire, which was neutral in the Second World War and by 1948 no longer in the Commonwealth.

by Ministers) that the goal foreseen for any of the Territories was national independence within the Commonwealth.

I am sure it was right for one man to combine the two jobs of looking after the Territories and representing HMG in dealings with the Government of South Africa. And when I arrived in 1959 the South African Government showed no sign of disagreement with that view. By 1963, however, when my time in South Africa was up, that Government had emphatically rejected it. Instead, I think they would have liked HMG to have two separate representatives – one diplomatic, the other a Governor in charge of the Territories. The diplomat (as they saw the position) would thus be solely concerned with fostering good relations between Britain and South Africa, not only as trading partners but as political allies in defence both of the sea routes round the Cape (against the Soviet Union) and of Western capitalism (against black nationalism in Rhodesia, Mozambique, Angola and elsewhere in Africa). Their hope was that the influence of the diplomat would prevail over the Governor's when there was any conflict of interest. So long as they had been able to assume that the Territories would in the end be transferred to them, they had been more than content that one High Commissioner should combine the two roles of diplomat and governor; for, in the rare cases of conflict, the diplomatic interest, the believed, would win. But during my time as High Commissioner the South Africans came to recognize that the Territories would never be transferred. They saw British policy in other parts of Africa move rapidly towards self-government and in the Territories evolve in that direction. They came to think that if Britain's diplomatic representative had no responsibility for the Territories, he would be more sympathetic to the South African point of view – about *apartheid* in particular. But of course HMG had, and was bound to have, only one policy. If HMG had had two representatives in South Africa, both of them would equally have tried to implement that policy and, if they had disagreed (as they might often have done), both points of view would have been telegraphed to London and settled there. I cannot believe that that would have been satisfactory, either for the British or the South African Government. As I alone had the two jobs to do, I had to make up my mind, set out the arguments in case of doubt and make one recommendation – and I can remember no case when London disagreed. But by 1963 one of the two jobs was about to disappear. The Territories were so near independence that the next year the High Commissionership could be

82

abolished and Resident Commissioners (with a change of title) become responsible to HMG.

I was fortunate in having a sense of consistent support from HMG in London. Mr Macmillan was Prime Minister from first to last, though my own Secretaries of State changed fairly often: at first I had Alec Home, and then Duncan Sandys, for both parts of my job; then Home for the diplomatic part, with Iain Macleod and then Reggie Maudling for the other; then Sandys again, for both. I remember cursing my luck when the last of these changes was announced, for I had much enjoyed working for Maudling when I was Permanent Secretary of the Power Ministry and I was glad to be working for him again. But I need not have cursed. Sandys proved to be a friendly and highly conscientious Minister; he gave me all the time I asked for and allowed my obstinacy to wear down his own. He was reluctant to spend thousands of pounds transferring the capital of Bechuanaland from Mafeking; but it was thanks to him that, when the new state of Botswana was born a few years later, its capital was not outside its national frontier but at a new-built Gaberone (with water all the year round).

My own mind became increasingly clear about the Territories. There could be no question of ever handing them over to the South African Government. What we must do was prepare them for self-government in the near future, and meanwhile spend much more money on them.

Preparation for *partial* self-government had already gone some way by the beginning of 1959, especially in Basutoland. A Basuto delegation had visited London in 1958 and I had been a fly on the wall during the negotiations with HMG which ended in agreement on a new constitution. I had been greeted enthusiastically by Chief Leabua Jonathan, but his handshake did not suggest to me (I must admit) that seven years later he and his conservative following of chiefs, the National Party, would secure at a Basutoland general election the absolute majority (though a majority of only one) over the radical Congress Party and all other rivals. Still less did I expect that in 1966 Leabua would be the first Prime Minister of an independent Lesotho (as Basutoland decided to call herself) and still be Prime Minister in 1980.

The gradual change in the South African Government's attitude to the Territories did not surprise me. By 1966 Dr Verwoerd had abandoned any claim to incorporate either Basutoland or Bechuanaland in the South African state. He chose to regard British policy towards the Territories as virtually indistinguishable from his own for 'separate development' of the Bantu homelands. So in 1966 he invited Prime Minister Leabua Jonathan of Lesotho to a discussion of future relations between their two countries. This friendly chat was concluded by a public statement from both Prime Ministers. The purpose of their meeting had been 'to establish how good neighbourly relations and co-operation could be arranged . . . We are pleased to say that our meeting took place in a spirit of good will and that it is quite clear that there is no desire for our states to interfere in one another's domestic affairs, but that friendly relations between these two independent neighbouring states will be preserved.'

Dr Verwoerd was assassinated in the House of Assembly soon after the publication of this statement. But his successor Mr John Vorster quckly reaffirmed the same policy when Bechuanaland became the independent sovereign state of Botswana, with Sir Seretse Khama as its President. Here, because of previous history, the change in South African policy was more dramatic. In 1948, when Seretse married Ruth Williams, the South African Government had at once declared him a prohibited immigrant; but they reversed that decision in 1965 when he became the first Prime Minister of Botswana. Next year Mr Vorster publicly stated that Botswana's independence was not a development that caused concern but was in keeping with South Africa's own policy. Indeed it was suggested, though not officially, that the future of a sovereign Botswana might lie within a confederation of Southern Africa, consisting of 'white' South Africa and a number of black homelands.

Seretse publicly rejected this suggestion: Botswana was not a Bantustan, and never would be. Its future was to remain an independent state within the Commonwealth. To join a Southern African confederation would prevent Botswana from having ties with black Africa and acting as a bridge between north and south. But this did not mean that Botswana would not maintain its economic, currency, transport and customs links with South Africa. Its policy was to maintain friendly relations with all neighbouring states.

Our policy for Swaziland was essentially the same as for Basutoland and Bechuanaland: to move towards sovereign self-government within the Commonwealth. Economic prospects were already bright in 1959 and by 1963 they were much brighter. Asbestos had long been a profitable export industry and, thanks to the Colonial Development Corporation (and in particular to its chairman, Evelyn Baring), forests and forest products, citrus and sugar had attracted investment from outside Swaziland and prospered. Now long negotiations over the export of iron ore at last

84

produced a large-scale ten-year contract with Japan, the deepening of the harbour at Lourenço Marques and the first railway from Swaziland to the coast (I managed to blow the first whistle of the shunting-engine, the 'Sir John Maud', in 1963).

But constitutional progress was bound to be harder going in Swaziland than in either of the other Territories, for two connected reasons: the division of the Swaziland population into black and white, and the great respect in which Sobhuza was held as the traditional 'king' of the Swazi people. Swaziland was a multiracial society – in fact a microcosm of South Africa. Its population of nearly 290,000 consisted of the one Swazi nation and some 6,000 whites (sixty per cent English-speaking and forty per cent Afrikaans-speaking) who between them owned about half the land, scattered in a patchwork quilt over the whole country. Was there a chance, here in Southern Africa, to prove that black and white could work successfully together? If a multi-racial society was found practicable here, then *apartheid* was not the only answer.

From the first I had a fine man as Resident Commissioner. Brian Marwick had come to Swaziland in 1925 as a young administrative officer and spent eleven years there before his transfer to Nigeria. He came back to Swaziland in 1941 and, except for spells of duty in Basutoland, stayed there till his retirement in 1964. He was devoted to the Swazi and his authoritative book about them★ shows how well he knew these people. They, and Sobhuza in particular, respected Marwick, and most of the white Swazilanders continued to respect him throughout our efforts at constitution-drafting. But the going was never easy, and past history, littered with concessions, broken promises and misunderstandings, delayed till 1968 the grant of sovereign independence. In 1963, however, the last stage before independence could begin, and under the new constitution Brian Marwick became Her Majesty's Commissioner for Swaziland, directly responsible to the Secretary of State – as Peter Fawcus also became in Bechuanaland the same year.

Sobhuza is one of the most remarkable Africans that I know personally. I am not thinking here of his innumerable wives (who used to come in bus-loads to celebrate the annual Feast of First Fruits) but of his personal ideas of a democracy. He told me once of his admiration for General de Gaulle, who seemed, he thought, to share his own convictions. 'When the question of selling cattle arises,' said Sobhuza, 'I would not dream of reaching a decision till

★ B. A. Marwick, *The Swazi*, Cambridge University Press, 1940.

85

I had called the leaders of the tribe and asked their opinion. But when they had all had their say, I would not dream of counting heads: I would reach my own decision in the light of their opinions. That is what I call democracy.' On another occasion, when my wife asked him whether he read many newspapers. 'Of course,' he said, 'but I prefer the *Observer*.' Under the agreed Independence Constitution of 1968 Sobhuza became King of Swaziland, and in 1980 he still reigns.

Botswana is the only one of the three Territories where *more* than stability has been achieved since independence – and none of the three has had a greater challenge from outside its borders. Parliament, with an Opposition questioning the Government, has never ceased to function; the constitution has never been suspended; there are no political prisoners in Botswana and political parties have not been banned. Remarkably enough, for the fourteen years of Seretse's Presidency, his Government was on friendly terms both with the Republic and with the black African states of the Organization of African Unity. Seretse was himself accepted as one of the 'Front Line Presidents' (with Kaunda, Nyerere and the Presidents of Mozambique and Angola), while Botswana, despite great provocation, stood firm in the very eye of the Rhodesia/Zimbabwe storm.

Nor have political problems prevented great economic progress. Throughout my years as High Commissioner we strove with no success to find resources (other than the cattle industry) on which a sovereign state could some day live. At one time the export of brine looked promising; draining the Okavango swamps remained an outside possibility; tourism was clearly worth developing. But when I left in 1963 no sign of future self-sufficiency was in sight. No sooner was my back turned than these prospects were transformed. Miraculous discoveries of nickel, copper and diamonds have now attracted the investment of international capital on such a scale that, unless frustrated by politics in the surrounding countries, Botswana's economic future seems assured.

In January 1960 Mr Macmillan rounded off his African tour of Commonwealth countries by a three-week visit to the Union. He was the first Prime Minister of Britain to be the guest of the South Africans and his visit marked a turning point in the relationship of the two countries to each other.

In private conversation with Verwoerd, and in the speeches he made during brief visits to the Territories, he made plain the British policy of giving each of the Territories independence

86

within the Commonwealth, not immediately but as soon as this could be done with reasonable prospects of stability. I do not think this was particularly distasteful or surprising to Verwoerd. Strijdom, his predecessor as Prime Minister who had died in office in 1958, had held the traditional South African view that the Territories belonged to the Union and ought to be handed over. But Verwoerd was not only a realist who knew that it would be futile even to discuss transfer with Mr Macmillan, but I know (though he never said so to me) that he saw the Territories as in some sense prototypes of the Bantustans which, in his reformulation of *apartheid* policy, would be established in the homelands and justify the permanence of white rule in South Africa.

The significance of the Macmillan visit went of course far wider than the Territories. It culminated in a speech on the morning of 3 February 1960 to the two Houses of Parliament which made explicit, for the first time and once and for all, Britain's rejection of the South African Government's racial policy. White South Africans had long been aware that there were people in Britain who disapproved of their attitude to blacks, Asians and coloured people; but the great majority associated such disapproval exclusively with long-haired socialists (barely distinguishable from communists in white South African opinion). It had not occurred to them (with the exception of individual South Africans) that no British politician of any major party could any longer defend racial discrimination, whether in South Africa, Rhodesia or elsewhere.

What Mr Macmillan said on 3 February was an encouragement to every South African who hated his Government's racial policy: not only blacks, Asians and coloured who were the chief sufferers from it, but various groups within the white population – editors and journalists, dons and students, politicians in the Progressive party, women of the Black Sash protest movement and leading members of all the Christian churches, including a few gallant dissidents within branches of the Dutch Reformed Church. Many of these people were day by day risking their livelihood by making no secret of their opposition to government policies. To know now that Britons of all parties were on their side was an encouragement that they had never had before. And it was this that Verwoerd could not forgive.

Macmillan had told Verwoerd the line his speech would take but he had not shown him a copy of the text. The speech was broadcast live from the Parliament building and Verwoerd's unscheduled reply was also broadcast. After a formal and courteous thank-you he launched into a half-hour impromptu speech in

English, seeking to correct Macmillan's alleged misunderstanding of South African government policy. It was a characteristically courageous effort and left no-one in doubt of how momentous Macmillan's speech had been.

Macmillan categorically stated: 'What we think right derives from a long experience both of failure and success in the management of our own affairs . . . This experience of our own explains why it has been our aim in the countries for which we have borne responsibility, not only to raise the material standards of living, but also to create a society which respects the rights of individuals, a society in which men are given the opportunity to grow to their full stature – and that must in our view include the opportunity to have an increasing share in political power and responsibility, a society in which individual merit and individual merit alone is the criterion for a man's advancement whether political or economic.' This presented a stark enough contrast to existing South African society and Verwoerd did not argue that no such contrast existed. But he passionately believed that his policy of separate development was the one way in which a mixed society such as South Africa could achieve Macmillan's purpose. The only way in which both black and white men could grow to their full stature was to keep them apart – and that was the way South Africa had rightly chosen.

Macmillan had gone on to argue in his speech: 'In countries inhabited by several different races it has been our aim to find means by which the community can become more of a community, and fellowship can be fostered between its various parts.' He gave Malaya as an example, '. . . where Malays and Chinese make up the great bulk of the population, and the Chinese are not much fewer in numbers than the Malays. Yet these two peoples must learn to live together in harmony and unity . . .' He quoted from a speech made by the British Foreign Secretary (Selwyn Lloyd) to the United Nations General Assembly the previous September, as summing up the United Kingdom attitude: 'Our policy therefore is non-racial. It offers a future in which Africans, Europeans, Asians . . . will all play their full part as citizens in the countries where they live, and in which feelings of race will be submerged in loyalty to new nations.' In other words, the British Government could not agree with Verwoerd that separate development was the way to peace in South Africa.

It was for the South African Government to decide what it thought right, but there must be no doubt about this difference of opinion. He therefore spelled it out: 'As a fellow member of the Commonwealth it is our earnest desire to give South Africa our support and encouragement, but I hope you won't mind my saying frankly that there are some aspects of your policies which make it impossible for us to do this without being false to our own deep convictions about the political destinies of free men to which in our own territories we are trying to give effect. I think we ought, as friends, to face together, without seeking to apportion credit or blame, the fact that in the world of today this difference of outlook lies between us.' After that speech relations between South Africa and Britain were never the same again.

The 'pass' which every black African was compelled by law to carry was the long-standing symbol of racial segregation. So when the Pan African Congress (PAC) declared 21 March 1960 an Anti-Pass Day and called on all Africans to observe it by leaving their passes at home and surrendering themselves to the police, there was a big response in many parts of the Union. The demonstration was to be non-violent but those taking part were advised by the PAC to accept no bail, offer no defence and pay no fine. On 21 March at the township of Sharpeville in the Transvaal a huge crowd of Africans converged on the police station. When ordered to disperse, they smashed the gates of the security fence around the station. The police opened fire; 67 Africans were killed and 180 wounded. All public meetings were promptly banned, a state of emergency was declared and innumerable arrests were made throughout the country.

Sharpeville was only one of several episodes when black African passive resistance to Government policies broke surface. One day before March was over I was playing one of my regular games of 'diplomatic golf' near Cape Town with the Canadian High Commissioner, Jim Hurley, and two Cabinet ministers. Something unusual was in the air that morning. No Africans were working near the course, and we decided half-way round to leave the game unfinished. Vincent, my Zulu chauffeur, and I had not gone far when we found ourselves driving towards a solid column of Africans, quietly marching in good order twelve abreast. Vincent drove slowly on behind the Union Jack as the marchers made room for us, and I learned later that no damage of any kind was done in Cape Town. The marchers (some thirty thousand Africans) had been told by a Government spokesman that if they returned to their location in Langa, their leader (Philip Kgosana, a young Cape Town student) could next day see the Minister of Justice. He came back next day – and was immediately arrested.

In consequence of world outcry over Sharpeville, a resolution was introduced at the Security Council of the United Nations deploring *apartheid* and requesting the Secretary General to make 'such arrangements as would adequately help in upholding the purposes and principles of the Charter'. This United Nations intervention helped to rally South Africans behind their Government. Once more, it seemed, the United Nations, ignoring its own Charter, was interfering in the domestic business of a sovereign state. 'Why pick on us?' asked the South Africans. In the communist world there were persistent breaches of the Charter, but the UN did not try to intervene.

Though United Nations action was some help to the Government, the whites were scared. When Paul Sauer, second only to Verwoerd within the Cabinet, stated boldly at Hermanus: 'We have turned a page of history; things will never be the same,' white opinion was inclined to think him right. And there was talk that a new leader might be needed. In fact I heard a Cape Town businessman remark: 'Are you ready, Paul? You may have to take over' – and Paul Sauer shut his friend up with a grunt. That was in private on 8 April 1960. Next day, in the full glare of publicity, when the Witwatersrand Agricultural Show was being opened, a bullet entered Dr Verwoerd's head. It had been fired at point blank range (for personal reasons) by a mad white farmer – and it seemed that the Prime Minister was dead. But he survived, by the narrowest of margins: the hand of providence had clearly intervened. Verwoerd's prestige, which for a fortnight had been sinking, now rose to an unprecedented height. His miraculous recovery continued – and Paul Sauer chaired the Cabinet in his place.

No change of any kind was made in Government policy – least of all in the Republican campaign. A referendum was to be held on 5 October 1960. The Government had always claimed that a South African Republic could automatically remain within the Commonwealth. They therefore asked the Prime Ministers' Conference in May 1960 to confirm this claim. The Conference declined to answer what was still a hypothetical question, but the Government did not withdraw their claim. Ninety per cent of the white electorate voted in October and the 'yes' votes prevailed – but only just.*

The narrowness of the majority did not deter the Government. The next step must be agreement by the Commonwealth that Republican South Africa could retain its membership. Dr Verwoerd at once asked for this agreement: correspondence, he

* The majority of 'yes' votes was 74,580 (out of 1,626,336 votes cast 775,878 voted 'no').

suggested, would suffice. As Macmillan judged that only at a Conference of Prime Ministers could Commonwealth agreement be secured, Verwoerd said that he would personally attend one in London in May 1961, and Mr Macmillan now set himself to get from that Conference consent to the South African request. He approached several Prime Ministers, imploring doubters (in particular the Canadian, Mr Diefenbaker) to postpone public commitment, and by the time the Conference started at least this had been achieved.

Meanwhile South Africa had made no change in racial policy, nor at the Conference could Verwoerd give any hint of change. He stood pat by his original contention: South African racial policy was the business of no-one outside South Africa. When other Commonwealth countries had become Republics, they had remained in the Commonwealth without argument. South Africa had raised no objection, however unfriendly to her such countries might have been, and South Africa should be treated in the same way. But when he saw he could not win, he changed his tactics: South Africa would leave the Commonwealth.

When I went to meet Verwoerd at the airport on his return from London, he was receiving a hero's welcome from the crowd. He assured me that there was nothing to regret. He had withdrawn his application because he wished to save Macmillan from embarrassment; South Africa and Britain would now be closer friends than before. In his heart, I think, he really was delighted: the Commonwealth was no club for Verwoerd.

The South African Government's racial policy was inconsistent with the multi-racialism which all other Commonwealth countries professed. However difficult Britain and other members might find the avoidance of racial discrimination in practice, there was a fundamental difference between South Africa and the rest. The South African Government regarded racial discrimination as *right* and therefore a proper foundation on which to build the laws of the country; the rest of us regarded it as *wrong* and therefore deplorable whenever it occurred. Then was Britain right to try to keep the Republic in the Commonwealth? I still think she was, and chiefly for one reason: continuing contact with other members of the Commonwealth was more likely than isolation to induce South Africans to change their ways. For example, if South Africa stayed in the Commonwealth, her Government would surely have to welcome High Commissioners from other member States. It was right that Verwoerd should have the chance to confirm these expectations. So far from doing so, he was not prepared to make any promise about receiving 'non-white' High

Commissioners in Pretoria, nor to agree that *apartheid* could even be questioned, let alone discussed, at a Prime Ministers' Conference. It would have astonished me if Verwoerd had taken any other line, but I shall never regret that Mr Macmillan gave him every chance to do so. As Verwoerd chose to be totally uncompromising, he could not expect the Commonwealth to accept his application for continued membership and he was right to withdraw.

This result, as things turned out, was very fortunate. Stormy times were ahead. Had the Republic been a member of the Commonwealth through the 'sixties and 'seventies, the prospects of peace in Southern Africa would now, I think, be worse than they are.

My Government asked me to stay on in South Africa. So when, on 31 May 1961, the Union became a foreign country (as the South African Republic), I became the first British Ambassador. But I continued to be High Commissioner for the three Territories, with responsibility to the Colonial Secretary, Iain Macleod. I found in practice little difference between my new position and the old one, but I had much more to do. There was no precedent for an independent Commonwealth country becoming foreign and some unusual negotiations were now needed between us and the South Africans. Citizenship was one of the most difficult, and another concerned 'fugitive offenders' from the Republic to the Territories. But both sides were anxious to agree and in the end we did.

There was one change which was bound to have difficult implications. So long as the British Sovereign was South Africa's head of state, it was the Governor General who represented the Sovereign in South Africa. For many years it had been the South African Government that advised the Sovereign on who the Governor General should be, and since the appointment of Patrick Duncan (in succession to Lord Clarendon, the Governor General when I first visited South Africa) the post had always been filled by a South African. The new State President would now inherit most of the Governor General's duties, but one of them would simply disappear. This was a garden party, to celebrate each year the Sovereign's birthday, to which the Governor General had invited leading citizens.

I too, as High Commissioner, had of course celebrated the Queen's birthday. In 1959 and 1960 I had given two parties on the Queen's birthday as Percivale Liesching, my predecessor had done, a morning one for the diplomats and South African Government representatives, and a garden party in the afternoon for British citizens. It had not been easy to decide who should be asked to the garden party, but each year we made progress in finding Britons who were leading citizens regardless of the colour of their skin. In 1961 I followed the same pattern as the year before. Verwoerd showed special courtesy by coming to my morning party and emphasizing his hope that our two countries would in future have even more friendly relations than in the past.

In 1963 I gave a diplomatic party in the morning, but to the afternoon one – whom should we invite? In recent years the Governor General had conformed with Nationalist party dogma and invited only whites to his garden parties. But the Queen whose birthday we were to celebrate was the Head of a multi-racial Commonwealth. Was I to feel myself compelled, by local racialist convention, to ask no-one but 'whites' to my Queen's party? It seemed to me unthinkable and, as HMG agreed, our guest list treated colour as irrelevant. We gambled on fine weather and, to make more room for guests, enlarged the lawn. Almost all our invitations (to whites and non-whites) were accepted, and eleven hundred guests came and shook hands. The weather kept us in doubt to the last moment – but in the end decided we were right. The Royal Marine band (white and non-white musicians) performed throughout the party. Towards the end the Mayor of Cape Town made a brave speech proposing the Queen's health, and I thanked him, before proposing the health of South Africa. Old Cape Town residents, as they took their leave, said with emotion, 'This is just as it used to be.'

But that was not the end of the story. Later in 1963, when I went to take my formal leave of the Prime Minister, the interview was exceptionally long. Dr Verwoerd, for the whole hour that I spent with him, denounced what I had done at my last Queen's Birthday Party. My Embassy, he recognized, was extra-territorial and I was free to use it as I liked. But I had flouted South African convention by entertaining guests of more than one race, and he must leave me in no doubt of my offence. I replied that what I had done was in accordance with instructions from my Government and I would of course report to them what he had said. I greatly regretted that he felt as he did and briefly explained my Government's attitude. Though Verwoerd as usual listened to me with courtesy, he did not conceal his anger or show the slightest sign of understanding my point of view.

It was in fact high time I left the country. In arguing with HMG about the man to succeed me (and successfully objecting to the first name proposed), the South African Minister, Eric Louw, had referred, by way of contrast, to my own behaviour: though his

Government was well aware of my objections to *apartheid*, I had given no offence by what I said. But Mr Louw's Cabinet colleagues did not agree with him: they were fed up with me because they knew I hated racial discrimination.

At the last annual dinner given to the diplomatic corps by Mr Louw that I attended, I sat at a small table with Paul Sauer and other members of the Government. At a late stage in the evening when conversation had become more intimate than diplomatic (and the wine had flowed), Paul lent across the table and said something like this: 'You are the most intelligent man, John, that your country has ever sent to represent her here – and no-one has done more harm to her relations with South Africa.' He never spoke to me again.

The leading Afrikaans Cape newspaper, *Die Burger*, published a friendly supplement about me before we left, under the headline 'Controversial Ambassador'. The editor, Piet Cillie, was a man I greatly respected and what he said about me was discerning. I had (he wrote) made many speeches up and down South Africa and had been careful to say nothing to which the Government could object. But the controversial ambassador had often 'needled' the Government, and too often the needle had gone home.

I would not have chosen to be serving anywhere but in South Africa during the four and a half years that we were there and, though it was a relief when my official duties ended, we were involved in Southern Africa for life.

The spell had first been cast when we reached Cape Town on our honeymoon. We had experienced the great kindness of South Africans to strangers: of white farmers in the Free State and the Transvaal, white Catholic Fathers in Basutoland, white academics in Natal. In Sophiatown, a suburb of Johannesburg where both blacks and whites were then allowed to live, we had stayed with my sister Dorothy and her fellow workers and had met Africans as naturally as whites. The friends we had made since 1959 in the three Territories were men and women, regardless of their race. But in the Republic colour-blindness was forbidden, and in consequence our non-white friends (apart from servants) could be counted on the fingers of one hand. Fortunately the white friends that we made there are among the finest people that I know, and admiration for their courageous integrity is the first thing I still feel as I look back.

Of all the politicians I have known personally – in Britain, the United States and South Africa – Helen Suzman is the one I most admire. A brilliant speaker and a marvellous mimic, handsome, intelligent, with a great sense of humour, she could have led a very comfortable life. Instead she chose to be an active politician – and to persist in opposition to the Government for twenty-seven years. In 1959, when I first met her, she was a member of the official Opposition, the United Party (UP); but before the year was over she and her radical friends in Parliament had left the UP and formed a new Progressive Party. In the 1961 General Election she was the one Progressive to be elected, and for the next thirteen years in Parliament she was alone. But in 1974 she and six other Progressives were elected; the Party became the official Opposition and was joined soon after by another splinter group, to form what is now the Progressive Federal Party. Helen Suzman's choice of an uncomfortable life shines like a good deed in a naughty world.

So do Laurence Gander's brave editorials in the *Rand Daily Mail*. So do the Roman Catholic, Anglican and Methodist church leaders – and the dissenting heroes of the Dutch Reformed Church. So do the great universities, continuing to protest against the laws which forbid them to admit non-white students or staff. And here I think specially of Ernie Malherbe, Principal of Natal University for nineteen years, and his wife Janie – Afrikaners born and bred, who have been unrelenting critics of the Nationalist Party.

If admiration for liberal white South Africans is one feeling that has never left me, indignation is another. Each year I lived in South Africa, I was more shocked. I was shocked by the cruelty of driving people from their homes by legislation, of separating members of one family and segregating husbands from their wives (my chauffeur Vincent had to leave his wife in Zululand). I was shocked by the hypocrisy of claiming that urban Africans – voteless and with no share in economic power, who constituted a majority of all blacks in South Africa and were indispensable to national prosperity – could be treated for all time as 'honoured guests'. I was shocked by the folly of supposing that all who fought against the Nationalist creed were 'communists' and must be treated as enemies of the State.

Even in 1963 I was convinced that there was hope for South Africa. Verwoerd's *apartheid* was in the long run self-destructive: not only unjust and hypocritical but incompatible with economic growth, for 'separate development' is a contradiction in terms. But what would induce a majority of the white voters to reject Verwoerdism? In 1963 I could not see this happening at any time in the next ten years, and said so in the valedictory despatch to my Government. Nor has it happened yet. But I had not foreseen the collapse of the Portuguese empire in Mozambique and Angola, the emergence of Zimbabwe, or the scandal that rocked the Nationalist Party and removed Verwoerd's successor from the scene.

The Nationalist Party still rules South Africa in 1980 and the statute-book is much the same as it was. But the foundations of Verwoerd's *apartheid* have been shaken. P. W. Botha, since he became South African Prime Minister, has said things about the Mixed Marriages and Immorality Acts that would have scandalized Verwoerd, and in Namibia the laws on this one point have actually been changed. But the constitutional power to make fundamental changes is still in the hands of the one white Nationalist Party. Will the electorate (as they did after Sharpeville) retreat into the *laager* and decide to shoot it out? Or will they tell Mr Botha to go further and faster in a new direction, recognize urban non-whites as citizens of the Republic, and work for a new Union of confederate states?

CHAPTER 8

Post-war Oxford, 1963–1976

When I became Master of University College on 1 August 1963 Jean and I had been away from Oxford for what seemed longer than twenty-four years, and I was determined to remember that ten years as a pre-war don could not make up for ignorance of what Oxford had now become. We were both of us also determined not to regard the happiness of our close but hierarchic relationship with our colleagues in the High Commission or the Embassy as any guide to the 'open house' relationship that we wanted between the Master's Lodgings and the whole college – dons, undergraduates, graduates and staff. As time went on, we found that there were certainly differences between Oxford now, in the 'sixties and 'seventies, and Oxford then, in the 'thirties. But the differences were less important than the continuities – and almost all the changes were improvements.

Univ, with some four hundred junior members and nearly forty dons, was now more than twice as big as when we left it. The juniors included some eighty graduates now working for a second degree, and many of them had come on to Oxford after graduating overseas or in some other British university. Several of the dons were not full tutorial fellows but held research fellowships created since the war. More significant than this increase in numbers was the greater specialization of the dons. Between 1929 and 1939 I had been the only fellow elected to a new subject (politics), and my colleagues had then included only two scientists (in physiology and chemistry), no mathematician, no physicist or engineer, no-one in English or any other modern language. By 1976 we had three philosophers and three historians, two economists and two lawyers, a modern linguist (in Russian) and a psychologist, three chemists and a bio-chemist, two physicists, two physiologists, two mathematicians, two engineers, two English dons and a musician.

But almost more important than this growth of dons was the new intellectual standard of the undergraduates. Every under-

graduate place in College was now competed for (as only scholarships and exhibitions had been before the war); and this had
transformed the catchment area from which undergraduates
came. Before the war young men competed hotly for the few
awards the College offered and they came from all kinds of
grammar school, both public schools and those supported by a
local authority. But even if you won a College scholarship, unless
your parents were comparatively well off, you needed another
one to supplement the first. So the great majority of undergraduate
places were filled by candidates whose parents could afford to pay
all fees and maintenance charges. They did an entrance examination, to satisfy us that they were up to reading for an honours
degree, but there was no competition for 'commoner' membership of Univ.

When I was at the Education Ministry after the war, we did two
things of revolutionary effect. First we encouraged local education
authorities (the councils of all counties and county boroughs) to
make sure, by supplementary grants, that everyone winning a
university award could take it up. Then we went much further:
we encouraged local authorities to do the same for *everyone* that
universities were ready to admit and, when 'encouragement'
proved insufficient, we made them (subject to a means test) pay all
the fees and maintenance grants required.

In consequence, admission to Oxford and Cambridge (and all
other universities) was thrown open for the first time to those
judged the best candidates. Competition for a place has now
become as keen as competition for an award before the war. Each
college is as free as ever to judge candidates on merit, but
candidates are no longer limited to those with private means to
pay for their maintenace and fees.

There is still a strict limit to our choice, set by the potential
candidates themselves and the advice given them at school. How
could we persuade a school which had never sent boys to Oxford
that we would welcome the chance of examining its pupils? And
how persuade such boys that they would be happy if they came
to us? First, of course, by taking trouble to seek out such
schools – by sending a don or two to visit them and inviting heads
of their departments to visit us. Then through collective action by
a group of colleges – inviting a cross-section of all kinds of school
to Oxford, discussing their problems and ours, listening and
asking questions. This has led on to various experiments: to solve
particular problems of inner London schools and boys with special
disadvantages, or to collaborate with groups of schools in Scotland or West Yorkshire, or to make offers of a college place

98

conditional on subsequent success in national examinations. Oxford has set itself deliberately to widen its actual catchment area year by year and, in particular, to make itself increasingly available to boys from comprehensive schools of various kinds. We still have a long way to go, but we have made progress; meanwhile we could not take more trouble to be fair.

In recent years at Univ. we have only had room for some two out of every five candidates for admission, and we have used some five criteria to judge by. The most important is the examination which our own dons set and correct. Next is the interview between each candidate and the dons who would teach him if he came to us and studied the subject of his own choice – say, history, philosophy or mathematics. Next, perhaps, is the account of each candidate given by his school. This is invaluable when written by someone who clearly knows a lot about the candidate and writes with candour, but nearly useless when it reads like a catalogue of virtues. Partly to redress the imbalance, we have added a second, arm-chair interview with a single don, which throws some light on the man's personality and attitude to Oxford. Finally, if he has done the General Certificate of Education, there are the 'A level' grades he has achieved. This last test has the merit of objectivity – but also the snag that no-one knows who set the papers or marked them. In practice there is no serious doubt about either the best candidates or the worst: those falling between the two are the real problem, especially when competition in one subject (say, medicine or law) is a great deal hotter than in some other (say, geology or classics).

I know we made mistakes during my time as Master, but only a tiny fraction of those we took dropped out or failed their finals. Each year some ninety per cent of those taking finals got a first or second class honours degree, and in three of the four years from 1975 to 1978 Univ. was judged (by a sophisticated and perhaps misleading formula invented some years ago by President Norrington of Trinity) the most successful of the Oxford colleges. But no-one knows how many candidates we ought not to have rejected. I know one. He was my godson, so I declared my interest and took no part in the debate. When Univ. rejected him I spoke up for him to New College – who took him and gave him a scholarship after his first year.

Univ. has now deleted the thirteenth-century statute which read: 'no woman may be a member of the college'. In 1978 the first woman was elected to a Univ. fellowship, and next year women were first accepted as undergraduates or graduates. But by 1963 women had become more normal parts of Oxford than they had been before the war. In 1924, when Jean and I became undergraduates of Somerville and New College, each college was confined to men or women but Oxford was already co-educational, with all degrees, examinations and lectures available to either sex. And as a pre-war don I had undergraduates of women's colleges as pupils, 'sent out' to me by their tutors for certain subjects.

Jean and I saw a great deal of each other as undergraduates and by 1926 I had decided to marry her if she agreed. But in several ways she was a quite unusual undergraduate. She had already had two years at the Royal College of Music (RCM) and qualified (with an ARCM) as a performer. Her master was the great Bach pianist, Harold Samuel, and with encouragement from him and Sir Hugh Allen she had decided to make music her profession. I first met her when she was brought in by the OUDS, exceptionally and by special leave of the authorities, to play a harpsichord in the wings of the New Theatre for the Society's performance of *Peer Gynt* (and her first sight of me was playing a lunatic in that production). Later I shared rooms in the old tithe barn in New College Lane with Alan Ker. He had a grand piano which he encouraged Jean to come and play. So we saw much more of each other than was common among female and male undergraduates, at a time when members of Somerville were not supposed to meet male undergraduates without a chaperon. Maurice Bowra, for example, complained that when he called on me he always found me in strange company – not only Jean but dark-skinned members of the Student Christian Movement and sometimes my father (then Bishop of Kensington): 'When you call on Maud, you find nothing but black female bishops.'

By 1963 there were no chaperons, even in theory. Undergraduate colleges were still male or female, but the Union, the OUDS and almost all College and University societies had members of both sexes. Except between midnight and seven am you found so many girls about the quad that no stranger would think the College single-sexed. Clothes and hairstyles no longer distinguished validly one sex from the other; beards were the only certain guide, and I had to remind myself quite often that no moral significance attached to length of hair. After all, as Peter Strawson once put it: 'New student is but old undergraduate writ long-haired.'

On the other hand, it was still true that the proportion of women to men at Oxford was far smaller than the national average for universities. There were only five colleges for women undergraduates and over thirty for men. So it was much more difficult for a woman to get a place at Oxford than for a man, especially in subjects such as English, history and modern languages. One way to redress the balance was to create new colleges for women, but where could the money be found? Meanwhile five men's colleges agreed with the five women's colleges a one-way scheme whereby a limited number of women would be admitted to the five men's colleges over a period of five years. The University endorsed this plan but declared a moratorium: for five years no other college was to become mixed and then, in the light of that experience, there was to be consultation between the University and all colleges about the future.

Univ. had decided in 1969 to ask its old members for £400,000. This was to solve the 'lodgings' problem. Traditionally our undergraduates spent in College the first two of their three or four years' residence in Oxford, and lived in lodgings for the remaining one or two. But Oxford city's population had been expanding fast since the industrial revolution between the wars and the growth of the Morris motor industry. The landladies of Oxford could now find tenants for longer periods than the three eight-week terms when undergraduates needed lodgings. So where were our junior members to live? Must they be driven further and further from College or else pay rents much higher than they could afford?

The College had made up its mind to solve this problem. For some years past we had been acquiring land, by judicious penetration into one part of north Oxford. Here we must equip ourselves with our own new buildings, and these must enable us to offer accommodation to all our members, undergraduate and graduate, married and single, throughout their time of residence in Oxford. The time had now come when we must ask our old members to help us. But there must be no question of a fraudulent prospectus: if we meant to change our statutes and admit women, we must tell them so – in case they disagreed.

Since our foundation seven centuries ago in 1249 the full name of the College has been 'the Great Hall of the University'. That was our name because the intention of our founder was to create a residential college where young and older men could live together and be members of the University. Merton and Balliol had been founded for the same purpose (and about the same time), other colleges had followed over the years and Oxford had become a collegiate university. Was it not right (some Univ. fellows argued) that the first part of Oxford to be residential should be the first to become co-residential? And as well as doing justice to the women, would not this raise the intellectual standards of the college? Co-residential Univ. would attract able young men and women whose co-educational schooling predisposed them to a mixed college rather than one of single sex. No, it was argued on the other side, the onus of proof lay with those who now sought to change a pattern which had proved its worth over seven centuries. No-one could reasonably say with any confidence what the effects of such a change would be on college life. And as for justice, women had fought their way into the University by an heroic struggle over the years against male chauvinism; they had established their own colleges and achieved intellectual standards that were now the envy of men's colleges. Was it just for the men's colleges to use their wealth, and their inheritance of prestige and gorgeous buildings, to bid against the women's colleges for their brightest candidates?

Debate was prolonged and consistently good-tempered, but when we voted the result was clear. There was no majority, still less a two-thirds one, in favour of change. Those who did favour it agreed that nothing should be said to our old members about the possible admission of women. They also agreed that, as this silence ruled out change for some few years at least, further debate must be adjourned.

It was not resumed till 1976. By then the appeal had been successful, the new buildings were up and we were able to offer college accommodation to all members of the college who wanted it. Meanwhile the five-year moratorium had passed and, when the Univ. governing body resumed debate, a two-thirds majority now favoured change. Almost all other colleges, including three of the five women's colleges, took the same view. The University therefore decided that all colleges who wished to change their statutes could do so. The way was open for the chauvinist male pigs of yesterday to plunge down the Gadarene slope into the Sea of Equal Opportunity. In 1980 only two women's colleges and one of the men's remain available to those who still prefer, within the context of a co-educational university, a home-base that excludes the other sex.

I think myself that we have gone too fast in scrapping the single-sex pattern of Oxford colleges. But certainly we have been too slow in making other changes: in particular, too slow to modify college sovereignty and improve the procedures of a collegiate university.

Soon after our return to Oxford, the University decided to appoint a seven-strong body under the chairmanship of Oliver

102

Franks, then Provost of Worcester College, and ask them to examine, as if they were a royal commission, the constitution and functioning of Oxford. All colleges and all departments gave their views, largely in public. This meant that Univ., for example, spent a great deal of time debating answers to the exhaustive questions asked by Franks, and in the process we had to reconsider what our relationship should be to the University and to other colleges.

This rigorous self-examination was very good for us. It was particularly valuable to me, a freshman Master, anxious to learn from colleagues and to understand how their minds worked and what they wanted done. As public debate developed we became increasingly aware of much agreement and much disagreement between the colleges and the University.

What became clear to me was a great divide. On one hand, there was the professorial view of some scientific departmental heads who hated college loyalties and saw them as the enemies of research; on the other hand, a passionate attachment of most dons to their own colleges. The 'professorials' thought of the dons in their departments (say, the physical chemists) as having an over-riding commitment, whatever college they came from, to the physical chemistry laboratory, which belonged to the University and was the centre of graduate research and undergraduate teaching for all physical chemists. They regarded college claims on the time and energy of dons as interference with this primary commitment. So they disapproved of dons who accepted college appointments such as senior tutor, tutor for admissions or dean. Yet each college had to have dons who undertook these offices and took them seriously. Were science dons to leave this crucial part of college life to non-scientific colleagues? Alternatively, should this work cease to be done by colleges and pass into the hands of university administrators? Eventually, should colleges become mere halls of residence and dons have done with all but teaching and research? Should Oxford go for all available economies of scale and use professional bureaucrats for a much larger part of its administration? Should it become more like the civic universities of England, continental Europe and the United States?

The Franks commission, reporting in 1966, came down unanimously against this professorial view. Oxford must certainly remain collegiate in the traditional sense. But if the college system was to sustain itself within the modern context of large government support for higher education, the colleges must look to their business: they must ensure their own future by helping Oxford to become *more* of a university. And they must find new ways of doing this. If colleges insisted on retaining all the vestiges of college sovereignty, they would find themselves losing the substance. They must enable themselves to speak with a single voice on certain subjects or their anarchic voices would cease to be heard. And the University must itself speak with authority in national debate with central and local government – and speak in time to influence national decisions.

The strength of college opinion clearly ruled out the possibility of a permanent Vice-Chancellor for Oxford (such as almost all other universities in Britain had), but Franks produced convincing arguments for strengthing the Oxford Vice-Chancellor's position. In consequence he or she is now pre-elected for a four-, not two-year term; becomes an *ex officio* member of the university's governing body two years before assuming office and remains a member for two years after ceasing to be Vice-Chancellor. So in effect he or she has eight years of major influence.

In the old pre-Franks days the post was always offered to the person who had been longest in office as his college head. Not only is he now elected but anyone can be a candidate. However, *plus ça change* . . . Alan Bullock, Master of St Catherine's, would have been Vice-Chancellor under the old arrangements and was the only candidate under the new. His two successors as Vice-Chancellor have both been college heads, and the election of neither was contested. In each case we not only got an excellent Vice-Chancellor but the best man available on any reckoning. Long may such luck continue.

Only one major innovation proposed by Franks was not accepted. This was for a Council of the Colleges. Each college would have one representative, and the Council would be able to take effective decisions which were not unanimous. It would complement Hebdomadal Council (as the University governing body of twenty-four elected dons is still strangely called) and would be built into the constitution of the University. Congregation, still consisting of all resident senior members, would continue to be the parliamentary body to which Hebdomadal Council was responsible, but the colleges would for the first time have a council of their own.

This was too much for the colleges to stomach – because it would limit their individual sovereignty. It would, of course, also give them a new collective power and a new protection against university interference in defined areas, but that was not inducement enough for colleges to swallow the whole dose. Instead we agreed on a one-year experiment. We created an experimental, temporary *Conference* of the Colleges. Two representatives of each

104

college (two could be trusted rather more safely than one) would meet under a chairman of their own choosing, with no constitutional status or statutory powers, and discuss anything that they thought worth discussing. No-one could find reason to suppress such boldness. We met twice a term, at first under the chairmanship of Kenneth Wheare, Rector of Exeter College, a recent Vice-Chancellor of high repute and long experience, who was also an acknowledged expert on federal government. Before the year was up it was quite clear that the Conference was not a waste of time, and we agreed, without dissenting voice, to continue the experiment a second year. The University, which never viewed the Conference with much favour, found it to be useful in one small respect: where the University was required by statute to consult all colleges, the Conference could be used for this purpose – but with a separate voting procedure to remind us that for all other purposes we were outside the covenant.

Before our second year was over we decided, again unanimously, to extend our life for yet another year, with the proviso (in case annual extension became a habit) that no-one should be chairman for more than two years. I succeeded Wheare as chairman for two years, and in 1980 the Conference is still meeting on the same precarious basis of renewal.

I thought this upstart body useful from the first and I hope it will soon achieve some constitutional respectability. In my time most heads of colleges attended it, as one of the college's two representatives. Debate could be inhibited by the sense that speakers were mandated by their colleges and unable to let argument affect their views. But this was not always so. We naturally voted as we had been told to vote on questions previously discussed in college meetings, but we also spoke our minds and argued like the reasonable men or women most of us were. The great snag was that no college felt itself bound by any decision that it disagreed with; but the Conference enabled progress to be made on several serious subjects.

One of these subjects was inelegantly called the non-don problem. The essence of a collegiate university like Oxford is that you cannot be a member either of college or university without also being a member of the other. This applied without exception to all undergraduates and everyone working for a second degree, and it applied to every don who was a college fellow. But it did *not* apply to those with university appointments who were not fellows of a college. These non-dons were of several kinds: scientists appointed by university departments; those holding appointments in the department of educational studies, or in the medical school or in university administration. These men and women were rightly judged by the university to deserve the same status as college fellows, and they had votes in Congregation. But most of them were people whose services no *college* needed, so how could each one of them be found a college fellowship?

Part of the answer was to create new colleges for graduates. All Souls for centuries had been such a one. Nuffield had been established just before war broke out. St Antony's had followed shortly after; Linacre, St Cross and Wolfson still more recently. These new colleges had greatly contributed to solving the non-don problem, but it would not disappear unless *old* colleges also contributed by offering fellowships – and only their own governing bodies could do that. The Conference of Colleges had of course no power to compel, but we worked hard to persuade. By 1976 almost everyone who was 'entitled' by the university to a college fellowship had been offered one, with the important exception of those with appointments in the medical school. For these people a new graduate college has now been created: Green College, named after a generous benefactor and headed by Sir Richard Doll who was effectively its founding father while still Regius Professor of medicine.

But of course much more important than this or any other bit of constitutional framework are the people Oxford attracts as dons, graduates and undergraduates and the kind of life they live. Most of our Univ. dons, in 1929 to 1939, were married and lived out of college. Though this was still true in 1963 to 1976, we had at least half a dozen bachelors living inside. This was to some extent a lucky accident but partly a deliberate change. An old member of the college, Harold Salvesen, gave us money to pay for one or two junior fellows who would live for a few years in college as bachelors and strengthen the link between undergraduates and dons. For quite different reasons, other benefactors have endowed science research fellows who have also been bachelors. Again, the appointment by the college of a young assistant chaplain, Joel Pugh (while the chaplain fellow was away on sabbatical leave) proved so successful that he stayed three years with us. When he returned to the United States (and later came back to marry our daughter Caroline), the college found David Burgess, another bachelor, to succeed him – and that has been our practice ever since.

One of the secrets of university education (which led William of Durham to found Univ. in 1249) is that older and younger scholars should share a common life under one roof. This idea of a college implied that dons and junior members should eat together,

106

and before the war a don's emoluments included dinner in college hall each night of the three eight-week college terms. But by 1963 this excellent fringe-benefit had grown in scope. Among the many benefactions of my predecessor as Master, Arthur Goodhart,* is a fine room in college (named after Giles Alington, a much loved fellow and dean who died too young), and here, or in the senior common room, all dons are able to have lunch together – and most of them do. The common table, let me add, both for lunch and dinner, is now available not only during full term but throughout the year. This extension of the old idea of meals as meeting-places is, I believe, one of the reasons why dons nowadays know each other better and take a more effective part in college life. Post-war Univ., despite its larger size and more heterogeneous mix, is *more* of a community than we were then.

It would have been inconceivable in the old days to stage a college entertainment, invented and performed by dons, graduates, undergraduates and Master – at moments marginally blue but so well acted, good-natured and funny that no reasonable man could take offence. Needing no precedent to justify his daring, the physical-chemistry don John Albery went to work. He mobilized dramatic talent in all parts of the college, converted college hall into a Globe Theatre, filled it with members of the college and their women friends, and produced an unforgettable revue. 'Come into the garden, Maud' had to be followed a year later by 'O Maud our help in ages past' and my last year was commemorated by 'In Memaudiam'. A new tradition had been established: that older and younger members of Univ. could mock each other with Aristophanic licence – and no-one's feelings need be hurt.

Relations between young and old were pretty good because we knew each other personally. Undergraduates met tutors every week and produced work for personal discussion with them. It was generally accepted that your main purpose at Oxford was to work at subjects of your own choice, and time was short. As your final examination for a first degree comes usually at the end of your third year (though, in some cases, of your fourth), whatever fun and games you may engage in, time must be strictly husbanded if your main Oxford purpose is to be served.

Besides your tutors you may get to know personally at least five other senior members of the college: the dean, the senior tutor, the chaplain, the domestic bursar (if you have doubts about your solvency or diet), and the Master, who has assured you on arrival

* See Appendix III (3) for what I said about him at his memorial service in Oxford.

as a freshman that he would like you to consult him, on or off the record, whenever you think that might be worth your while.

Many of the other dons you may never meet or know by sight. But you may find yourself sitting beside any of them at a dean's luncheon (to which from time to time you are invited), or at the dinner given to all freshmen your first Friday in residence (when your hosts are all the dons and all the officers of college clubs).

Becoming an Oxford undergraduate has always brought a momentous increase in freedom – freedom from family, from schoolmasters, and from a timetable made by someone not yourself. Probably for the first and last time in your life, you are free to dress, eat and drink in any way you like. If you want to work through the night and sleep all morning, your college servant will protest but no-one stops you. This is as true today as in 1924 when I went up to New College. But the undergraduate is now even less bound by rules than in those days. Except when going to the schools for examinations, he need not wear a gown or put on academic dress. He can use a key to come into college after midnight, instead of climbing a barbed wire entanglement. He can go to a pub without risk of challenge from a proctor's bowler-hatted bull-dog. He can go home or to London during term-time without leave or serious risk of impeachment. He can make music, except when neighbours ask him to stop, at any time of day or night.

And, quite apart from this absence of negative constraints, his opportunities to do what he wants are wider than when I was young. Learning to row, for example, in a college eight. Pre-war Univ. had always been a great rowing college. But during my ten years as a pre-war don no-one at Univ. rowed who had not been an oarsman either at school or at another university. So most college rowing-men came from the same kind of school and, though they were friendly enough to land-lubbers, they formed a race apart. Today we have some six boats on the river every year, and at least half the college boat club members never touched an oar before they came to Univ. The seasoned rowers make time to coach the novices; everyone, whatever school he came from, has a chance to row. We lose the boat race against Cambridge much less often, and rowing plays a new part in college life.

Music is another example of more positive undergraduate freedom. Fifty years ago I asked some of the dons whether they thought it would be worthwhile trying to found a college music society. They all favoured the idea but doubted its feasibility; Univ., they said, was not that sort of place. However, some undergraduates (including the captain of boats and the rugger captain) joined me in writing a letter to propose the idea. We announced a first concert in hall – by Steuart Wilson, tenor, and Jean Hamilton, pianist. That concert was a triumph. The society grew steadily in strength, survived the war, and now has a larger membership than any other club. Undergraduates continually make music for themselves – at a freshmen's concert in their first term, in choral and orchestral concerts, usually in college but sometimes in the University Church or Town Hall. They also have the chance to hear great artists at concerts sponsored by the society; for from the start professionals have been generous in accepting modest fees (or even refusing to be paid). And since 1976, when Arnold Goodman succeeded me as Master, the college musical society has been richly blessed. It still has its all-purpose home in the Master's Lodgings, with the Master's concert-grand in constant use; and it now also has a second one in college hall. Its main purpose is still to make music, of all kinds and of increasing excellence; but the Master now brings to college audiences great artists who come only because he invites them: Menuhin and Söderström and the Russian violinist Guidon Kremer (on his first visit to England).

Undergraduates now also have a much better chance of acting. The OUDS productions are still available, as in my day, but women undergraduates as well as men can now take part. The University Opera Club has come into its own. Today the University has its own Playhouse and some weeks in the term this is available for undergraduate work. Much more important, college societies (such as the Univ. Players) have been founded and all undergraduates have the chance of a part – as actor, director, stage-manager or electrician. Colleges now compete each year in 'drama cuppers', each putting on a one-act play of its own choice.

Another kind of undergraduate freedom increased during the later 'sixties but since then has become less noticeable or publicised – freedom to run the place. During my time at New College, no-one wanted to spend time serving on college or university committees or in amending the syllabus of Greats. But by the end of the 'sixties a great change in undergraduate interests had appeared. Students demanded a part in all decision-taking: about what subjects the various honours schools should cover and how the different subjects should be taught; what disciplinary rules must be accepted; how the University should now invest its funds. Such demands had become strident in America, in continental Europe and in some non-collegiate universities of Britain.

There learning, teaching and research often became impossible; protest and violent disruption took their place. Such troubles took a milder form in Oxford but we took them seriously. The University was wise enough to appoint a strong committee to look into them, and persuaded Herbert Hart to take the chair. Herbert and I had read Greats at New College; when he succeeded Goodhart as Professor of Jurisprudence, he had become a fellow of Univ. and remained one of my colleagues till his election some years later as Principal of Brasenose College. His liberal sympathies, and his distinction in philosophy as well as law, made him the right man to chair this committee and draft its wise and eloquent report. In consequence undergraduates now have representatives on almost all university bodies, with a say in many academic decisions (through membership of joint committees established by the various faculties) and a chance of sharing in judicial functions too.

These opportunities were never, I think, seriously wanted by many graduates at Oxford or by more than a very few undergraduates. In practice the great majority have not troubled to make use of them, and many of the minority have found more interesting ways of spending time than in meetings with more experienced elders.

Some years before the University took action, many colleges had been trying out new forms of consultation between undergraduates and dons. Our Univ. innovations were substantial. The result was that we took no college policy decision (on membership of women, for example) without asking the advice of the undergraduates and discussing it with them in a college meeting. This of course slowed up decision and made college meetings longer; but it also meant that everyone knew more about the college and got some valuable experience of decision-taking. We gained on balance from these formal interchanges, and it was right that they developed as they did. But what really saved our happiness through the troubled 'sixties was nothing institutional or new: it was the old informal friendliness of all concerned.

Graduates, at least those working for a second degree outside the natural sciences, had a poor deal in pre-war Oxford. Some of them have a fairly poor deal still, but much has been done to adapt what used essentially to be a university for British undergraduates and make Oxford more worthy of its international reputation. We have developed a new pattern of second degrees and new types of examination for them. We have modified the traditional tutorial system to match graduate needs. One college after another has added to the traditional two common rooms (the senior one for

110

dons, the junior for undergraduates) a third for graduates, their wives and friends. So, besides sharing in sport and other forms of college life, graduates have their own meeting-place, their own table in hall and their own entertainments. Univ. and many other colleges now also appoint one of the dons as 'dean of graduates', available to any graduate in need of help.

Headship of an Oxford college must have been, nearly always, one of the most enviable forms of life. No doubt at some times less than at others. In the seventeenth century, for example, Univ. was deeply split on issues of church and state, with Master Obadiah Walker celebrating the Roman mass in a room in the front quad next the chapel, while in the chapel itself his colleagues used the reformed service. And once, in the eighteenth century, the governing body was so divided that two Masters were simultaneously elected and the Lord Chancellor was left to pick the winner. Nor in the nineteenth century can Bradley have been a happy Master when undergraduates screwed up the dean inside his college rooms and, as no-one confessed, the whole college was sent down. (Nor do I envy Bradley when the culprits confessed and the whole college was invited to return.)

Before the war Univ. had a convention that when a new Master had to be found it was the dean who called the other fellows into conclave and himself (however junior) took the chair. This was because one (or perhaps several) of the senior fellows might himself be, or think himself, *papabilis*. So when Michael Sadler warned us that he wished to resign the Mastership, I found myself (aged twenty-nine) responsible for action. There were then several fellows who had given long service to the college and not unreasonably thought their turn had come. Sadler had been a Christ Church undergraduate and no part of his distinguished life, at the Board of Education or at Leeds as Vice-Chancellor, had given him a special link with Univ. Colleges try not to make the same mistake twice running; so they tend over the years to choose their heads alternately from inside and outside their own fellowship. We certainly thought it was an insider's turn. But which one? No-one declared his hand. We all knew two or three who would love to be Master, but which of them did a majority of us want? If none of them, whom from outside? After straw votes galore, we found ourselves unanimous. We wanted Dr A. B. Poynton, our classics don – but not for an indefinite period (the statutes were then silent on this point): only for two years, till he reached seventy.

So quite soon Poynton's successor must be found. It was my business to re-convene the conclave and it was soon clear the pendulum had swung: this time we must look outside for a Master. The problem of such search is Pistol's in *The Merry Wives of Windsor*: 'Why, then the world's mine oyster . . .' All you can do is first assume that anyone you want will accept election – and then decide who in the world to choose. Our trouble was that no name anyone suggested was of a person many of us knew; and could we invite someone to come and meet us, without commitment on our side or his?

Beveridge, for example, then Director of the London School of Economics, was someone few of us knew well. Douglas Cole offered to sound him out, without committing us to a firm invitation. He did so, and reported 'Beveridge is willing'. That turned the scale and in the end, though Beveridge remained a blind date for most of us, we all agreed to take a chance. Years later, I was an even blinder date. (I was in Africa, and only three fellows who had been colleagues of mine before the war still had a vote.)

It is not easy to describe a Master's job. You are in the chair at every college meeting, at almost all committee meetings and at all college dinners, whether in hall or senior common room. You live in college, at least during all three terms of the academic year, and that pretty well exhausts all items of your formal duty. The job itself, of course, is altogether different. It is to feel yourself the one person responsible for the whole life of the college during your mastership, especially when anything goes wrong; to see the college as a lively part of Oxford and Oxford as part of the world society of learning. So the demands on you are literally infinite – and impossible for anyone to meet.

But you are also almost totally dispensable. Some fellow (one of your colleagues, appointed by the college as an 'officer') is directly responsible for each part of college life: undergraduate selection, arranging of tutorials, discipline, college finances, graduates, the work and welfare of the staff. Yet these concerns of theirs are also yours. So you must understand all kinds of college business. Best of all, you must establish in the minds of all your colleagues and all members of the college that you are available at almost any time.

When we came back to Univ. in 1963 the college servants were the part of the college that seemed to have changed less than any other. They had been a most important element in pre-war Univ. and their continuity was one reason why Univ. was fundamentally the same college that we had left in 1939. This was a reassuring fact, and I was specially glad to find that my old friend Norman Dix was now one of the senior and most respected members of the staff. But there was a new head porter, Douglas Millin, who had come first to Univ. on demobilization and was now firmly ruling from the Lodge (a commanding position to be sharply distinguished from the Master's Lodgings). For the next thirteen years this formidable, forthright, delightful man was one of the two people who did most to teach me my job as Master. The other was Gwynne Ovenstone. Like Douglas, she had come to Univ. on demobilization, but the post of College Secretary that she came to fill had not existed before the war. Nor had the College Office – a couple of rooms on the ground floor in the Radcliffe quadrangle which had become the heart of college life, with a constant inward and outward flow of people through it – and Gwynne presiding, with one colleague, at the centre. Here I found something we had never had before the war: a single source of current information about every member of the college, whether in residence or an old member. Much better still, here was a person (of catholic taste but very firm opinions) who was devoted to the college, past and present, and could not only remember names and faces with infallible precision but was prepared to let me know what she really thought of them. Here, with adaptations to fit the difference between a college and a government department, was the realization of my own ideal of a Permanent Secretary: discreet, wise, entertaining, incorruptible.

College meetings were not at all like meetings of the Cabinet. We voted often, on trivial questions as well as the most serious ones. Often of course there was no need for voting. But when I decided that a vote was needed, I would propose something and amendments could be moved. I seldom used my own vote at college meetings but, when I did, I often found myself out-voted. If votes were equally divided, I had a casting one – and hardly ever used it; but at all other times the youngest fellow's vote had the same weight as the Master's – and I remember this was true before the war. Soon after Beveridge resigned the LSE director-ship and became Master, there was hot debate about a fellowship election. All but three distinguished candidates had been elimi-nated; but which of the highly commended three should we elect? The issue was long in doubt – till Beveridge, forgetting that he was no longer at the LSE, declared that one of the three candidates 'he would not have'. The effect of this veto was dramatic: all fellows were immediately at one. David Cox, the man the Master 'would not have,' was soon elected – and has proved, for forty years, how right we were.

Fellowship elections are the most important of all college acts. If you elect the wrong man (or woman, nowadays) when he is aged, say, twenty-three, you may have him for the next forty-four years; for though his first three years are probationary and he then comes up for re-election every seven years, re-election (until retirement at sixty-seven) is almost automatic. All full fellows take part in all elections (in most cases with the help of outside experts who represent the University). But at each election only a few fellows have expert knowledge that is relevant and, if those few are in no doubt about the best candidate, other fellows are likely to concur. But if, as often happens, those appointed by the University think three or four candidates equally acceptable, then choice is shared by all fellows, expert and amateur alike; subjective judgment of personalities is then decisive, and the man best qualified on strictly intellectual grounds may not be picked.

We followed much the same principle whatever we were doing: debate was open to any don who chose to intervene, nor was decision left to a small inner group of senior citizens. (I soon learnt never to introduce a subject by remarking that a committee had already spent hours discussing it.) The governing body was still just small enough for this procedure to work, but quite a marginal increase in our numbers would have made more delegation unavoidable. (In this, Cambridge, with its much larger colleges, has long since led the way.) If Univ. follows, time will be saved but something of real value will be lost.

The job of every college head is to do what he can not only for his own college but for Oxford, and this can take many forms. One is to seek (and seek successfully) election to Hebdomadal Council, the General Board of the Faculties, or some other statutory part of Oxford government. Another form is to attend (and sometimes speak) in Congregation – arguing the case for treating nearby teacher-training colleges as part of Oxford or (once more in vain) the case against truckling to the Government when we were told to charge students from overseas more than we charged Britons.

Another job, outside the formal structure, is to address branches of the Oxford Society (in various parts of Britain or abroad). This I did fairly often, trying to dispel the more fictitious kinds of rumour and to keep old members of the University in touch with modern Oxford.

But my first priority was of course Univ. I set out as Master to know everyone involved: dons, graduates, undergraduates, college secretaries, scouts (as we call college servants), porters, kitchen staff, men in the maintenance department, and all their spouses – a total of about seven hundred souls.

I had been happy in Whitehall and in South Africa. But a Master's life is unlike a Whitehall mandarin's and, though it has something in common with a diplomat's, in my experience it is unique – and there is nothing to touch it. My wife and I never achieved what we set out to do, but we were both equally involved in the attempt. I think it was our mutual indispensability that made this the happiest part of my life.

We entertained a lot. Drinks, meals and music all played their part. At the beginning of each academic year, once I had seen all freshmen individually (the excuse for this was that each had to sign the college admissions book), we asked them to small parties, with girls and a few dons to add spice to the dish. Before each party we made good use of a freshmen's photograph, taken each year before they went in academic dress for the Vice-Chancellor to make them members of the University. Each summer term we asked all who were going down to similar small parties in the garden. And every term we lunched as many junior members as we could, including the elected officers of undergraduate and graduate common rooms and of the college sporting and other clubs and societies. We watched almost all college boats competing on the river. We watched the college teams at rugger, soccer, hockey, cricket, tennis and squash – Jean much more frequently than I, in pouring rain and gumboots ('a woman for all seasons', as a colleague's speech at a rugger dinner once described her). We watched the plays performed by Univ. Players, whether in competition with other colleges or simply for pleasure. The musical society held meetings round the grand-piano in the Master's Lodgings. And Jean (as a committee member) would exert influence on her friends (Britten and Pears, George Malcolm, Curzon and others) to come and perform for the society.

The dons' wives (and wives of college guests) she had to dinner each time their husbands feasted in the hall. She would involve them (and undergraduate volunteers) in jumble sales. She rounded off our last college revue (the 'In Memaudiam') with a startling first appearance as a singer and self-satirist. Meanwhile, near single-handed and wholly without a husband's helping hand, she had made the small Master's Garden one of the sights of Oxford.

The ideal Master of an Oxford college must be deeply interested in the past, present and future of his college, in all its members and all their concerns. If he gives absolute priority, first to his college and secondly to Oxford, he can do anything else that comes his way or takes his fancy. But he must give his college the first place in the disposing of his affection, time and energy. And he is fortunate if someone alongside him does all these things better than he.

CHAPTER 9

Local Government, 1929–1979

'Sewage without Tears' was the sub-title given by friends (who never read it) to the first book I ever wrote.★ And it summed up the sense of boredom that most of my more intelligent friends (including my wife) have always felt about a subject which I fortunately still find fascinating.

It was certainly great luck for me that I got landed with the subject early on. No-one can seriously pretend that education or health or the environment are not important, or that in Britain and most countries these things are not the stuff of local government. But the subject is not in the same class as philosophy, physics, chemistry or mathematics. Compared with them it is a subject anyone of average intellect can understand and think about coherently. So it suited me well enough – as an interesting, neglected, not too exacting field of study. There were certainly few rivals in sight either in 1929, when the Home University Library asked me to write on English local government, or in 1934 when the Johannesburg city council asked advice from W. G. S. Adams, then Warden of All Souls, about a municipal historian from Britain to celebrate their fiftieth civic birthday.

The Council proved to be ideal clients. They gave me access to all their papers and a local research assistant of my own choice (first, N. B. J. Huijsman and later A. D. Davidson), and they encouraged me to do what I wanted: to write a book whose theme was not merely Johannesburg and whose method was to proceed from detailed examination of one city toward the problems of city government in general. So I was able in the preface of the eventual book to thank the council for doing everything in its power to help me: 'It gave me freedom to treat the subject as widely and as critically as I might choose, and never in the three years which I have spent upon the work has it sought in any way to hurry or

★ *Local Government in Modern England* by John P. R. Maud, Thornton Butter-worth, 1932.

embarrass me. It would have been impossible, indeed, to attempt a critical appreciation of Johannesburg municipal history without this patience and dispassion on the council's part'.*

As things turned out later, it was great luck for me to have this chance of starting to learn about South Africa some twenty-five years before I went there as British High Commissioner. It was instructive to study the effects of excluding from the franchise, because their skins were black, half the population of a so-called self-governing city of a million souls. It was a valuable corrective, if later one were tempted to blame Afrikaans-speakers or the South African Nationalist party for *apartheid*, to see for oneself what pre-war South Africa was like. And I made many friends who were still there when I came back. Most valuable of all was what I learnt of local government – and some of it was relevant to English local government reform.

For before the Anglo–Boer war ended in 1902, Johannesburg was given a quite new form of city government. This owed much to Lionel Curtis's experience as a junior official of the London County Council but it was in some respects much better than what we still have in England. The local taxation system, for example, was derived from British practice and relied on a single rate levied on the value of fixed property. But from the start assessments were based on capital, not annual rental, values; it was the owner, not the occupier, who paid; and land and buildings were valued separately. Indeed, after 1919 rates were levied only on site value; buildings and 'improvements' escaped altogether. Lloyd George's historic description of the English rating system in 1913 did not apply to Johannesburg, as to some extent it still does to us in England – and still would in part apply if we changed from rental to capital valuation for rating purposes, as the Layfield report recently proposed.†

One respect in which Johannesburg had the better of Britain even more decisively was geographic. In 1902 the new city council was given, at its own request, an area of some eighty square miles, larger than the municipal jurisdiction of any city in the world save Tokyo. The old *stadsraad* of Kruger's day had operated within an area of only five square miles, and this did not include land owned by the mining companies; but the new boundaries embraced the whole mining area and all undeveloped land within a six-mile radius. This was a brilliant innovation. It was of course bitterly

* *City Government* by John P. R. Maud, p. vii, OUP, 1938.
† *Local Government Finance, Report of the Committee of Inquiry.* London, Cmd. 6453, May 1976, p. 144.

opposed by the mining companies and by the speculative land-owners of adjoining townships, but Milner (now Governor of the Transvaal as well as British High Commissioner) accepted the arguments put forward by Curtis, who had been appointed acting town clerk in 1901 ('until,' to quote the minute book, 'a suitable man can be obtained from England'), and the council got what it wanted.

Enormous advantages flowed from this decision. As population increased (from nil in 1886 to a million fifty years later) their needs were the business of the one city council, in startling contrast to our English experience wherever similar developments have occurred. In Tyneside, for example, which in 1936 had an area almost exactly the same as that given to Johannesburg in 1902, the Royal Commission that studied local government there found sixteen separate local authorities at work, six of them with police forces and nine with fire-brigades. The Commission unhesitatingly recommended that all should be amalgamated and that a new 'Newcastle-upon-Tyne' should become the single municipality for the eighty square miles.* No action followed for thirty years. In 1969 another Royal Commission found itself driven to the same kind of conclusion and three years later Parliament sought to repair the damage done.† At last the metropolitan county council of Tyne and Wear came into existence, with eighty square miles and 1,209,000 people to serve – but still with a second tier of five district councils to help or hinder it. Lucky Johannesburg!

Another instructive feature of Johannesburg's history was its relations with the Transvaal Government. When Kruger was President of the Transvaal Republic, the Johannesburg *stadsraad* was virtually without independent power. In 1901, before the Anglo-Boer war ended, when Milner became Governor of the Transvaal and went to live in Johannesburg, he determined to foster the town's prosperity and make it a self-governing centre without waiting for the war to end. He appointed an executive council of leading white citizens who worked with such effect that in 1903, when elections became possible (the franchise, deplorably, still confined to whites), almost all of them were elected to the new town council. Curtis was appointed to an important post under the Transvaal Government and was succeeded as town clerk by another great public servant, Richard Feetham, later a high court judge and Chancellor of Witwatersrand University.

This new council got pretty well all that it wanted out of the Transvaal Government: not only the huge municipal area and the

* Cmd 5402 of 1937, § 128.   † By the Local Government Act, 1972.

financial set-up, but wide powers to provide roads and transport, electricity, gas, water, drainage, sewage disposal and an abattoir. Johannesburg was then a unique Transvaal town and its new pattern of self-government was tailor-made to match its own taste. Other municipalities gradually came into existence along the reef but Johannesburg has ever since remained in many ways unique.

It has also remained almost completely self-supporting in finance, with no substantial subsidy from provincial or national government funds. Whereas an average local authority in Britain nowadays gets from its local ratepayers only about a third of what it spends (the rest comes as a subsidy from the national taxpayer), Johannesburg got (and still gets) practically nothing from either provincial or national funds. So it has partly paid for local government out of its own version of the local rate, and partly by charging its inhabitants for the services they use – electricity, gas, transport and sanitary services.

And this contrast goes wider than finance. From the beginning of the century Johannesburg not only paid its way: its own elected council was allowed to govern it. When the council wanted new legal powers from the Transvaal Government, it almost always got them in the end. And there was virtually no supervision from the centre. Administration was the business of the council, with no Whitehall to approve or disapprove. This was no doubt partly because Johannesburg spent only its own money, but there were other reasons. The chief one was the conviction of Milner and his men that Johannesburg and its gold mines were crucial elements in the future prosperity of both the Transvaal and South Africa, and that Johannesburg self-government was an essential means to this end. This faith of Milner's has not been shared by any government in Britain. Politicians of all parties, especially when in opposition, constantly profess their faith in local government but few of them in this century have really believed in it or proved in office that they mean what they say. Nor is it hard to explain this inconsistency. The functions of city government in Johannesburg were very different from those of English cities. They never included education, welfare, house-building, police or official policy towards non-whites, for these were the preserve of national or provincial government. In Britain, by contrast, there has been no such clear division of labour. Our local councils have long been responsible for police, education, housing and many social services; but national government has always shared with them these crucial functions, partly because local finances were inadequate but also because of their national importance.

119

In the United Kingdom local self-government in the traditional sense was in suspense from 1939 till the war ended. Local authorities became agents and outposts of central government, and in their new role they were indispensable to the war effort. For instance, though food distribution and rationing were the sole responsibility of the Food Ministry, the national system would have been unworkable without food offices up and down the country and the local authorities which ran them. Air raid wardens, the emergency fire service and the Home Guard were part of national government and at the disposal of Whitehall departments and of their representatives, the regional commissioners. But their incalculable value was due to the British volunteers, part-time or whole-time, who did the front-line work. The same was true of those who taught in the schools (and fed the children there), of the Womens Voluntary Service (who helped to feed survivors from the blitz, in Coventry or any other shattered area) and of the organizers of evacuation from the towns. The war revealed the British genius for coping with crisis when almost everyone wanted to help. Inadequacies of pre-war local government structure were not allowed to matter. What was to happen to them after the war?

The national structure of local authorities dated back to Acts of 1888 and 1894. Most towns which in 1888 had had a population of more than 50,000 were county boroughs, their councils responsible, since 1902, for education and every service that Parliament from time to time had asked local authorities (or told them) to provide. That was simple enough. But the rest of England and Wales had two main tiers of authority: the county council as first tier and, as second, the borough, urban district and rural district councils, dividing between them the services which in a county borough were the one council's business. And each rural district contained a third tier, at parish level.

Since the 1888/1894 pattern was first formed, the motor car had steadily been blurring the difference between town and country. Each year more people moved their homes out of the town to the new suburbs, or farther still, so that they no longer lived, worked, shopped and entertained themselves in the one local government area. And the town population was all the time becoming a larger proportion of the whole.

But why did not the urban local government areas expand in sympathy? Because their rural neighbours did not want them to. And why? Because no local authority could raise money save by the rates and none wanted to lose rateable value to its neighbour. That was why rural districts would not yield land to boroughs or

1. The author

2. The Earl of Woolton

3. Ellen Wilkinson

4. Benjamin Britten and Peter Pears, outside Southwark Cathedral after their first London performance of *Saint Nicholas*, 1949

5. Gilbert Murray receiving a bronze portrait head from Julian Huxley in Unesco House, Paris

6. Harold Macmillan with the author in Basutoland, 1960

7. BBC *Brains Trust* in 1958: Noel Annan, Isaiah Berlin, Norman Fisher (chairman), the author, Violet Bonham Carter

8. Dr Hendrik Verwoerd proposing the Queen's health in High Commission House, Cape Town, 1961

9. The Queen's Birthday Party in the garden of the British Embassy, Cape Town, 1963

10. Helen Suzman after receiving Hon. DCL degree from Oxford
    University in 1973, with the author

11. Sir Seretse Khama, the author's wife, the author and Lady Khama,
    outside Government House, Gaberone, Botswana, 1972

12. The author and his wife in the Master's Garden, University College, Oxford, in 1976

urban districts. But there was a special reason why counties could not stomach losing land to county boroughs. When boundaries for the election of MPs were changed so that they corresponded with local government boundaries, the political balance would tilt in favour of the Labour party whose strength had always lain in county boroughs rather than counties.

Councils of each five types had their own powerful group to battle for them against encroachment: the county councils association (CCA), the association of municipal corporations (AMC), and those of the urban districts (UDC), rural districts (RDC) and parishes. There was no one group to see the importance to all five of an effective local government structure – no one group to reconcile the conflicting interests of county and county borough or speak with one voice to central government.

A royal commission under Lord Onslow's chairmanship had sat for seven pre-war years (from 1923 to 1930), received conflicting evidence from all sides and produced three reports. The result? Only one change of any substance: boroughs in future had to have populations of at least 100,000 (not 50,000) before applying for county borough status. So the structure became still more inflexible.

Before the last war ended the Government did what it could to start the process of local government reform: it appointed an outstanding expert, Malcolm Trustram Eve (later Lord Silsoe), as chairman of a local government commission. But in doing so it made one fatal mistake: it used the word 'boundaries' in the commission's title and terms of reference. What needed doing, and what the commission set itself to do intensively, was to examine all types of local authority throughout the country and make recommendations, not about boundaries only but about functions – about the work that each authority should do. By 1948 the commission finished its work. Its report recommended a new pattern of local government, including the abolition of complete separation between counties and county boroughs.* Aneurin Bevan, the Minister to whom this report was made, disliked it for various reasons and rejected it, on the grounds that it was outside the commission's terms of reference. Instead he set his ministry to work on a quite different plan, but this never saw the light of day. The 1950 General Election so much reduced the Labour government's majority that no local reform could be attempted.

By 1958 the Conservatives had done their best to get agreement between the local government associations. The result was inevit-

* Report of the Local Government Boundary Commission for the Year 1947, HMSO, 1948.

able: a new commission. From 1958, till it was wound up in 1966 by the new Labour government, it heard evidence and drew conclusions about one part of the country after another, on the assumption that piecemeal improvements could do the trick.

But though the local authority associations could not agree on change of structure, they knew that they were falling down on their job. And in 1955 the first woman ever to become permanent secretary of a major Whitehall department had become head of the Ministry of Housing and Local Government.

Evelyn Sharp was the most able civil servant I have ever known, and the most endearing. She was also one of the most formidable, whether as ally or opponent. Set in her handsome face the blue eyes left you in little doubt of her opinion about what you or someone else had just been saying. But she was too intelligent to stop listening or to close her mind to argument – until she thought you had closed yours. She was intolerant of bullies, especially when bullying someone who could not answer back, and ruthless in fighting incompetence, cant or dishonesty. She never gave offence gratuitously but if offence was taken – well, that was just too bad. What distinguished her from many of her Whitehall colleagues was a passionate personal concern for causes she thought good. And one such cause was local government reform.

Soon after I got back from South Africa in 1963 Evelyn brought me up to date. The local authority associations, she explained, at last agreed on something: they were about to ask her Minister to appoint two high-powered local government committees with the plain purpose of self-improvement. They were all dissatisfied with their own present performance. They all wanted something done to improve the internal management and staffing of local authorities of every type. In particular, how could local government attract into its service more people of high personal quality? Most members of both committees would be suggested by the four associations, but they both needed independent chairmen without commitment to any of the four. Would I accept chairmanship of the committee on management? A three year job, she thought. Good people to work with (the associations would persuade their best people to serve). We would appoint our own secretary, meet round the corner in congenial offices, make whatever use we wanted of the government social survey unit. Expenses, but no salary. An irresistible temptation? I asked my colleagues in the Univ governing body what they thought of it. They said 'no possible objection' and left me to decide. So I told Evelyn Sharp I would do it if she was quite sure the local government people wanted me. Apparently they did.

122

Though the Food Ministry owed much of its success to local government officers I had had nothing to do with local government as such throughout the war. Seven post-war years at Education had given me some experience, under Ministers who genuinely believed in local self-government, of a working partnership between local elected councils and Whitehall. For the next six years, at Fuel and Power, I was involved in a quite different kind of partnership – between Whitehall and the boards of nationalized industries, appointed by Ministers and responsible to them. Then in South Africa I had seen what happens when the majority of citizens have no vote in what purports to be democratic city government; and in the High Commission Territories I had been part of the unsuccessful struggle to convert local government by chiefs into local democracy. So my conviction about the need for local government, and about its difficulties, had been confirmed.

The Local Government Management Committee was a good one, though larger than I wanted; but if we were to include elected members of both main parties, appointed officers and some people from outside local government, we could not number less than about eighteen (for weightier reasons Prime Ministers never succeed in keeping the Cabinet as small as that). What mattered most was the quality of some half-dozen of my colleagues. They included Andrew Wheatley (the Hampshire county clerk), Peter Mursell (ex-chairman of West Sussex county council), Philip Dingle (town clerk of Manchester), Harry Watton of Birmingham (a highly respected Labour city councillor), a shrewd businessman of real originality (E. B. Mayne) and a most intelligent journalist (T. S. G. Hunter). We were lucky to find in succession two first-class secretaries – an ex-colonial administrator and, to succeed him, Michael Saville, another of his kind. Dr Hedley Marshall gave us invaluable help by planning and co-ordinating our research work. In particular, when we looked abroad and found an almost complete lack of information about local government in action, he visited six countries on our behalf and brought back exactly the report we wanted. We met about once a week in London; paid a few visits inside this country and abroad; and in three years produced two readable reports, unanimous except on one important point.

In 1964, before the first of the three years was up, the thirteen years of Tory government ended and the six years of Harold Wilson's Labour government began. This made no difference to us; what did make a difference was Dick Crossman's change of mind. As Minister of Housing and Local Government he first took the view, which Labour and Tory Ministers had held for years, that changing the basic structure of English local government was not a starter. He was reported, plausibly enough, as saying that 'anyone who thinks you can abolish the relationship between county and county borough needs his head examined'. But by 1966 he had had second thoughts. The time had come (the Government now declared) for fundamental local government reform. Two Royal Commissions, therefore (for England and Scotland respectively), would be appointed, with wide terms of reference, and asked to recommend what should be done.

Dick Crossman was still responsible for English local government, and for chairmanship of the English Commission he first wanted a judge. The Commission's task, he thought, was not to waste time touring the country. It was to weigh the well-known conflicting views of the contenders (counties, county boroughs and the rest) and come up with a judicious scheme which could become law before the next general election. Abandoning search for a judge, he scraped the barrel and eventually asked me.

The main work of the management committee was finished but we had several months' drafting ahead of us. I told Crossman it was absurd to think the Royal Commission could report in two years' time and (if I was to be chairman) we must be free to take whatever time we needed. But the management committee had already generated corporate energy. If some members were now to join the new Commission, this momentum of reform could be sustained. Crossman agreed; my college told me to accept the chairmanship; and the management committee provided five of the eleven members of the Royal Commission. Still more important for our chances of success, Dame Evelyn Sharp (who had just finished her Civil Service career) agreed to join us; and as our full-time secretary we got James Douglas who was our first choice in Whitehall.

We started work the same day that our appointment was announced. At that first meeting one of our members, Derek Senior, gave each of us a copy of his recently published book *The Regional City*.★ When I had read my copy I shared with Jean a prophecy: 'Unless this book is our report, there will be at least one memorandum of dissent.' Three years later ten of us signed our report (unanimous on all essentials) and Derek signed a dissenting memorandum.

It was of course illogical to enquire first about the inner working of each local authority (as the management committee had done) and then about the national pattern that authorities of

★ Longmans, 1966.

124

different types should form. Why not consider the national pattern first and then the way each unit should manage its business? Because no-one but HMG could start a national enquiry and HMG would not do so till local government had given a lead: there was no practical alternative to two enquiries in the wrong order.

Simplicity came to be one of our chief goals as the debate developed. The evidence presented to the management committee (about people's present attitudes to local government) was overwhelming: for the most part they had no idea what services it dealt with, what councils were responsible, or who the members of their council were. In a county borough (say, in Oxford) there was no excuse for this ignorance: one council was responsible for all the services. Outside the county boroughs three separate councils were elected, on different dates and for various terms of office, to provide each citizen with various local government services: was it surprising if no-one knew who was responsible for any of them? So long as this continued to be true, it was hypocrisy to call the system democratic. Whatever other faults we sought to cure, this was the one which seemed to underlie the rest. Search for simplicity was the main reason, I believe, why all but one of us plumped in the end for one all-purpose authority for every part of England outside four metropolitan areas – London, which had already been reformed and was outside our terms of reference, and the areas round Liverpool, Manchester and Birmingham. Having agreed on the all-purpose principle we were determined to make as few exceptions as possible. That was sound reasoning on our part as a Commission, but I now think both Labour and Tory governments were right to propose an increase in the number of metropolitan exceptions.

If you are going to improve local government you want a plan simple enough for people and parliament to understand. But you want simplicity for another compelling reason: one body of local representatives must be responsible for jobs that have their own peculiarities but need linking together. Education, housing and the other social services (for the elderly, the handicapped, the single-parent families) may all be concerned with different members of one household. It is mad to make separate authorities responsible for any one of them in the same area – and that was what the old local government structure did. The more we looked at the various functions, the more convinced we became that in each place the 'personal' ones ought to be in the same hands. It was difficult enough to co-ordinate the work of different specialists – teachers, social workers, housing managers – even in county boroughs where the same council (though through different committees) was responsible. We became determined to unite responsibilities wherever we could.

And we found powerful allies. Frederic Seebohm, Lady Serota and other experts were already at work in a committee on 'local authority and allied personal social services'.* They implored us to recommend that one single authority in each area should administer the housing, education and personal social services.

None of us could seriously dispute this argument. All but one of us thought it pointed further still: to one authority in each part of England not only for 'Seebohm' but, wherever possible, for all main local government services. Derek Senior thought otherwise. He saw England (and in his mind neither the Welsh nor Scottish boundaries were sacrosanct) divided into regional cities, most of them already visible but some of them (round Ashford in Kent, for instance) only potential, and in each regional city more than one tier of local government. To have more than one tier was for him essential, for several reasons but especially because he thought all parts of the National Health Service (NHS) must become part of local self-government. He listened patiently to all the evidence that came to us. The evidence from education, especially from the Inspectorate, pointed emphatically to areas too large to fit into his scheme, so that at times he spoke of education as a cuckoo in the local-government nest. If it were thrown out, Seebohm could not have his way, and local government would lose more than half its present business. Too bad, but national health would be some compensation. He knew that none of us would agree to leave education out (and he never seriously asked us to agree) but he was deadly serious about bringing the health service in.

The rest of us were all determined that the new local government pattern should prove a better link with national health than the old one, but we all knew there was no chance of a local government takeover. The medical profession would not have it and no government would try to compel them. In any case the NHS must be financed from national funds. All we could insist on was that the area and district health authorities of the new NHS should *not* have boundaries that cut across those of the new local authorities and *should* include local government representatives in their membership. Those two conditions were in fact satisfied eventually.

* The Seebohm Committee was appointed in 1965 and reported in 1968. Cmd. 3703.

Ten of us in the end reached unanimity. And how did this come about? By hard bargaining between county and city councillors? Between people with Labour sympathies and people without them? Between enthusiasts for particular services – planning, housing or education? Of course each of us ten had his or her special convictions and all of them had to be reconciled. Jack Longland fought throughout for areas large enough to satisfy his and the Inspectorate's educational experience, while Reg Wallis was convinced that the small education authority could be very good. Peter Mursell knew from experience that a wise county council delegated authority to district offices and could defend itself against the charge of 'remoteness'. Frank Hill's experience of city government, on the other hand, inclined him to want smaller (and more numerous) authorities. These differences explain the one or two notes of reservation which individual members added to the report we all ten signed. But unanimity was not achieved by bargaining, appeasement or compromise on any point of principle. The final pattern was in none of our minds when we began our work and came from no witness who submitted evidence. It was something new, formed out of the process of discussion, and its final shape was largely due to the continuous hammering that Derek Senior gave it. It was the hardy brain-child of the whole commission. How was it brought to birth?

We looked at one part of England after another and in each case asked ourselves whether a single elected council could reasonably be asked to do *all* the expensive work of local government: education, the Seebohm personal services and the environmental ones (planning the use of land, road-building, traffic control and transport). By 'reasonably' we meant a combined answer to two complementary questions about size. First, was each area (its shape and population) about right in the sense that the skilled manpower and equipment needed to provide it with local services could be found without unreasonable cost? Was it, in other words, *big* enough to be efficient? And secondly, was it *small* enough to give local democracy a decent chance? Our examination of each service led us to conclude provisionally that an area with fewer than some 250,000 inhabitants would be too small for efficiency, and that one with more than about a million would be too big for democracy. So what we asked ourselves about each part of the country was whether a main area could be found with a population somewhere between 250,000 and a million.

This detailed search led to one clear conclusion. Around Liverpool, Manchester and Birmingham were populations larger than a million that, in each case, needed one council to do certain things (strategic planning, transportation and the like). Here, then, we could not satisfy conditions needed for a single all-purpose council. But here, for the very reason that ruled out a single council, there was room for a second tier of councils which could serve populations of at least 250,000. In these three metropolitan areas, therefore, we decided to follow the pattern set by the Herbert Royal Commission on London: a county council for certain services (comparable to the Greater London Council) and a tier of district councils for the rest.

Elsewhere in England we found that a single main authority seemed feasible. Elected 'local councils' would also be needed, to represent the wishes of each borough and urban district within the new main area, but their role would be different from that of existing district or borough councils. It would be representative, not operational: to strengthen democratic links between citizen and main authority, and to make articulate the distinctive wishes of their part of the main area.

In June 1969, almost exactly three years after our appointment, we published our report. We doubted whether many members of the public would find time to read it or the still longer memorandum of dissent by Derek Senior (enviably readable though it was, compared with the collective work of ten of us). But we were anxious for the general public to know what we proposed. So besides writing a detailed summary for the press and other media, we published a 'short version' of the report and of Derek's volume of dissent. On the day of publication the BBC and independent television did us proud (exposing me in half a dozen separate programmes), and the press did us still prouder that day and the next. This was a mercy, for the poor Stationery Office was so paralysed by a strike of warehousemen that in many places the report was unobtainable for days.

We ceased to exist as a Commission once our report was published. It was now for the public, the politicians and the Government to consider what they thought of our advice. We had examined some two thousand bits of evidence, and the Government now received two thousand comments on our work. Members of the commission were of course free to take part in this continuing debate and several of us did so. During the next nine months I stumped the country, making some fifty speeches and jousting happily with any group that wished to listen, cross-examine or abuse.

The Women's Institutes and many parish councillors became almost enthusiastic. Rural district councils were unanimously indignant (we had proposed their abolition). Municipal corpora-

128

tions gave me a generous hearing at their Association's annual conference. Some county boroughs and some counties cautiously walked round our report – and found things to their taste; but neither of their Associations came out on one side or the other. As for the politicians, no party could make up its mind whether it would gain or lose. I sensed that the Conservative local government conference (at which I spoke in 1969) thought us too radical, perhaps because the national swing in recent local elections (against an earlier swing which favoured Labour) had put Conservatives in charge of most existing councils. When I explained our report at the Labour Party Conference that year, I found them sympathetic but far from any sign of unanimity. A mass meeting in the Bradford town hall (which the local newspaper had organized) was one of the liveliest I have ever talked to, but there was no sign of consensus. At Stoke-on-Trent an all-day conference gave me the same impression of great interest combined with disagreement.

In the autumn of 1969 the House of Lords had an excellent day's debate on the report and, for the first time, I began to think that Parliament might actually do something about local government reform. Labour spokesmen (on behalf of the Government) were polite enough but prepared only to tell the House how deeply they were studying the subject. They did not go further than the friendly remarks made by the Prime Minister when he had laid our report before the Commons the day it was published. What pleased and surprised me was George Jellicoe's speech from the Opposition Tory front bench. I can still hear him as he gave us a picture of himself on holiday in the Mediterranean, snoozing over the Commission's report. As he read on, he told us, he came nearer and nearer to approval – but the issue was too important to decide in such circumstances and he could therefore assure the House only that his party would continue to give serious thought to our proposals.

Meanwhile Tony Crosland had become Secretary of State for 'local government and regional planning' and taken over from Dick Crossman responsibility for advising the Cabinet on our report. The change was welcome but I had no idea what the result would be. Nor could I guess what Peter Walker was thinking. I only knew that he was a member of Ted Heath's shadow cabinet and was canvassing opinion in the country.

On my sixty-fourth birthday, 3 February 1970, Crosland sent me a copy of the Government's White Paper on local government reform, with a note hoping that I would think it a nice birthday present. It said nothing about our proposed provincial

129

councils – inevitably, because the Government's wish to cool off Scottish and Welsh nationalist fervour had led them to appoint in 1969 the Crowther-Kilbrandon 'commission on the constitution', with regional government in England thrown in for good measure into its terms of reference. The Labour White Paper added two metropolitan counties (West Yorkshire and Southampton–Portsmouth) to the three we had proposed. It gave education to the metropolitan counties, not (as we wanted) to the metropolitan districts. And it spoke of the need for neighbourhood councils of some kind. But on every point of principle it accepted our report and promised legislation to effect it.

I was, and I still am, convinced that our report was about right. I was, and shall always be, delighted that Wilson, Crosland and the Labour Government accepted it. They were courageous, it still seems to me, to stick their necks out and commit themselves. There was no chance of getting Parliament to legislate before the next election and little chance that their commitment to reform would help them win.

Within a few months of Labour's acceptance of our report there was a general election. Wilson was out and Heath was Prime Minister. To my surprise, and to my great relief, the new Government quickly committed itself to local government reform of some kind, with Peter Walker as the Minister responsible. He asked me out to lunch and encouraged me to tell him what I would do if I were in his shoes: a Tory Minister, committed to 'two tiers everywhere' but otherwise open to persuasion. There was now no chance of the reform I wanted ('two tiers everywhere' had destroyed that). But there was still a chance of something much better than the *status quo* – and if that chance were missed, how long should we be stuck with things as they were? I was determined to help Peter Walker make the best of his two-tier commitment.

After nine months' gestation, a new child was born: the Tory alternative to our report, published in a White Paper proposing local government 're-organization' (though 'reform' crept into an early page of the text and constantly recurred).* It was a child of no great beauty, with some features more plainly 'political' than others. Though the commission's concept of a metropolitan county was adopted – and extended to three areas not proposed by us (Tyne and Wear, West Yorkshire and South Yorkshire) – the historic shires had to be preserved – Lancashire,

---

* Local Government in England: Government proposals for Reorganization, Cmnd 4584, HMSO, 1971.

Cheshire, Hampshire in particular. They were the Tory strong-holds and had mounted powerful attacks on the commission's report. So to preserve Cheshire, for example, the new metropolitan counties of Merseyside and the North West had to be tightly confined to built-up areas; and to preserve Hampshire, Labour's proposal to make Portsmouth and Southampton a metropolis was dropped.

Nevertheless here was an end to the ring-fence round the old county-boroughs and the disastrous split of the whole country between county boroughs and counties. Old rural and urban districts were to be merged in a new second tier, no longer based on an out-dated difference between town and country. The principle was accepted that the great conurbations (which *did* need two tiers) should have counties for the whole area and within them districts large enough for the main personal services. So to denounce the Bill as worse than useless was a glamorous option I was not prepared to choose. In any case I was dead against delay. No party has ever thought local government reform a vote-catcher – and yet here were two Governments, Labour and Conservative, prepared to go for it. Such luck would not last. So for me there was no real alternative. Most of the shortcomings of the Walker plan were ineradicable because their cause lay in the two-tier principle (requiring Plymouth, for instance, to become a district in a new Devonshire county with Exeter its county town). But some of its defects we could at least try to cure.

Both Houses of Parliament spent months over the Bill. A few faults were removed in consequence, but most of the changes were for the worse. The size of metropolitan areas was further restricted and the power of metropolitan counties further reduced. Division of functions between county and district everywhere became more indistinct and the national pattern harder to understand. The Government rightly held to the principle that social services and education in the shires must stay with the county but, to appease the districts, gave counties power to use district councils as 'agents' for many other services. By the time it reached the statute book the Bill was worse than when it started. Could it be made to work? I was (and still am) convinced it could – on one condition: that we refuse to reorganize local government for some ten years.

On April Fool's Day 1974 every English and Welsh local council (save in parishes) 'ceased upon the midnight with no pain'. Few of my friends noticed any change. For out of the ashes of this unprecedented bonfire there had arisen, phoenix-like, a complete set of new authorities – county and district councils, elected twelve months before, which had been quietly sitting on the sidelines and now took on their full responsibility. While on the sidelines, each council had equipped itself with whole-time officers and staff, appointing (or disappointing) members of the existing local government services, at salaries and on conditions nationally negotiated.

Since then, a lot of nonsense has been talked about that April Fool's Day. No doubt some officers who were too good for local government to lose then left the service. No doubt some of the new councils played too safe and failed to put the best people available in the top jobs. No doubt some officers who stayed, and some who left, got salaries or compensation higher than was warranted. But I believe that a great debt of gratitude is owed to the whole local government service for the smooth, painless transition from 31 March to 1 April that year.

It would be best for all of us if Parliament and Ministers now left local government alone and let each individual council make the best of it. The worst would be to suspend another sword of Damocles over the present structure. Eventually we must have a new deal: Commissions must take another look at England and Wales, and Parliament must again make up its mind on national structures. Perhaps by that time final decisions will have been taken about Scottish and Welsh devolution – and Britain will be more firmly part of Western Europe.

Past history warns us, surely, against piecemeal tinkering with national structure. The Bill which became the County Councils Act of 1888 excluded originally some of the great cities, for the Government could not bring itself to put Birmingham, Manchester and a few others under the jurisdiction of the proposed new county councils: so less than ten cities (and they alone) were to become counties in their own right, called county boroughs. But while the Bill was before Parliament, more and more members pressed the Government to extend the list and convert their own cities into county boroughs. In the end, therefore, the Act excluded more than sixty boroughs from county council jurisdiction. From that time onwards it was the goal of every town to gain county borough status and the goal of every county to prevent this happening. At last the 1972 Act had seemed to end that war. But no. In 1979 Mr Callaghan's Labour Government pledged itself to legislation that would give nine of the ex-county-boroughs freedom to reinstall themselves as islands, for major services, outside the shire counties to which they belong.* Call

* *Organic Change in Local Government*, Cmnd 7457, HMSO, 1979.

this organic change if you like. It is in fact renewal of the old war declared in 1888.

Peace is what local government chiefly needs: in each county between county and district councils, between neighbouring counties (especially across metropolitan frontiers) and between the three national associations (metropolitan, county and district). This peace can be made more precarious by national government or parliament, but only local governors can make it secure.

Of course by the word peace I do not mean agreement. Between separately elected county, district and parish councils, there will often (and rightly) be disagreement. And as elections are increasingly fought on lines drawn up by party politicians, county and districts will often disagree on party lines. The likelihood of such disagreement only makes it the more necessary that county and district councils within each county should meet, consult and understand each other. And though all functions call for collaboration of some kind between county and district, this is essential where councils of each type have concurrent powers. It is already happening in many places. In West Glamorgan, for example, county and district councils have drawn up and agreed an 'arts development' plan. This links the county's education service with what Swansea and the other districts do to support music festivals, drama, dance and the visual arts. Education in schools and colleges is recognized as an essential part of arts support; county and district play into each other's hand. Norfolk is another example: there county and districts have agreed a single plan for museums and galleries.

Regional arts associations (which now cover almost all parts of England and Wales) enable neighbouring counties to collaborate across county boundaries. Regional sports councils too have proved the value of this type of structure. The case for statutory provincial councils, put forward in 1969 by the Royal Commission, has now gone by default (the more's the pity): it must be reconsidered when the time comes for the next general review of local government. But meanwhile, without parliamentary action, there are many ways in which neighbouring counties can concert plans and help each other.

And can peace between local and central government be stabilized? In two ways certainly. First, local government itself must close its ranks. The chance of having one organ of consultation and one local government voice has for the present vanished. But metropolitan, county and district leaders can do much to bring their associations into line: that is the only way (till the three bodies federate) for them to have valid dialogue with national government.

Secondly, Ministers must do more than clap their hands when asked if they believe in local government. They must trust local

133

democrats to spend national money. If (as I guess) they will never trust them with power to impose a local income tax, they must trust them to use grants from national taxpayers. They must cut more of the distrustful Whitehall strings that strangle freedom and responsibility. They must let daylight into the darkness of the rate support grant and give citizens a better chance to understand. The Chancellor of the Exchequer must of course have the last word about the share of national taxes local governors can spend and about totals of local capital expenditure. But if he and his Cabinet colleagues want local democracy to work, he must whip in his Treasury hounds. He must leave local councillors more free to make mistakes and let local electors hold them to account.

CHAPTER 10

Chairmanship

The first time that anyone asked me to chair anything outside my own college was in 1937. By then I had sat hours a week for six years under chairmen of Oxford city council committees – under my old philosophy tutor H. W. B. Joseph, for example, who succeeded in getting the education committee to accept on all important questions the advice of an exceptionally bright education officer, Alan Cameron (husband of Elizabeth Bowen, the novelist), or under Bursar Gill (of Merton College) who with equal skill prevented the electricity committee from interfering with the professional handling of light and power supplies.

I had also sat under the chairmanship of Michael Sadler at agreeable college and committee meetings in Univ. At none of these was anyone present save Sadler and the fellows. As our absolute sovereignty over all college business must be protected at all costs, we fellows must share the labour of decision-taking, even the recording of decisions taken, with no-one who was not a fellow. So one of us must take the minutes, write them out in longhand and read them aloud at the next meeting. This quaint procedure had unintended but important consequences. One was that the fellow responsible for a particular part of college business – the estates bursar, domestic bursar or dean – shared with the rest of us only such knowledge as he chose to share (and that was not much, while A. B. Poynton was the estates bursar), so that the governing body remained ignorant about substantial areas of college policy and, in effect, delegated to individual fellows much of its corporate responsibility. Another consequence was that we all spent much time on college business which could have been saved by using a college secretary and typewriter.

Still more time would have been saved if Sadler had been less scrupulously courteous in urging fellows to share with colleagues their own doubts and fears. Just as we neared the point in a discussion when everyone seemed ready for a vote, he would ask the history fellow, Kenneth Leys, whether he wished to speak before we voted. Invariably we were then back where we began.

In 1937, after some years of preparation in England, Europe and the United States (under the leadership of William Temple, J. H. Oldham, Reinhold Niebuhr, Paul Tillich and other theologians) there assembled in Oxford for two weeks a conference on 'Church Community and State'. Delegates came from many countries, representing all the main Christian denominations except the Roman Catholic (and even some Catholics came as observers). The main work was done in commissions which reported to plenary sessions before the close of the conference. Preparatory work for the economic commission had been done by various well-known people of sharply differing views; but which of them should be asked to chair the commission? None of them, thought the conference organizers; better have someone never heard of – such as me.

At the first meeting of this commission we had a general debate on the draft document circulated beforehand for discussion. All that became clear was that, although a quite new draft would need to be written as the commission's ultimate report, there was general agreement about the line to be taken. But one delegate, Professor Sergius Bulgakoff, had not opened his mouth (or even shown it). He had made a late but impressive entrance after discussion had begun: tall, with a long black beard, whiskers and moustache, in the black cassock of the Orthodox Church, wearing a black hat like the inverted cooling-tower of a power-station. Before the meeting ended I asked him (remembering Michael Sadler) whether he would like to comment on the discussion. He said he would – and, to my great relief, gave briefly his unqualified assent. As the meeting happily broke up, I heard the leading American delegate's comment to his neighbour: 'That was certainly an experience: to hear that bunch of whiskers open up – and find they were on your side.'

For the next ten days we wrestled in a small drafting committee to find words that the commission could endorse as our report to the full conference. The chief wrestlers were Niebuhr, T. S. Eliot, Tillich and John Baillie, the Scottish theologian. We had two admirable secretaries, John Bennett (who later became head of Union Theological Seminary, New York) and Archie Craig (eventually the first Moderator of the Church of Scotland to pay an official visit to the Pope). The report that finally emerged was amended only in detail by the full commission and

136

'commended' by the conference for consideration by the churches.*

I still think it as good a statement of the relevance of Christianity to problems of pre-war Western society as I have ever read.
Certainly it was a huge improvement on the pre-conference draft.
It embodied the insights of several wise and good men but it was
rather more than that: it was the creature of a group in travail.
Thoughts which at the outset were in no-one's mind emerged out
of intense discussion between serious people who were determined to understand each other, learn from each other and change
their minds only when convinced. It was the first time in my
experience that such a thing happened. Since then (especially since
chairing the Royal Commission on English local government) I
have become firmly convinced that in some circumstances such
things are possible: the artist's creative spirit does not work only
through individuals. Subsequent experience has also confirmed
what my first chairmanship taught me: a chairman's part in
committee work is sometimes crucial, but members of a group
can make do with almost any chairman, however ignorant or
inexperienced, if they work hard enough and have the right
secretaries to help.

Timing, however, is in the hands of no-one but the Chairman.
He must decide the order in which questions are discussed and the
length of discussion. Here lies his power and the art of chairmanship largely consists in his use of it. I have been told that once
when Churchill wished to defer discussion of a foreign policy
question, he started business by drawing the Cabinet's attention to
that morning's report of an incident in which someone had run
amok in a ducal residence and shot two menservants. Deploring
this occurrence, he commented that it was none the less encouraging that in days like these it was still possible to bag a brace of
butlers before breakfast, and he invited the Home Secretary to tell
his colleagues what action was proposed. This led on to various
other questions and enabled the Prime Minister to adjourn the
meeting before the foreign policy item was reached. Less eminent
chairmen than Churchill have used similar techniques in less
extraordinary circumstances.

My first experience of an official international conference was in
May 1943 at Hot Springs, Virginia. The post-war problem of
food and agriculture was our theme and I was made chairman of

* *The Churches Survey Their Task*, Report of Oxford Conference on Church,
  Community and State, Allen and Unwin, 1937.

137

one of the commissions through which the conference did its business. This was also my first experience of 'simultaneous translation' – the miraculous device by which delegates can speak their own language and have it translated in a number of glass boxes by several interpreters at the same time, so that the other delegates (using headphones) can hear the speaker in their own language. Once you have learnt how to use your headphones when, say, the Russian delegate is speaking, and how to speak into the microphone slowly enough for the interpreters to understand your speech, you can experience what the New Testament records of the first Pentecost: 'And they were all amazed and marvelled, saying one to another, Behold, are not all these that speak Galileans? And how hear we every man in our own tongue wherein we were born? Parthians and Medes and Elamites . . .'

I was an apprehensive chairman at the first meeting of that Hot Springs commission, but once we got going everyone became anxious to agree. Cubans, South Africans, even the French, seemed in conspiracy with delegates from Britain and the United States. Towards the end, however, when the commission came to consider its draft report to the full conference, a discordant note was sounded by the distinguished Australian delegate. Dr Coombs in effect asked whether the Emperor had any clothes on: was the draft report more than a bunch of truisms? This question was addressed to the chairman and was too near the truth for comfort. I was about to make the mistake so characteristic of an inexperienced chairman and try to reply, when Sir Girja Bajpai (of India) caught my eye: 'The honourable delegate of Australia is quite right,' he said; 'but let us not treat his shrewd summary of our report as if it were disparaging. For what is a truism, honourable delegates, but a truth that we too easily forget? Let us have courage, honourable delegates, and remind the world of too long forgotten truth.' Dr Coombs nodded assent, and we were home and dry.

My next experience of chairing an international body was quite different. It was for a whole year, 1949–50, and it was as president of a permanent body, the executive board of Unesco. This board, Unesco's governing body, was elected each year by the Unesco general conference, which consisted of delegations from all member-states, meeting in those days once a year in Paris (Unesco's permanent headquarters) or in some other capital (Mexico City, Beirut or Florence). The board's main duties were to propose to the general conference Unesco's annual budget and, from time to time, the name of some person to be full-time director-general (the head of the secretariat). But between meetings of the general conference the board was responsible for supervising the management by the director-general of all Unesco business and, in some sense, 'controlling' him. It therefore met regularly for a fortnight or so two or three times a year in Paris, and also at general conferences wherever they were held. I had been elected a member of the board each year since 1946, and when the board elected me its president, the director-general was Jaime Torres Bodet.

He was an enchanting Mexican, a poet with long political experience (he had been Foreign Secretary and Minister of Education in Mexico at various times), with a great reputation as a man of letters (his French was perfect) and with a friendly French-speaking wife. He spoke little English but was determined to learn. Passionately dedicated though he was to Unesco, the concept of a 'permanent civil servant' (doing what he could to persuade his political masters and then making the best of whatever they decided) was totally beyond his comprehension. Of course it was. He had never met such an animal before meeting me. He could not have treated me with more consistent courtesy, and the last time we talked together (celebrating in 1971 Unesco's twenty-fifth birthday in Paris) he made it plain beyond peradventure that, whatever differences of opinion there had been, we were still friends. In 1950, however, when the general conference refused to vote the budget that he wanted, he did what he had often threatened: he resigned. In the end I got him to withdraw his resignation; but he always kept it handy and continued to treat it as the joker in the pack.

The executive board of Unesco in my time was a group of eighteen men (no woman even stood for election during the 1946 to 1952 period) and we came to know each other well. Neither the USSR nor China was as yet a member of Unesco, nor had the new African states of the 'sixties yet emerged. But India joined Unesco in 1947 and each year sent an outstanding delegation to the conference, for six years in succession under the leadership of Sir Sarvepalli Radhakrishnan, who was elected a member of the executive board and eventually its chairman. He was a fellow of All Souls and held an Oxford philosophy chair (before becoming Vice-President and later President of India), and we became close friends. I never saw him lose his temper, but he could be shocked (by the director-general, Julian Huxley, for example) and as chairman he often retired into meditative silence (and sometimes sleep). His chairmanship was always just and everyone respected him, but he made no pretence to detailed mastery of the documents that we discussed.

No-one contrasted with him more strongly, in dynamism or style, than one of his Indian colleagues, Homi Bhabha. Homi, a young Fellow of the Royal Society, had been a Cambridge science don. He became the founding father of the Indian atomic energy commission, but he was also a leading Indian painter (a poster reproduction of one of his less attractive works was outside Burlington House throughout the London post-war exhibition of Indian art) and a musician in his own right, with an exceptional knowledge of Western music as well as Indian. He symbolized the many-sided purpose of Unesco, and I shall always be grateful to Unesco for our friendship. He commuted between India, the United States and Europe and died tragically in an Air India plane smash at the height of his career; but he left his mark for good, on Indian history and Unesco's.

Paulo Carneiro of Brazil, another member of the original Unesco board, was a major influence in the early days – and long after them. Eloquent in French, English, Spanish and Portuguese, with a slow beautiful contralto voice and Latin looks that no-one could resist, Paulo was the most effective of the board's chairmen that I knew. Other chairmen had to fit visits to Paris into a timetable mainly filled with business in their own country, but Paulo lived happily in Paris as his country's permanent delegate to Unesco. He made it his whole-time job to know the director-general and key members of the secretariat, and I doubt whether his government troubled him with instructions – or he them with advice. Unesco was financed, like the United Nations, on principles intended to reflect the relative wealth or poverty of each member-state, so that in practice the United States contributed much more than any other state, with Britain and France next in generosity. Brazil could therefore expect to gain rather than lose from the kind of increased budget for which Torres Bodet and all other directors-general fought consistently. Paulo well understood that it was British Treasury instructions, not my personal meanness, that made me invariably oppose expansion of the budget; and in any case no difference of opinion could prevent his treating me with affection. He was the most beguiling of my Unesco friends.

Ronald Walker's chairmanship of the board had little in common with Radhakrishnan's or Carneiro's. He was a large Australian economics don turned full-time diplomat. A good linguist and a prodigious worker, he was full of flat-footed Anglo-Saxon common sense which had uncommon value for the Unesco of his time; but he was abrasive enough to madden one director-general after another. Nor did he always keep his cool while in the chair.

140

No Frenchman chaired the board in my time, but no-one was a more significant member of it between 1946 and 1952 than Roger Seydoux, a career diplomat with a distinguished career ahead of him. The French government, in striking contrast to the British, attached serious importance to Unesco from the start and used it as an instrument of French cultural policy for all it was worth. For this purpose, and fortunately for me, Roger saw Britain as France's most important ally and we soon became friends. (Though he was no less determined than any fellow countryman to make French the post-war language of diplomacy, he never hesitated to use his excellent English in conversation with me.) We often disagreed officially – about the budget, about elections to the director-generalship and about the United States – but nothing inhibited the growth of our friendship. As a member of the executive board he was near faultless – excellently informed over the whole field of Unesco (he was much helped by another brilliant Frenchman, Pierre Auger, who headed the scientific division of the secretariat), witty and eloquent, realistic in negotiation and loyal once bargains had been struck.

The strength of United States influence in the early days of Unesco had deeper foundations than finance. It rested on the enthusiasm of Americans in many parts of the country and many walks of life: the universities and churches and the world of journalism, radio and television. And this enthusiasm was institutionalized. Under the Unesco constitution each member-state was bound to set up a national commission for Unesco, consisting of citizens not chosen by state or federal governments but representative of 'science, education and culture'. Alone of all such national bodies, the United States Commission soon established its authority. Dean Acheson, when United States Secretary of State, viewed it with barely concealed disfavour, for he rightly judged that its purpose was to develop an effective instrument of public opinion quite independent of the State Department and potentially hostile to aspects of official foreign policy. But in 1945 the assistant Secretary of State, with responsibility under Acheson for cultural affairs, was Archibald Macleish. He came that year as chairman of the United States delegation to the London conference at which the structure of Unesco's constitution was provisionally agreed, and in 1946 he was elected the first United States member of the executive board. A graduate in the class of 1914 at unreconstructed Yale, he had enlisted in 1917 as a private in the US army, taught government at Harvard, then practised law in Boston. But from 1923 he became a whole-time man of letters (he and his wife had lived in Paris and he spoke perfect French), and by 1939 he was Librarian of Congress. By 1945, when I first met him, he had become a powerful orator (as well as poet), and his charm was irresistible. But the secret of his influence on Unesco was his conviction that here was an institution that could at last do something positive for the peace of the world. This was what made him pre-eminent at each Unesco conference and established his position as the one prophet who could lead Unesco into the promised land. If circumstances had been different, he would have become the first director-general of Unesco. In any case his lifelong friendship with Acheson made it unlikely that the United States national commission for Unesco would be prevented by the State Department from getting off to a vigorous start. I think it was in fact Archie Macleish (and the enthusiasm he generated in his own country) that made the United States a more powerful influence on Unesco policy during its early days than either France or Britain.

The head of an Oxford college is a sitting target for anyone in search of a chairman. My colleagues in the Univ. governing body (of course I consulted them before agreeing to be shot) invariably left the decision to me, with the proviso that it should not involve my death. The consequence was that I often meekly complied – when the Royal College of Music asked me to be chairman of its Council and the British Diabetic Association to become its president, and when Conservative and Labour Governments made me the chairman of three local government enquiries and the first chairman of the Schools Council.

I enjoyed all these chores. Each job was worthwhile in itself and none of them was boring. All of them taught me a great deal about subjects I find intensely interesting and introduced me to people who became friends.

The fact is that I enjoy sitting round a table with people who share an interest in a tough subject, have various kinds of relevant experience at the outset and gradually get to know each other's point of view. I specially enjoy the moment when one or two of them lose patience and become cantankerous, for that may bring out a crucial issue which needs deciding one way or the other, either at once or after passions are spent. At such times the chairman must decide how long the fight should last, how to contain it within reasonable limits, and when the gong should sound.

Whether a chairman enjoys himself or not, it is part of his job, I think, to keep his colleagues happy, for if they are they will turn up at meetings, read written evidence submitted and find time to think about it. But agreement at the end of the day is still more to

142

be desired. A report with several notes of dissent (such as Kilbrandon on the Constitution) is more certain to be ignored than if it is unanimous. But the purpose of an enquiry is more than agreement: it is to judge rightly what needs changing and what should not be changed. The door must therefore be left open for dissent; and in the end dissenters may be proved right. In 1911, for example, the Webbs recommended the break-up of the poor law (in a minority report of the 1909 Royal Commission); twenty years later that recommendation was accepted by Parliament and the poor law guardians were abolished by the Local Government Act of 1929. Again, in 1928 the chairman of the Hilton Young commission was over-ruled by his three colleagues (under the leadership of George Schuster) who wrote their own report opposing the chairman's concept of an East African self-governing dominion.* Subsequent history seems to confirm their view.

In any case there is no doubt that, before an enquiry finishes, members dissenting from their colleagues have the right to say so and declare their own views as part of the report. For example, Arthur Goodhart (my predecessor as Master of Univ.) wrote his own memorandum of dissent from his colleagues in the Royal Commission on the police and recommended the nationalization of all local police forces.† Derek Senior did likewise (but on a still grander scale) in dissenting from the rest of the Royal Commission on English local government in 1969.

Apart from such major cases of dissent there are almost always points on which individual members of an enquiry, though they go along with their colleagues in signing the report, wish to express a personal reservation. Andrew Wheatley, for example, though he signed the report of the local government management committee, wrote an important note of reservation explaining why he opposed our recommendation of an executive board as part of a large local council's internal structure.‡

Judging the time when hope of agreement must be abandoned is perhaps the crucial test of chairmanship. In Wheatley's case, what the management committee recommended in the end was a radical departure from local government tradition. From start to finish we all gained enormously from Wheatley's critique of what we had in mind. I was in no doubt as chairman that the debate must continue till it was clear that all but one of us were in

* Sir George Schuster, *Private Work and Public Causes*, D. Brown and Sons, 1979.
† See Appendix III (3).
‡ *Management of Local Government*, Vol. I, Report of the Committee, Ministry of Housing and Local Government, HMSO, 1967, pp. 154–7.

agreement. At that point we took a vote and Wheatley drafted his own reasoned note of reservation.

In Derek Senior's case I found the chairman's task more difficult. Long before his decision that he must write a memorandum of dissent, the patience of some colleagues was exhausted. Had he been an expert witness, we would have spent time considering his evidence and cross-examining him, but in the end we would have rejected his conclusions – and I think we would have saved six months or more. However, without him as a full member of the commission the other ten of us might never have agreed, for by defending his own views against the rest he helped us to agree among ourselves. It was only when ten of us had reached agreement that the time had come to go our different ways.

More commonly the chairman has to handle a problem of a rather different kind. By the time a group reaches the last phase of discussion, most of its members will have modified their original views and, perhaps reluctantly, made some concessions. But nearly always, in my experience, one or two people round the table will have made fewer concessions than the rest; and if they declare when time has almost run out that unless this or that further point of theirs is met they will have to dissent and write their own report, their colleagues may well reply that in that case they must themselves withdraw the concessions they made earlier. This means that the game must start again from scratch – and that is very seldom possible. The situation can only be saved if both sides wish to save it – and in my experience that is what they do.

Select Committees are appointed by the House of Lords for various purposes and in most respects their working does not differ much from that of other kinds of enquiry. But traditionally their reports cannot include notes of dissent or reservation by individual peers. In consequence, when disagreement cannot be resolved by discussion the chairman must eventually ask the Committee to vote for or against the relevant part of the draft report. The result of the vote is then entered in the Committee's minutes – which in due course are published. Members of the Committee can thus make public their dissent and, in addition, when the House debates the report they can elaborate their reasons.

When Lord Wade's proposal of a Bill of Rights came up for second reading in February 1977, the House decided to commit the bill to a Select Committee with instructions to report back to the House an answer to two questions: was the enactment of a Bill of Rights desirable? If so, what form should it take? Philip Allen, sometime permanent head of the Home Office and now, as Lord Allen of Abbeydale, an Independent peer, became the Committee's chairman, the other members consisting of four Labour, four Conservative, one Liberal (Lord Wade) and a second Independent peer (myself). We heard evidence from many distinguished legal and other witnesses, starting with Lord Hailsham and ending with Leslie Scarman (both in favour of a Bill) but including Kenneth Diplock and many other powerful opponents. Philip Allen was a faultless chairman. He handled all witnesses, the grander and the less grand, with equal courtesy – and kept most of them to the point. He read all written evidence submitted to us and could cite the relevant passages at will. Neither to witnesses nor colleagues did he reveal which side he favoured – till it was time for a vote.

Starting with a strong prejudice against any Bill of Rights (I had tried my hand at drafting one when Basutoland was nearing independence), I came to the conclusion that those who shared my prejudice protested too much – and were in the wrong. By ratifying thirty years ago the European Convention on human rights and fundamental freedoms our government had, in effect, signed an international treaty which guaranteed all rights spelled out in the Convention to all our citizens. And subsequently we in Britain had agreed that a citizen who thought himself aggrieved could take his case for decision by the European Commission and the Court at Strasbourg; but no citizen can take it to any court in Britain – until our Parliament makes the Convention part of United Kingdom law. I came to think it was high time that this was done – and that until it was done, most people in Britain would remain as ignorant of the rights guaranteed them under the Convention as I had always been. Some who opposed the Bill feared that our judges would often prove oldfashioned and reactionary. But was there reason to suppose that the Strasbourg Court, manned largely by retired legal luminaries from other states, was more enlightened than our own courts? In any case, an individual citizen could not be worse off, and might gain, if the Convention became part of UK law; and he might get a decision quicker than a certain Mr Golder – the UK citizen who had had to wait five years for a favourable decision from the Strasbourg Court.

When the Select Committee came to the crunch, we were unanimous that if a Bill of Rights were thought desirable, its form must be the incorporation of the Convention in UK law. But there agreement ended. Six of us thought it desirable to incorporate the Convention; five of us, including the Chairman, thought it was not.

It would have been ludicrous to submit a report which recommended that the House should endorse the majority view, leaving peers to discover only from the minutes (and the last sentence of the report) that the Committee was irreconcilably divided and that five of the eleven members rejected the main recommendation. Thanks to the chairman and the reasonableness of all concerned, such nonsense was avoided. The report set out what each side thought were the main arguments in favour of the Bill and against it, and recorded the number and names of the peers on each side.*

There was an excellent full-dress debate on the report for several hours on 29 November 1978. The motion, introduced by Philip Allen, was simply 'to take note' of the Committee's report; but an amendment was then moved by Lord Wade in favour of incorporating the Convention in UK domestic law. When the Lord Chancellor (Lord Elwyn-Jones) summed up before we voted, he made it clear that the Labour Government was against a Bill of Rights. It was encouraging for those who were in favour that the House supported us – by a majority of roughly two to one.

In 1979, after the change of Government, Lord Wade took up the cudgels once again and introduced another Bill on the same lines as the earlier one. Lord Hailsham, who was now Lord Chancellor and spokesman for the Government, warned the House that HMG could find no time in their present legislative programme for a Bill of this kind; but he made plain that his own views had not altered. Though the Labour party was still opposed to legislation, their spokesmen did not ask the House to vote against the Bill and it passed through all its stages in the Lords.

This illustrates, I think, the continuing value of the Lords for certain purposes. Here is a subject of importance and great difficulty, which cuts across party lines and needs debate. The House of Commons has no time for it, but the Lords include some of the most distinguished lawyers and also a broad cross-section of relevant experience. Through their select committees they can consult opinion outside as well as inside Parliament, and can work out the form that legislation might take.

I had my first experience of chairing a Select Committee of the Lords in 1978. Lord Byers, the Liberal leader in the Lords, had introduced the Foreign Boycotts Bill. This would forbid com-

* House of Lords paper 176, HMSO, p. 40.

pliance by British citizens or companies with any boycott that foreigners imposed against another country, unless the United Kingdom Government approved it. Lord Byers made no secret of the purpose of the Bill: it was aimed at the Arab boycott of Israel. It was on the same lines as legislation passed by the United States Congress for this purpose, following promises made in 1976 by Mr Carter during his Presidential campaign. The Lords concluded their debate by giving the Bill a second reading on condition that it went to a Select Committee which would hear evidence from interested parties and report back to the House.

The Committee which I was asked to chair consisted of nine members: three Labour, three Conservative, two Independent and one Liberal (Lord Byers). The secretary was Paul Hayter, one of the permanent officials of the House. I had first known him some years earlier when he was secretary of the Select Committee on Sport and Leisure and played the chief part in writing our two reports (of 1973). I was also very lucky in my colleagues, but only one of them was an old friend (Harold Caccia), and I was scared at the prospect of the chair. I need not have been. The Committee showed their maiden chairman the indulgence that the House showed me when I made my maiden speech.

Written evidence was received from more than forty individuals or bodies and oral evidence from fifteen. We published with our Report all these submissions, whether written or oral, except when witnesses asked us to treat their evidence as confidential or were unnamed at their request. The Trade Department, the Foreign and Commonwealth Office and a dozen or so of the chief organizations involved in commerce, banking, insurance and other services, whether with the Arab States or with Israel, were among those whom we asked to come and give us oral as well as written evidence.

Besides giving us valuable information, these long sessions taught me a lot about the other members of the Committee and their mutual attitudes. One lesson we all learnt in the end was that when cross-examining witnesses you must concentrate on hearing what they say and not start arguing among yourselves. Luckily too, towards the end of our work, we found we must go to Brussels and beard the European Commission in its den. Six of us went, and the twenty-four hours spent in continuous proximity did us a world of good.

When we had read and heard (sometimes in private) a mass of evidence, what we agreed on covered almost all the ground and greatly outweighed our points of disagreement. We were all against trying at the present time to make compliance with a

147

boycott illegal and we therefore recommended that 'the Bill should not proceed'. (The United States differed sharply from Britain, in its political attitude to Israel and its far smaller dependence on exports.) But we were all for bold positive action by all businessmen, despite the boycott, to expand exports to all Middle East countries including Israel by means already found successful by adventurous firms. Furthermore, as the boycott runs counter to basic EEC principles of non-discrimination, we were all agreed that a common European policy should be developed against it. We recommended that meanwhile our Government should cease to take any part, however tenuous, in the boycott process. In particular, HMG should cease authenticating negative certificates of origin.

Time almost ran out. If we did not report before the House went into recess, our work would almost certainly be wasted. Most of my colleagues agreed with me that we must complete our report without delay – and our luck held. Paul Hayter's drafting skill solved all our detailed problems, but two minor points of principle remained. On each of them both John Boyd-Carpenter (Conservative) and Bill McCarthy (Labour) disagreed with the rest of us. On the last day before the recess we voted (seven to two) on these two points, and on the rest of the report we were unanimous. We launched it at a well-attended press conference and the response of press and radio was generous.

The House was at its best, I thought, when it spent five hours (on 1 February 1979) debating the report, and Lord Goronwy-Roberts, replying for the Labour Government, was more encouraging than I had dared to hope. Since Lord Carrington took office as Foreign and Commonwealth Secretary he has had more important matters to consider than our Select Committee's report and the replies to Questions about the Arab boycott given on his behalf have so far (in mid-1980) been more polite than satisfactory.

The Foreign Boycotts Bill was a private *member's* bill, as distinct from one introduced by the Government. A *private* bill is something quite different. It is promoted neither by the Government nor by a member of the House but by some corporate body such as a local authority or university and the House has its own procedures for dealing with it. London University, for example, a few years ago promoted a bill to change its own constitution. Enquiries and discussions had been going on for many years, inside and outside the University, and this bill was the result. It represented a large measure of agreement between the many colleges and schools that constitute the University, but as it was

148

opposed by the Association of University Teachers (the AUT) it was referred by the House to a Select Committee, consisting of an experienced Tory chairman, Lord Derwent, and four other peers of whom I was the one Independent. We behaved like judges (in mufti); both London University and the AUT were represented by Queen's Counsel (in uniform, and not unpaid); both sides called witnesses and cross-examined them; proceedings were in public and took several days. We listened and asked Councel and witnesses whatever questions we liked. After discussing in private what we had heard, we found ourselves united in rejecting without hesitation all the objections raised by the AUT and we agreed a recommendation to the House 'that the Bill should proceed'. Without debating this report, the House then sent the bill to the House of Commons – where London University made some concessions to the AUT and the bill passed into law.

CHAPTER 11

The Spoken Word

I once came across an end of term report, made by the principal of a high school in the United States on one of his pupils: 'Homer excels in initiative, group co-operation and responsibility. Now, if only he could learn to read and write!' No laughing matter. Learning to read is one of the hardest lessons – and reading aloud is a separate and exacting art. Learning to write is even harder – and teaching any of these arts is harder still. But here (as I said earlier) I was exceptionally lucky: my mother taught me all these various arts. Each reading lesson was a fresh excitement, but meanwhile she was teaching me to learn by heart and, in the process, act and imitate. So before I could read or write, I had begun to learn public speaking and, once I could read, there were fresh opportunities to learn that art.

Acting and speaking what other men had written were important parts of life at school. For 'saying lessons' each week we learnt by heart some of the great English and Latin classics. We also learnt to read aloud (and perhaps remember for the next fifty years) passages from the 1662 authorized version of the New Testament (for example: 'That ye, being rooted and grounded in love, may be able to comprehend, with all saints, what is the length and breadth and depth and height, and to know the love of Christ, which passeth knowledge, that ye might be filled with all the fullness of God').

Reading the Bible in a church or chapel is a form of public speech that calls for something special. You must not over-dramatize but you must leave no-one in doubt of what you think the passage means. You must give open access to your under-standing but without imposing it on any of your hearers. And you must be heard in all parts of the building – by those who hear your words for the first time in their lives and by those who already know them by heart. For five years as a schoolboy I heard the lessons read in chapel by Dr M. R. James, then Provost of

Eton. When I listened to him (as I quite often did), there seemed to be no problem. It was when I tried reading aloud myself that I came to realize how many problems Dr James had solved.

Some radio programmes in which a critic is discussing works of literature make use of speakers other than the critic. This lets the critic off and makes life easy for the listener. But how much better, surely, if the critic dispenses with all voices but his own. There need be no problem for the listener: by changing his tone of voice the critic can make plain when he is quoting and when speaking for himself (just as when reading aloud from *Mansfield Park*, for instance, the voice changes when Mrs Norris interrupts Fanny Price). But not all broadcasters can read aloud, and I think programme-makers are right in thinking that many listeners prefer variety to monologue. A compromise has something to be said for it. Once, when I was to broadcast on Henry James, my producer first assumed that professionals should read the extracts I had chosen, but when I offered to read some of them myself she let me try. In the end I shared the reading with a professional actress – and the critics were friendly about both of us.

Broadcasting has introduced more and more people to the experience of hearing literature spoken aloud. And this has encouraged artists to offer the public live as well as broadcast readings of poetry and prose. Larger and smaller halls in many parts of England can nowadays be filled when readers and musicians offer combined practice of their arts. Constance Cummings, one of the artists who reads aloud and acts with the same magic, once asked my wife and me to join her in a performance of 'reading and music' at the Radcliffe Hospital in Oxford. She and I read, singly or together, pieces of prose and poetry, and Jean played two groups of piano music. I shall not forget Constance reading Mrs Bennet, with me as her husband, in the first chapter of *Pride and Prejudice*.

Reading aloud what poets, dramatists and novelists have written for you is difficult – but child's play compared with finding words of your own to speak. And few of us can nowadays escape this ordeal; sooner or later we must get up and use the spoken word. But how do we turn ourselves into creative artists? How do we start our search for the right words?

I try first to answer a quite different question: when the time comes and I stand up to face the audience, what am I going to hold in my hands? A complete script, to read from start to finish? Notes, that I glance at from time to time? Or nothing, so that I seem to the audience to be thinking aloud and finding words out of my head?

There are times when you must write down each word beforehand, if only because each word commits your colleagues –

and perhaps your Government. So sometimes you must make sure that nothing you mean to say seems wrong to someone else. Even so, the question remains whether to read a script or trust your memory. In either case you may need a written text of the crucial passages, to hand out to the press before you speak: so why not always use it yourself? Why put yourself to the extra sweat of memorizing and run the risk that memory will let you down? I think the right answer to this question is not always obvious.

When listening, I find spoken words much more persuasive if the speaker seems unbound to a script. However well a speaker reads his speech, attention quickens when he abandons it and speaks out of his head. And this is particularly true when he is quoting. Any quotation needs to be quoted slowly or it will not be understood; but if quoted by heart, it may be the one thing spoken that listeners would be sorry to forget. Nothing is more encouraging when a speech is over than to be asked where something quoted can be found. If the answer is 'Nowhere: the book is long out of print', and the stranger looks disappointed, I have found myself extracting from a pocket my own copy of the passage and gratefully presenting it.

South African experience convinces me that even when you are speaking as the spokesman of Her Majesty, you may have to pocket all signs of preparation and speak without notes. For sometimes what matters most is credibility. Here in Mbabane (or Serowe or Maseru) is a great company of Africans, sitting in the sunshine and prepared to listen. You are in the splendid fancy-dress of High Commissioner, with a microphone in front of you and an African interpreter to make the best of what you say. If you have a script (or even notes), your audience will listen but assume that what you say has been prescribed by someone else. Somehow you must persuade them to the contrary. My African interpreter was always happy to collaborate. I would pause after each point – and he would make the best of it, while I made up my mind what to say next. When I made a joke and English-speaking Africans laughed at it, the interpreter would try to get a bigger laugh himself. When he saw the end was near, his style would become doom-laden and rise to an ecstatic peroration.

Sometimes – say, for broadcasting in a programme with a time-limit* – there is no escape from writing out and using a full

* See Appendix II.

152

script. If your speech is to be taped and published later, you can speak without a script – but count the cost. Your hosts will send a typescript of the tape-recording and ask for leave to print it as it stands. You read it through and find your blood has frozen. No punctuation in half a dozen lines. No syntax. Little grammar. Repetition. As you read, you feel like Hamlet's father's ghost:

Cut off even in the blossoms of my sin.
No reckoning made, but sent to my account
With all my imperfections on my head:
O, horrible! O, horrible! Most horrible!

But though an accurate version of your unscripted speech is horrible, there is worse to come: you must rewrite the script before it can be published, and this costs you more time and frustration than if you had composed it in advance. And yet why lose the chance to captivate an audience? I have obstinately refused to change my ways.

There are times when you must write out what you mean to say – and read it. When a friend dies and you must speak at the memorial service, you cannot trust yourself to speak without a script.* All you can do is check the facts (including details of the service), write what you really think and read it aloud. When you have done your best and have a typescript, underline one or two words in each paragraph, some firmly and some faintly; read the whole script at the pace required by the building – and shorten it still further if you can.

Mistrust the man who tells you that you will not need a microphone (unless you think he really means that the public address system will not work). But if you plump for a microphone, make sure you know its ways. If it needs hanging round your neck, rehearse the halter-work in private – and somehow remember before leaving the pulpit to extricate your head.

Another gadget that deaf speakers must beware of is the hearing-aid. Mine tends to make me bellow and my instinct before speaking is to pocket it. But you must hear the criminal record that the Chairman reads out in introducing you, and you must have all aid available at question-time; so you must learn the fine art of aid-manipulation: out of the ear before you speak and back in as soon as you've spoken.

Before speaking at a dinner you can ask your host for advance

* See Appendix III for what I said about Oliver Woods, Ian Fraser, Arthur Goodhart and Seretse Khama – four friends who have done much to confirm my optimism.

warning of the length and order of the speech-list, but he must decide whether you bat early or late. If you bat fairly early, you can find dreamful ease in every speech that follows. If you come last, all will depend on the company's condition, the lateness of the hour, and how much the pitch has suffered. None of these things can be predicted: you must be ready for anything and, when your turn comes, adapt ruthlessly to circumstance. Your job can easily turn out to be impossible – but it may be uproarious fun.

The only rule I have for after-dinner speaking is: no script – and on the night no use of notes. Unlimited expenditure of time is the result of this decision. I read about the purpose of the dinner and the people who are likely to be there; I cover page on page with random jottings, and an outline can at last be written down. As the fatal date approaches and time begins to run out, gestation becomes steadily more painful: fear alone (or panic) drives me on. What will happen when I stand up empty-handed and cannot remember what I meant to say? when I dry up half-way through a long quotation? I rewrite the final outline on a post-card; reduce the long quotation by a half; and when my host has offered me my first drink, cast care aside and think no more until I speak. Once you get up you must betray no sign of agonizing: no-one must doubt that you are totally in charge. And everyone must know when you have finished – not simply that at last you have sat down.

Sometimes your speech must end with the proposal of a toast, coupled with the name of the next speaker. So whatever else you have forgotten when you reach your peroration, don't forget the title of the toast you are proposing – or some virtues of the man who will reply. At the start, besides the chairman you may need to greet your excellencies, my lord bishop, your worship the lord mayor, the lady mayoress, sheriffs, aldermen – in the same order that the toastmaster has followed. This catalogue must be treated with respect (or ignored completely by substituting, as George Tomlinson when Minister of Education often did, the one word 'Friends'). But its recital, with faint echoes of the toastmaster, has been known to get the speaker his first laugh. Still greater risks can sometimes be run safely when you are opening an agricultural show. Once, in South Africa, the air well charged with harmonies of bleating sheep and other fauna, I took a chance and started an ambassadorial speech: 'Mr Chairman, Excellencies, Your Worship, pigs, sheep, cows, ladies and gentlemen.' But such opportunities are dangerous – and rare.

Though a speech's top and tail are both important, they are not the parts that should be settled early. First, is there one serious thing I want to say? That depends partly on the audience and on what

154

brings them together: so let me lay hands on all the facts that I can find. Exceptionally, this may not be the first time I have addressed this company. If so, I must dig out the previous pile of notes and outlines and make sure that I use none of them again. Then on with new notes, new quotes, new final outlines. And here the tempter may present himself: why not, at this point or at that, lapse into dialect? Welsh, Irish, Scotch (unless my wife is there), South African, Sri Lankan, American, Australian, French, German, Norwegian, Dutch? There are undoubtedly strong arguments *against* impersonation. First, Mr Ustinov and Mr Yarwood have now set standards that no amateur can touch. And, secondly, if any member of your audience thinks you are making fun of him he may regard it as a joke in execrable taste. None the less, each time I disregard these scruples I find temptation harder to resist.

The word 'lecture', I suppose, should mean a 'reading'. But readings of a script are not always lectures, and most of my lectures were not read from a script. Lecturers, however, have one thing in common: they are paid.

In 1929 when I first lectured in Oxford no training was available. It was assumed you had learnt all that could be taught by being lectured at: only practice might make perfect in the end. During my undergraduate years at Oxford I had spasmodically listened to some lectures – not in the subjects with which my own lectures were to deal. At Harvard I had been copiously lectured at: lectures were the sole kind of formal education offered me, they were compulsory, and the marks given by lecturers throughout each term helped to decide the class of your degree.

Now back at Oxford I must teach myself to lecture. This, for ten years, I struggled painfully to do, without much method and with only marginal improvement as I worked on and learnt from my mistakes. I made myself accept whatever invitations came my way. Besides what I was bound to do (lecturing to Univ. freshmen about economics), I lectured once a week to anyone who wished to hear about English local government; and three years later this became a book. I went on evening pilgrimages to Burford and Watlington, lecturing (as part of Oxford's extra-mural programme) to all-age heterogeneous groups of local citizens. I took part, whenever asked, in broadcast programmes – symposia with Lowes Dickinson and Julian Huxley, and talks of my own. A group of Oxford dons put on a lecture-course on Personal Ethics, with one from me on politics and Christianity.* Sometimes I preached in College chapel on a

* *Personal Ethics*, ed. K. E. Kirk, OUP, 1935.

155

Sunday evening and from time to time (I blush to think of it) at Winchester, Uppingham and other boarding schools. Trying to interest a wide range of audiences taught me the versatility of the spoken word and how each type of audience needs special handling.

Except for broadcasting, in those days I never lectured from a script. I would have less to blush for if I had; and yet, even for academic audiences, without a script I think you can do something that no scripted lecture can. This is true even of special lectures, sponsored by some institution and given in memory of some distinguished person. All such lectures seem to demand a script and I used one for a Stevenson Lecture (on Southern Africa) at the London School of Economics and a Wilfrid Fish Lecture (on Professionalism) at the General Dental Council. But for the same kind of lecture at the Royal Free Hospital in 1978 I took a chance – and I would take it again.

Lectures abroad are the most rewarding form of lecture: they cover your travel expenses (and perhaps your wife's). And the chances are that none of your audiences has ever heard of you before. If you can get on terms with them and speak to their condition, what you say strikes them as new and relevant; and in any case by visiting their country you probably learn more from them than they from you. 'There never was a better bargain driven.'

My first experience of this happy kind was in Johannesburg in 1936, when my lectures were intended to celebrate the city's first fifty years of life (five minutes after the start of the first lecture the Vice-Chancellor, my chairman, fell asleep). After a lapse of forty years I had another invitation from abroad, this time from Canada: the Canadian Institute of Public Administration asked me to visit eight provincial cities and give the Clifford Clarke memorial lectures. Only one script was needed by the Institute – for publication in English and French – entitled 'Politics and the Art of Local Government'. This I wrote out and handed to the Institute, but I could not bring myself to give the same lecture more than once. So in each city (Halifax, Ottawa, Winnipeg, Vancouver, Victoria, Edmonton, Saskatoon and Toronto) I made myself adapt it to local circumstances.

I was invited back to Canada soon afterwards for an autumnal and less formidable tour – this time to talk about the arts and public patronage. On my first visit to Vancouver I had made friends with a formidable broadcaster, Jack Webster. He was still running the most successful of the local radio programmes and he asked me to collaborate again. So next morning at eight-thirty down we sat together. After some introductory dialogue between us, he invited listeners to phone in and ask me questions – for me to hear through earphones and answer off the cuff as best I could. From time to time the stream was interrupted for 'commercials', but for an hour and a half I was on call. I was learning all the time about Vancouver and I was greatly impressed by what I learnt, for the questions were friendly and intelligent – and with few exceptions clearly on my side. I shall always be grateful to Jack Webster for his kindness and his high professional skill.

In the nineteen-fifties I could not resist temptation when the BBC asked me to take part in a television programme called the *Brains Trust*. You had no idea what questions would be asked. You were told who would be the chairman and the other members of the panel, but that was all. You lunched exceptionally well, in a private room at a distinguished London restaurant, and talked of anything under the sun. No hint was given of the questions which would be asked two or three hours later (when nerves or hangover had reduced most of you to yawns). The BBC had of course selected, from the questions sent in by the public, those that were most likely to provoke their four invited guests; but as your three fellow-panellists were always polymaths (in science, literature, philosophy and art), there was no point in guessing what the questions would be.

We drove to the studio, the cosmetician did her best for our faces, and there was tea to wake us up. Then on to the set, where we were ranged around the chairman. He asked a practice question, with the light still green, for all of us to answer. Then the count-down, the red light, and we were live.

The chairman introduced us, read out the first question and invited one of us to answer. If the questioner wanted to know what existentialists believed and Ayer was on view to answer, the rest of us would not have much to add. The chairman would soon move on to the next question, which might be: 'I have a teenage daughter, and someone has sent me a copy of the full text of *Lady Chatterley's Lover*. Should I leave it aound, or conceal it?' I remember Marghanita Laski answered that one first. (Had she provoked the questioner to ask it?)

When I took part in sessions of the *Brains Trust* I was a civil servant and, before accepting a BBC invitation, I always asked my Minister's advice. In fact none of my Ministers, whether man or woman, Socialist or Tory, wanted me to say no; they thought it useful that their chief adviser should sometimes expose himself as a human being whose mind and lips were not permanently sealed.

157

When a question raised some controversial issue – say, the safety of a nuclear power station or the cost of laying cables underground – I had to watch my step. But that was true each time one spoke in public, and I do not remember any *Brains Trust* answer that made trouble for my Minister or me. Anyhow, it is no bad thing for a civil servant (who normally has time to think before he speaks) to find that he must sometimes take a decision on the spur of the moment.

I certainly learnt a lot from such experience. Those Sunday afternoons were an odd form of relaxation but I regret none of them. They gave me the misleading sense that there was nothing to fear from television, least of all when it meant answering live questions heard for the first time on the set. Years later, taking part in a full-length *Panorama* programme (in 1969 on local government reform), I thanked my stars for the *Brains Trust* experience.

The BBC radio programme *Any Questions* has many things in common with the *Brains Trust* – a chairman, a mixed team of guests and no pre-knowledge of the questions. Experience of both programmes was exciting in different ways. The chief difference lay, not in the contrast between radio and television nor in the kind of question asked, but in the live and breathing presence of an audience. The *Brains Trust* was a closed conversation, and the fact that viewers might overhear you was something to forget. In *Any Questions*, on the other hand, live people in the hall were involved in the performance and you were vividly aware of their reaction.

J. B. Priestley is an old friend and a man I much admire. So when he asked me to take part with him in a new television programme in the early 'sixties of course I said yes. The BBC had just got access to a second TV channel and had invited Priestley to give a series of small dinner parties at Television Centre. He and two guests who shared some common interest would have dinner on the set – and then relax over the port in conversation which would go out on BBC 2. Would I be one of his guests when the subject of post-prandial talk would be 'religion' and the other guest Professor Zaehner? I had never met Zaehner though I knew about him: Professor of Eastern Religions and Ethics, fellow of All Souls College, author of some eighteen books on various aspects of religion. The sooner we met, the better chance (I thought) of easy broadcast conversation; so I rang up and asked if I might call. We met in All Souls and sipped his sherry. Curled up in his chair and blinking behind thick spectacles, he seemed incapable of speech. I failed abysmally to find a single point of

158

common interest: Jack Priestley? Television? Zaehner? God? We found nothing in heaven or earth that we could talk about – and what would happen when the television cameras moved in?

Our next meeting was at Television Centre. We dined on the set – and dined extremely well. Jack was the excellent host that he is at all his parties. The wine flowed and Zaehner became a different person. His tongue was loosed. Words came cascading from him: drugs, mysticism, make-believe were all discussed. Zoroastrianism had its dawn and twilight; the Catholic church took her unique place among world religions. Here was a shy man (of quite exceptional ability) at last released from inhibition, talking of things he deeply cared about, in company he seemed to find congenial, completely unaware that we were watched and overheard by a large company of viewers. It was a miracle and (I heard afterwards) the BBC judged the programme a success. But the nightmare that it might have been still haunts me.

When you record the spoken word for broadcasting, you can re-record (with luck) in whole or part. But a live broadcast is something you must live with – and the less you enjoyed it, the longer it will live. One thing, and one thing only, can be done about it: you must contrive to see and hear your own performance. Self-viewing or self-hearing can be very painful, but it has helped me as nothing else has done. And it has led me to take very firm decisions. Avoid ingratiation like the plague. Smile if you must, but don't depreciate the currency. Sit firmly in your chair, beware gesticulation, and relax. Speak with authority and let no-one scare you. Never say 'if I may say so', or 'to be frank', or 'well . . .' Above all, let nothing stop you from enjoying yourself.

CHAPTER 12

Epilogue

So much for some of my experiences. And why do I call them experiences of an optimist? First, because no-one could fail to be an optimist who from the day he was born has had my various experiences of family life. After the great happiness of my own childhood I have lived for nearly fifty years with an incomparable wife who has borne me four talented and loving children. Three of them (Humphrey, Caroline and Ginny) have survived, married with fine judgment and given us grandchildren (one daughter, Pamela, died on the eve of her fifth birthday and one grand-daughter, Nancy, an only child, at half that age).

And I am an optimist because some things have hugely im-proved since I was born. Health, for example. When I was a child and one lung was put out of action by tuberculosis, some people could reasonably call my recovery miraculous, and now they would not. Now it remains to contrive that tuberculosis is no longer the killer that it still is in Africa and other parts of the world. Again, if my pancreas had begun to pack up before insulin was discovered, I should be dead; but since I did not become a diabetic until 1971 I can inject myself daily and still live a normal life. It remains to press on with research and meanwhile secure that the diabetic in the Third World benefits from what we already know. Or take education. I had five years at Eton, four at Oxford and one at Harvard only because I won scholarships. Now *every* boy and girl in Britain can go to a secondary school (at least till they are sixteen) and to a university with a local authority grant – if they wish to go and are thought capable of staying the course. It remains for us to ensure that higher education becomes available to qualified students from overseas (especially the poorer Commonwealth countries) who wish to come here but cannot afford the unsubsidized cost of a place.

Then there is my personal experience of institutions that I have known well at two periods of time – Eton and Oxford, for example. Both seemed to me so good when I first knew them that what I hoped for them was continuity, not change. Each of them of course needed a judicious mixture of both – and they have got it. So Eton and Oxford have both improved, though fortunately not out of recognition, since I first knew them. It is no longer true (as it was for me, alas) that after five years at Eton you can speak no language but your own, make nothing with your own hands, nor play an instrument of music. And Oxford now draws its much larger numbers from all parts of society, expects a much higher standard of work from all its members – and gets it from almost all of them. University College is an even better place of education than when it elected me a fellow – and now, I suspect, better than when I ceased to be Master.

And taking my lifetime as a piece of history, I believe that Britain's greatness has actually increased. We are no longer the super-power that we still were in 1906, but none the worse for that – and all the better since 1956, when the shadow of Suez saved us from at least some illusions. Out of the doubts and horrors of the nineteen twenties and thirties – the General Strike, three million unemployed, our deafness to both Keynes and Churchill, and the 'peace' of Munich – Britain emerged in the nick of time, made up her mind to stop Hitler, and became one nation. The gallantry of the young men and women in the armed services then disproved the pessimists. We became good neighbours to each other. There was less poverty and children were better fed than before. We even subsidized the arts. We reached a new height of excellence in the art of government, both inside Britain and in collaboration across national frontiers with other members of the Commonwealth, the United States and the Soviet Union.

Before the war ended, all Parties reached agreement on at least two crucial points about the post-war policy of Britain. First, whatever government the country might have (Conservative, Socialist, Liberal or Coalition), it would accept responsibility to maintain 'a high and stable level of employment', by a Keynesian policy set out in a detailed White Paper. This made no bones about the part that government must play but it also made plain that the success of the policy would not depend on government alone. Secondly, a new far-reaching Education Act was passed by Parliament. Thus, before the 1945 General Election put Mr Attlee's Government in power, Britain had not only proved her greatness throughout six years of extreme danger but had committed herself in at least two respects to become juster than she had ever been in time of peace.

Wartime *consensus* ended in 1945, and we rightly resumed our democratic right to disagree. But as I look back on the twenty-five

161

years of party warfare between 1945 and the 'seventies, what strikes me as most remarkable is our success in practising the art of peacetime government and securing national *consent* whatever government was in office. There were exceptions: we disagreed, for example, about iron and steel nationalization and comprehensive schools, and about Suez. But for the most part we agreed about continuities and about changes. We agreed, for example, to continue the traditional relationships between transient politician and permanent civil servant and between central and local government. And the changed purposes of government were also generally agreed: not only full employment but the new comprehensive welfare services. Successive governments did not reverse what had been done by previous parliaments but made the best of it – and tried to find answers to new and outstanding problems.

Edmund Burke defined statesmanship as: 'well to know the right time and manner of yielding what it is impossible to keep'. But statesmen can do more than yield to superior power: they can yield what they think *right* to yield. The conversion of Empire into Commonwealth is a good example of what I salute as British statesmanship. When Parliament passed the Statute of Westminster in 1931 we had been following Burke's advice for 150 years and we now left the white men in Canada, Australia, New Zealand and South Africa to run their own countries for themselves. But we could not make up our mind, during the 'twenties and 'thirties, about India or the still dependent Empire. We knew there must be change but what was the right pace and character of change? India had been united under our rule: could that achievement survive a transfer of sovereignty? Could Hindu, Moslem and the Princes learn to live in peace when we had gone? In East and Southern Africa, where white men had made their homes, on what terms could white and non-white share in sovereignty?

Between 1945 and 1980 we have resolved these doubts, with the agreement of all Parties, and a new Commonwealth of over forty sovereign states has been created, each one of which has *chosen* to belong – and South Africa to withdraw. Appalling things have happened in the process and innumerable problems remain unsolved. But no-one can persuade me that the present Commonwealth is a farce – or anything but an achievement of statesmanship unmatched in my lifetime. Except that English is its common language and the British Sovereign its head, Britain is now no more than one member of it. But Britain created it. We reached agreement with each part of it in turn before surrendering sovereignty. We were realists and recognized the limits of the possible, but we also came to believe that where the evidence convinced us that all parts of a community wished to run their own affairs, they must be free to try. Sometimes we reached agreement, as in Rhodesia, only 'at the last gasp of love's latest breath'; sometimes, as in Botswana, soon enough to avoid the arbitrament of force; and in all cases because individual statesmen won each other's confidence.

In 1971 the University of Oxford asked me to preach a sermon before it, and what I said is reprinted at the end of this book, for any reader who may care to know more about my personal faith.★ All that I wish to say here is this. I believe that the world of 1980 (and everyone living in it) is in process of re-creation or relapse into barbarism, as the world (and each living soul) has always been. We are all capable of rebirth and enlightenment, in the sense of knowing what we should do next and doing it; and whether the world improves or becomes more barbarous depends on us: we share in the unending process of re-creation or destructiveness. In some respects Great Britain *has* improved since I was born, both as a nation and as part of the world; and where she has *not* improved there are no grounds for despair. Indeed the gravity of the unsolved problems that confront us in 1980 – unemployment, the darkness of the so-called dialogue between North and South, the nuclear confrontation between Western democracy and Communism, our failure during the 'seventies to agree among ourselves – all this reminds me of the 'twenties and 'thirties. Had we been less slow to become enlightened, Hitler might have been stopped without a war; but even as things were, he *was* stopped. And that was not all. Since the war ended, we have not learned to pay our way but we have proved that great social changes can be made by peaceful means. No adult citizen of either sex is now excluded from 'the governing class' and, though other kinds of class distinction have persisted, they are on the way out. All kinds of art have grown in popularity; the standard of young performers has risen to new heights, and our creative artists have transformed our reputation in the world. Our scientists now win a disproportionate share of Nobel prizes. But we have still to learn how to produce and sell enough wealth (of goods and services) to pay for a juster and more civilized society, and how to live in an interdependent, vulnerable world of nation states. Now, as in 1940, the one thing we must *not* do is despair. We must do what we can.

On a stone tablet outside the church in Staunton Harold, Leicestershire these words are inscribed: 'In the year 1652, when

★ See Appendix I.

throughout England all things sacred were either neglected or profaned, this church was built by Sir Robert Shirley, Bart., whose special praise it was to have done the best things in the worst times and hoped them in the most calamitous.'

The University Sermon

Sunday, 24 October 1971 in St Mary's Church, Oxford

Witnessing to the Light

'There was a man sent from God whose name was John. The same came for a witness, to bear witness of the Light, that all men through him might believe. He was not that Light but was sent to bear witness of that Light. That was the true Light that lighteth every man, that cometh into the world.'

I want us to consider what happens if we try to think of these words as applying to you and me this morning in Oxford rather than to St John the Baptist. For myself, several of my personal convictions are implicit in them.

First, my conviction that there *is* light. Outside and beyond ourselves, at the heart of reality and as an eternal objective part of reality, there is transcendent Light. And some two thousand years ago, once and for all, that Light broke through the darkness that has also been part of reality from the beginning. That Light shone, and has been shining ever since, in our world of time and space; and the darkness has not been able to master it, either to overcome or comprehend it. ('Master' is the word chosen by Ronald Knox to translate the Greek *katelaben*, and it rightly covers the two possible meanings.) It follows for me that there *is* a real objective difference between good and bad, between beauty and ugliness. When cruelty makes you feel sick, that is not, I believe, simply because you personally dislike it. When you feel as you do about Michelangelo's Pietà in St Peter's or his painting of God creating Adam on the roof of the Sistine Chapel, that is not simply because you personally admire those works. Of course your or my subjective judgment may be wrong in any particular case; but there *is* a right judgment that *could* be made, because quite apart from all subjective judgments there is a real difference, in the nature of things, between better and worse, between light and darkness, and therefore between witnessing to the light and witnessing to the darkness.

My second conviction is that the transcendent Light is within our reach: it can shine through *us*, and therefore we can witness to it. We human creatures are capable of catching glimpses of it, here and now 'through a glass darkly' and in the end 'face to face'. We are *not* 'blind men looking in a dark room for a black hat that isn't there'. We are pretty blind. The world is pretty dark. But there *is* something there for us to find, and Light *can* shine through your darkness and through mine, through the irrationality and complexity and evil of the world we live in. You remember the words Shakespeare makes Lorenzo say to Jessica as they lie looking up at the night sky:

> There's not the smallest orb which thou behold'st
> But in his motion like an angel sings . . .
> Such harmony *is* in immortal souls;
> But, whilst this muddy vesture of decay
> Doth grossly close it in, we cannot hear it.

Well, I believe we can. And whether or not we *do* hear it depends on us. I refuse to believe that we have no choice: on the contrary, I believe that the nature and history of the universe is such that man has evolved as a creature possessing (and it is his most important characteristic) the ability, within limits imposed by his inherited genes and by his evolving environment, to choose darkness or to choose light. As the passage I quoted goes on to say about the Light that was incarnate in Jesus: 'He came unto His own, and His own received Him not. But as many as received Him, to them gave He power to become the sons of God – even to them that believe on His name.' So I reject determinism. I reject all forms of *pessimistic* determinism that foresee inevitable doom of one kind or another – the vision, for example, magnificiently expressed by Yeats between the wars:

> Things fall apart; the centre cannot hold;
> Mere anarchy is loosed upon the world,
> The blood-dimmed tide is loosed, and everywhere
> The ceremony of innocence is drowned.

And I reject all forms of *optimistic* determinism, that foresee inevitable progress towards universal harmony. Instead I believe that we have the tremendous responsibility of choice: consciously or unconsciously, in what we think or say or do we are affecting, in however infinitesimal a way, the issue between light and darkness.

But in at least one respect we are like St John the Baptist: we are *not* that Light. Our vision of the Light, and therefore our witness to it, is always distorted by 'the muddy vesture of decay', that is by our muddle-headedness, our self-deception and our blindness.

166

So we can never rightly claim that what *we* see is the Light: we cannot claim divine authority for our personal convictions. But we must none the less stand for those convictions unflinchingly. We must *struggle* for light; we must *refuse* to let the darkness master us; we must feel our way, step by step, without waiting for certainty or even expecting it. For very few of the actual issues confronting us are clearcut. As we struggle to see light in the concrete circumstances of day to day life, more often than not we find conflicting claims, with much to be said on both sides that we must respect; and yet a decision must be reached between them – and we must plump for what on balance we think the right decision. Whether Britain should join the European Common Market is not a bad example of such issues.

My third conviction implicit in the text is that we have a purpose in life, each one of us. We have been *sent*, from God, each one of us, for a unique purpose. And that purpose is to let the light shine through us, in the unique complex of confusing circumstances in which we find ourselves from day to day, in Oxford on this particular Sunday morning – and tomorrow morning and the day after. In our thinking. In our speaking. In our loving. In our praying. In our inner life. In our personal relations with everyone we have to do with. And in our more impersonal relations, with people at a distance, as citizens or members of any other social or political group through which the structure of society can be made more just.

And this purpose is not primarily anything to do with ourselves, our own happiness or self-satisfaction or self-fulfilment. As for St John the Baptist, so for us: our purpose is witness to the Light *so that other people* may see the Light and witness to it. 'For their sakes I sanctify myself.' One of the wisest things that Archbishop William Temple used to say was that the peculiar characteristic of the Christian Church is its concern for people who don't belong to it. When we meet here in the University Church or in our College Chapels, our chief concern must be the people who don't come to our church or chapel. Our appalling responsibility is to let our light 'so shine before men that they may see our good works and glorify our Father in heaven'.

And if we are to understand what witnessing to the Light should mean in practice for you and me as disciples of Christ in Oxford, it is most important that we should recognize the witnessing to the Light that has been given and is being given by those who don't regard themselves as disciples of Christ in any sense. It is a fact of my experience, and has been all my life, that most of my friends and many of the people I most admire are not professing Christians. If we are consciously trying to follow Christ, we are members of a very small minority, whether we think of Oxford, or Britain, or the world. We have to face this fact and come to terms with it. In one sense I find it most encouraging.

For surely every increase in knowledge of the truth – about the universe, about man and about society – must be regarded by a Christian as Light breaking through darkness. The explosion of scientific knowledge that has happened in our lifetime is part of God's revelation of Himself. So is the work of all the great creative artists that have ever lived. It would be *un*christian for Christians to claim a *monopoly* in witnessing to the Light. Maurice Bowra, for example, was a witness to the Light. To quote from a review of his last book, on Periclean Athens: 'His purpose was missionary: to reconvert a modern audience and readership for whom the urbane tradition of classical learning . . . has come to seem deeply alien, if not actually menacing in its humped posture of intellectual introversion . . . He saw his task (his Prefaces always contain the word) as a necessary and indeed heroic one . . . his last book is a final act of witness.'

Thank God, then, that in all branches of the humanities and natural sciences there are innumerable men and women, living or dead, who are witnessing or have witnessed to some aspect of Light. Oxford is full of them. There are the architects and builders of churches, such as this one, and of the buildings that surround us here in the heart of Oxford. There are the sculptors, painters, writers, makers of music. And there are interpreters, such as Kenneth Clark, who are concerned to help our eyes to see. If we seek as Christians to witness to the Light, we must acknowledge and receive as gifts of God what such men have to offer. And this means that a main part of the purpose for which we have been sent to Oxford is, on the one hand, rigorous intellectual discipline and, on the other, the development of every capacity to create or appreciate beauty that we possess. We fail in our Christian witness if we take for granted, or regard as irrelevant, the tremendous opportunities we here all have to sit at the feet of masters in the arts and sciences, the living masters and the dead, and let their inspiration work in us. Whether those masters are or were conscientious atheists, agnostics or Christians, is for us irrelevant: the Light to which they are witnessing is for us some aspect of the Light that is incarnate in Christ. Indeed, I believe that the distinction we so often tend to make between the secular and the concern of Christians, between the pagan and the holy, is fundamentally bogus. Certainly we make a great mistake if we think of our life in

168

Oxford as divided between sacred and profane activities. The *whole* of our life here is potentially a witness either to darkness or to light. We witness to *darkness* when we fail to concentrate on the work in hand – or scribble slogans on great buildings. We witness to *light* when we struggle to think clearly, to submit (in William Cory's words) to censure and refutation, to regard minute points of accuracy, to enter quickly into another person's thoughts, or to indicate assent or dissent in graduated terms.

Yes, but where specifically does Christ come in? Each of us of course must answer for himself. I believe that Christ came into the world with light for every man, over the whole range of human thought and activity. His particular kind of living and of dying, at a particular time and place in history, was, I believe, an 'explosion' of Light such as there has never been before or since. In that light we men have the capacity to *match* the discoveries of artists, scientists and technologists with increasing *wisdom* about the uses that should be made of those discoveries and with redemptive and creative *power* to direct and rule that use. His particular kind of loving, suffering and surviving death, was such that he could justly say 'He that hath seen me hath seen the Father'. And he could, I believe, have said: 'He that has seen me has seen what man and the world are meant to be'. His love, and the holy spirit which he promised would lead his disciples into all truth, can give us power to become the loving sons of God, and have eternal life abiding in us here and now: to live out, that is to say, in flesh and blood, a life that has a depth and breadth and quality which transcend dimensions either of time or space. *This* is where Christ comes in. His spirit only waits for our collaboration, not only to give us *knowledge* of ourselves, but gradually to *transform* us and gradually transform the world. As He, the Son of Man, and the transcendent Father are "one" (He in the Father and the Father in Him), so His holy spirit can be in us and we in Him – His spirit "enabling with perpetual light the dullness of our blinded sight".

Towards the end of a recently published lecture on John Stuart Mill, Isaiah Berlin said this: 'Yet what solutions have we found, with all our new technological and psychological knowledge and great new powers, save the ancient prescription advocated by the creators of humanism – Erasmus and Spinoza, Locke and Montesquieu, Lessing and Diderot – reason, education, self-knowledge, responsibility – above all self-knowledge? What other hope is there for men, or has there ever been?' Well, I would say self-*knowledge*, however difficult and however necessary, is *not enough*. Above all we need self-transformation, self-

169

transcendence if you like; and that the great men mentioned by Berlin don't offer us. Christ does.

'Wherefore,' as St Paul said in his Epistle to the Hebrews, 'seeing we also are compassed about with so great a cloud of witnesses, let us lay aside every weight and the sin which doth so easily beset us, and let us run with patience the race that is set before us, looking unto Jesus the author and finisher of our faith.'

William Temple: A Personal Impression

4 April, 1948 (BBC Home Service)

I wish William Temple could be giving this broadcast about himself. He was wonderfully uninterested in himself – almost as uninterested in himself as he was in what other people thought of him. But he always left me with the feeling that he knew himself quite exceptionally well: self-knowledge was one of the important facts about him. And of course he was one of the best half-dozen broadcasters were have yet had. I wonder if you heard the service broadcast on the evening of D-Day, immediately after the King had spoken? It was only arranged that afternoon. The message arrived asking Temple to take part in it just as he was about to take the chair at a difficult meeting (a thing, by the way, he did better than anyone else I know). So he had the motor-drive to the studio and the time it took to sing a hymn in which to decide what he would say in his address and in the prayers.

The fact was, he was a natural orator. And he never used emotional tricks. That was one reason why he could fill St Mary's Church in my time at Oxford with two thousand undergraduates whenever he liked. We would sit on the stone floor of the church (or stand, if the last stone as well as the last seat was occupied) and wait for those extraordinary logical sentences to roll themselves off the Archbishop's tongue. Eventually the sentence would end, just as you began to think even Temple's breath would give out. And then there would often be general laughter – not of amusement at any joke, but of sheer delight at the clinching of the argument. All the same, what made Temple so effective was not his intellect or his power of speech: it was the sheer goodness of a great man.

In those bewildering years between the wars I think he did more to help my generation than any other of our teachers – by making us feel we were wanted, and giving us hope. And the wireless brought him into living touch with thousands more of young and old, in this country and overseas. Of all the great religious leaders of history, he was the first who had the microphone to make the range of his voice world-wide. But though he cannot give this broadcast himself, what advice would he give *me* (I wonder) if I could consult him about it? He would certainly do his best to help, as he always did when you asked him a personal favour.

I can see him sitting there – ample, friendly, jovial, with his clear, ruddy complexion; genuinely wanting to hear what I had to say before talking himself; with no trace of pomposity (in spite of his gaiters and black smock), or any suggestion that time was short; beaming through his spectacles; alert and tranquil – yes, even when he released one of those sudden rolls of laughter, to go reverberating round the house and garden. 'Do bring out the fact that I had quite extraordinary good fortune,' I think he might have said to me. 'For example, my father: he was a bishop when I was born, and became Archbishop of Canterbury when I was fifteen. Partly because of that and partly in spite of it he and my mother gave us children the perfect home to grow up in. I went to school at Rugby.' ('One of the great schools,' he might have added, 'that are euphemistically called "public".') 'There I was admirably taught, and I made friends with people like R. H. Tawney who went on educating me all my life. Then there was a college Exhibition to take me to Balliol.' (There are two things here, by the way, that Temple would not have mentioned, but I will. He got first class honours in the two most exacting examinations Oxford can subject us to and he was elected President of the Oxford Union by his undergraduate friends.)

'Then Queen's College, Oxford,' he might go on, 'kindly made me a philosophy don – so that I had the chance to start earning my living at once, by doing the two things I most wanted to do: teaching and thinking.' Incidentally, the final verdict of the head of Queen's was that Temple was the most distinguished Fellow the College has had since 1341. 'But you didn't let yourself stay long like that,' we might interrupt: 'you can't pretend that it was luck that made you stop being a layman?'

'Oh but that wouldn't have happened without great good fortune,' I can hear him answer. 'My bishop refused to ordain me: he thought my views about God unsound, as no doubt some of them were. But Archbishop Davidson took the risk and did

172

ordain me. If he hadn't, I should probably have stayed a layman all my life.' If Temple had stayed a layman, what would he have been? A politician? That would be my guess – and Prime Minister? Probably – if he had survived the war.

He was only twenty-nine when Repton School made him their headmaster. But Temple took all the time he needed before making the two most important decisions of his life. He was not ordained till he was twenty-seven. He was thirty-five when he asked Frances Anson to marry him – and she agreed. The rest of his life triumphantly justified both those decisions. At forty (five years after burning his boats and resigning a good safe job for an unsafe one at one-third the income), Temple became Bishop of Manchester; and less than ten years later he was Archbishop of York. At sixty-one he was Archbishop of Canterbury – and not a day too soon: two and a half years later, in 1944, he was dead.

'O Jerusalem, Jerusalem, thou that killest the prophets and stonest them which are sent unto thee,' said Jesus Christ; 'how often would I have gathered thy children together, even as a hen gathereth her chickens under her wings, and ye would not!'

In this country too, we have sometimes killed our prophets. But not always. Temple was a prophet. But it is to the eternal credit of both Church and State in our day that Temple was a prophet honoured even in his own country: a prophet, in fact, who was made to take office very young at each stage of his life. And it is to his eternal credit that not even the highest office ever stopped him prophesying, declaring the truth as he saw it, giving us a lead or challenging our complacency, even when the Government of the day found this embarrassing, or even seditious. Now he was the champion of the unemployed or of the victims of the concentration camps. Now he was trying to break a deadlock between coal owners and miners. Next moment he would be patiently working (and with astonishing success) for the reunion of the Church – not only in Britain but throughout the world (including Germany, of course). Then, in 1943, he was second only to Mr Butler in getting agreement to the pattern of a new Education Act.

And constantly he was summoning us to examine our consciences. It was indeed our duty to love the neighbour next door, but that was not enough. Could we escape responsibility for the neighbour we never saw, whose life was deeply affected by faults in the economic system? Did not that neighbour demand action on our part, as citizens – action to make the system work better, and so make it a bit easier for our fellow citizens to live at their best? Love in our immediate personal relations, justice in our

173

remoter relations with other members of society, at home and abroad – those were the principles he was out for, in what he said, but also in what he did.

He passionately believed that men need not be divided – that they can be 'gathered together' and even behave like members of a family. But he did not believe this by shutting his eyes to facts: the obvious fact, for example, that men are selfish and in practice constantly behave like beasts. It was a gross fallacy, he thought, to suppose that the normal state of the world was 'peace, interrupted by occasional wars'.

'War is what happens,' he said, 'unless something effective is done to prevent it. Peace needs to be made.' And peace is not a mere absence of fighting: it is 'goodwill' (and these are his own words) 'goodwill effectively maintained against every form of greed'. He had no illusions about the difficulty of making this sort of peace. But he really believed that peace could be made, and he was always acting on that belief. This conviction of his was rooted in his personal experience, not in any mere theory or dogma: in his experience that we can forget ourselves – in work, for example (as we found in the war); work so absorbing that we have no time for self-consciousness, or self-pity, or even self-interest. But still more in his personal religious experience of losing one kind of self, and finding his *real* self, in the love of God and of his fellow men. I can say no more about the secret of his power than this. Whenever I met him, he gave me the sense of being a man under authority – a personal authority which he chose to be under – which asked everything of him (his mind, his heart, his will), but would take nothing from him that was not freely given. And, what is more, he treated the people he met as if they were having that experience of forgetting themselves – or at least as if he knew they were capable of it.

He had prodigious talents and of course he had faults too. But the real point of his life was neither his talents nor his faults but his humility, his right judgment of the importance and unimportance of himself. That was what really distinguished him from the other giants of our time. This humility showed very clearly in his dealings with other people. There was one thing which those of us who used to meet him quite invariably found – his courtesy. Of all his visible characteristics, I think that was the most obvious mark of his greatness. But he was ruthlessly tough with himself. Tough with his body – he was racked with gout, and quite often, especially towards the end, he was in terrible pain. He allowed this to make incredibly little difference to his work; but he knew he must give it every possible chance of being cured; so he schooled

174

himself to an austerity of diet that I think came less easily to him than his teetotal habits.

The use of his time was another test of his self-discipline. He did not care much for games or science, but he was naturally drawn to almost all the other human activities that take time – music, walking, poetry, prose, including detective stories ('provided,' he would add, 'the body comes in the first chapter'). And he found it much too hard to say 'no' to anyone who wanted to see him or make him speak in public or sign a letter to *The Times*. But Temple always seemed able to beat the clock. I can hear him interrupt here and insist that he constantly mismanaged his engagement book and left too little time free. That may be so. But what he did secure was time to pray and read his Bible. That was an absolute priority for him, day after day.

When one of his young friends – Ronald Poulton, the rugger player – was killed in the war, Temple said of him: 'I have never known anyone with so perfectly clear a grasp of all that matters most. He will not do on earth the work that we had hoped. So we must do it for him. We shall not do it so well. But we can see the sources of his power and take care never to sin against them.' I feel the same about Temple.

I shall always remember the end of his Mission to Oxford in 1931. He gave us his last address on Sunday night. On the Monday morning early, there was a final service in St Mary's and the church overflowed with the people who had been sitting at his feet through the previous week. When we reached the Epistle, Temple announced and read it. I can hear his voice: 'Be ye doers of the word, and not hearers only, deceiving yourselves.' And he closed the book. He was a doer of the word. He did great deeds – incomparably more than any broadcast talk can cover. But he died too soon to do on earth the work that we had hoped. 'So,' as he said of the dead soldier, 'we must do it for him.' But we shall not do it so well.

1. Oliver Woods (of *The Times*)

Philosopher and wit with a relish for life and truth

When Oliver Woods was around, the atmosphere always seemed to have something of a party about it: he was such marvellous company – a wonderful host (and you cannot think of him as host without thinking also of Joan Woods as hostess); but he was equally good as a guest, making the best of whatever food and drink was going, wringing his hands, twinkling through his spectacles and squirming with delight at anything funny, listening, and responding with quick, invariably unmalicious wit.

All of us here have our own unique memories of him – at Marlborough, or New College, Oxford, or the Garrick, or fighting in the desert, or working for *The Times*, or on visits to Africa or to pretty well any other part of the Commonwealth. But in my experience whenever Oliver turned up, it was always a party; however serious the business, he found something to be amused and amusing about, and his gaiety was infectious and irresistible.

What makes this meeting of his friends unique is our grief – the appalling sense of the loss of his physical presence. There is no denying that. But even so it is not the whole story. 'Lord, I believe; help thou mine unbelief.' I do most firmly believe that Oliver would wish us to do more than feel stricken this morning: he would want us to give thanks, and to renew our faith in the power of redemption through suffering and love.

Oliver had that faith, and he lived it with zest. He went about doing good, and he left the world a perceptibly better place than he found it. He loved life, and he hated suffering, other people's suffering and his own. But he was a brave man, in every moral and physical sense, and a realist, and he knew from experience that to come at the truth, to do creative work and achieve a measure of justice or beauty in this world, you have to struggle and suffer, in body and soul.

He proved this triumphantly in battle. He proved it triumphantly in time of peace – for example, when politicians or administrators who were his friends, and had trusted him with their inner thoughts, made grave mistakes and Oliver's undeviating integrity compelled him to say so in published articles – which inevitably made them angry at the time, though sometimes they were great enough to admit later that Oliver had been right.

His courage and loyalty were never more triumphantly vindicated than when he had to die. Shakespeare might have had Oliver in mind when he wrote:

> Love thyself last: cherish those hearts that hate thee;
> Still in thy right hand carry gentle peace,
> To silence envious tongues. Be just, and fear not.
> Let all the ends thou aimst at be thy country's,
> Thy God's, and truth's. Then if thou fall'st,
> Thou fall'st a blessed martyr.

Oliver Woods had many natural gifts and much good fortune. He had the wide intellectual power that could profit from rigorous training in Greek and Latin, ancient history and philosophy at the hands of distinguished Oxford tutors and contemporaries. Even at the undergraduate stage, when his interest was deeply engaged, for example when writing about the battle of Marathon in the light of a study by someone who had been an infantry officer in the First World War, he could reveal first-class quality to a discerning tutor.

The consequence of this training was that he went on learning all through his life, as only well educated people do, who have acquired 'the habit of attention, the art of expression, the art of entering quickly into another person's thoughts, the habit of regarding minute points of accuracy'. But he also had bowels of compassion: he really cared about people, not only his personal friends but acquaintances of every kind and colour, public figures and whole communities, in this country and in the developing Commonwealth and wherever his travels as a professional journalist took him. So he combined a ruthless search for truth and the facts with a profound concern for principles of justice and deep, unemotional involvement in judgments of value. This combination, of the clear head and the warm heart, was the basis of his success as a highly professional journalist; for in addition he wrote like an angel, and rewrote like an artist. But it was well said of him by an experienced colonial governor that Oliver was more than a journalist or editor; 'he was scholar, historian, geographer, philosopher, clairvoyant all rolled into one, and spiced with that penetrating wit that underlay so much of what he wrote and said';

so that proconsuls were 'more dependent on him for insight, wise comment and brilliant forecasts of what was to come' than he was on them for news of events.

Nor was it only proconsuls that gained from working with him. Car drivers who drove him here or there, secretaries who worked for him, men who served under him, all who had any discernment responded to his 'gentleness' and loved him. And he had a flair for encouraging the young, especially recruits to his profession, spotting capacities the man did not know he had, boosting his morale, giving him a push at the right moment.

During the last year and a half of his life he had his first chance of showing how this extraordinary mixture of talents could be deployed in full-scale literary work, and his success in using the new freedom makes it all the more intolerable that he was taken from us when barely sixty-one and clearly at the height of his powers. What a book we should have had from him, if only he had had more time for recollection in tranquillity, for drawing together the threads of his first-hand experience, and describing that travail with which the new Commonwealth was born during these postwar years!

The great consolation is the happiness which marriage brought him sixteen years ago. There can be no doubt that it was his wife who gave him a new inner strength and certainty and enabled him to radiate a sense of ease and serenity that he had never shown before. What unites all Oliver's friends this morning is gratitude to her, and our common desire to help her and her daughter Sarah in whatever ways we ever can.

Joan is a large part of the reason why when we sum up our thoughts of Oliver we can rightly repeat what Francis Bacon said some four hundred years ago: 'Certainly it is heaven upon earth to have a man's mind to move in charity, rest in providence and turn upon the poles of truth.'

2. Ian Fraser (Lord Fraser of Lonsdale C.H., C.B.E.)

Westminster Abbey, 4 February 1975

Nothing is here for tears; nothing to wail
Or knock the breast; no weakness, no contempt
Dispraise or blame; nothing but well and fair
And what may quiet us in a death so noble.

Milton had been completely blind for twenty years when he wrote those lines, just three centuries ago. They come from a poem, about a blinded soldier, which is the finest testament I know to man's conquest of despair and his capacity for resurrection. They say exactly what I feel about Ian Fraser this morning, and though he might shrug some of them off as going a bit far, he would like the last line – 'what may *quiet* us in a death so noble' – for he always regarded worry and fuss as great enemies, and he would like us to take his death quietly.

He was proud of his Scottish descent, and especially of a turbulent ancestor Simon Fraser, Lord Lovat, who was hung, drawn and quartered for his part in the 1745 Jacobite rebellion; and someone who knew Ian intimately as a boy is probably right in thinking that the Fraser motto 'Je suis prest' (I'm ready) sums up what was one of his great qualities from the start, at Marlborough College and at Sandhurst: his immediate and sometimes fanatic readiness to help anyone in trouble.

In 1916 it was his King and country that needed help. Off he goes, with the King's commission, to lead his men into the Battle of the Somme. And before his nineteenth birthday he knows that he's totally blind for life: the sniper's bullet in the eyes has just failed to kill him but it has finished the career of his first choice – just when the regiment needed help from a fully-trained born leader of men.

Now, at eighteen, he must start to learn something quite new and appallingly difficult: the art of letting *other* people help *him*. He learnt it. And characteristically he went on at once to the next stage: the art of *helping* other people to help him. When we come to a road-crossing and there happens to be a stranger there, waiting like us for a break in the traffic, and he happens to be blind – don't ask, 'Can I lead you across?' Wiser, says Ian, to say, 'Let's cross the road together.'

Then he goes on to talk about the crucial relationship between the handicapped person and his guide: 'I find it best', he says, 'to take hold of his or her arm, rather than have the guide take *my* arm. That means, you see, that you are always a few inches *behind*, and if a step is coming from the pavement down to the street, the guide will take the step a split second before you have to, and you're warned that it's coming.'

Well, there we have the chief secret of his success story – and perhaps the first thing which his friends want to thank God for this morning. He found the perfect guide. He fell in love, at first sound of her (to use his own words), with the girl who wore the smoothest and most beautiful kid gloves that he had ever felt. And she married him. *He* took *her* arm. For all his unquenchable instinct for leadership, he schooled himself to be always just a few inches behind. For all her infinite respect for him, she took each step a split second before he had to. And the consequence was (to quote his words again): they lived happily ever after.

She had been nurse, reader and guide to Sir Arthur Pearson, the Founder-Chairman of St Dunstan's; so it was Sir Arthur from whom Ian Fraser inherited her. It was Sir Arthur too who gave Captain Fraser his first job on leaving hospital – and who died a few years later, to be succeeded by Captain Fraser, aged twenty-four, as Chairman of St Dunstan's. So thank God this morning for Sir Arthur Pearson: for the twin blessings that he brought to Ian (his wife and his first job), and for the half-century of blessings that have followed for the rest of us.

When a brave thoroughbred steeplechaser has a brave rider with highly sensitive hands, there's no stopping them. There was certainly no stopping the Frasers. One fence after another, regardless of the occasional stumble. There was the *personal* fence – Ian Fraser learning to do without sight, and instantly starting the life-long St Dunstan's job of helping others to do without sight (he stayed Chairman till he died). Then, only a year later, the *political* fence – into the London County Council at twenty-five, and into the House of Commons at twenty-seven, with twenty-eight years ahead of him as an MP and sixteen more in the House of Lords; fighting for the ex-servicemen whatever Government was in office; with a leading role in establishing an independent British Broadcasting Corporation, and some splendid election fights in St Pancras. ('Don't you suffer from the delusion, my friend,' he said to one heckler, 'that I can't see right through you.') Then, when he loses an election in 1929 and looks round for another fence to jump, he goes for the Inner Temple and, a year later – over all the law exams and called to the Bar.

But no – instead of practising as a barrister (he would have become a QC and a judge in record time), back to the House of Commons and the BBC. And what next? Over the big business fence now, in Britain and South Africa, with directorships ahead of him and chairmanships galore. None of these posts, mark you, *because* he was blind but because he *beat* blindness, by ruthless self-discipline, by exploiting a marvellous memory, and by endless methodical work.

How did he achieve all this? Chiefly, I think, through the near perfect understanding between the two of them, the husband and the wife: that was the common factor in this astonishing series of successes, in private enterprise and so many kinds of public service. But what were the secrets of Ian's personal contribution to the partnership?

Well, he *laboured*, night and day, with a fierce concentration of courage and ambition. 'There's no discouragement Shall make him once relent His first avowed intent' – and that intent was to *help*. 'No foes shall stay his might, Though he with giants fight' – the giant temptations of self-pity, impatience, ill-temper, sleeplessness. He never stopped casting away these *works of darkness*, treating the giants in the path as fancies that must be made to flee away – and now they have fled.

But he not only cast away the works of darkness: he never stopped putting on the *armour of light*: the armour of compassion, hopefulness, zest for life. Of course he was deadly serious about any *work* he had to do. But he was also gay, un-pompous, light-hearted. He rejoiced in family life (and was pleased as Punch when his grandson got an Oxford doctorate). Wonderful parties they were when the Frasers entertained their friends – no fuss, but every detail meticulously planned. And he loved smoking-room gossip (red, white *and* blue) in both Houses of Parliament, and especially with political opponents. He loved riding across the veld in the sunshine of South Africa. He taught himself fly-fishing in his later years, and loved that. He enjoyed a game of bridge (provided no-one tried signalling under the table). And he loved argument.

How right that the man who spoke of him in Cape Town Cathedral the other day was Colin Eglin, not only Vice-Chairman of St Dunstan's South Africa (of which Ian was the President), but also leader in the South African Parliament of the Progressive Party (whose only parliamentary representative till recently was Helen Suzman and whose multi-racial policy is a long way left of Ian's). How right that Colin Eglin should describe 'this beloved Rooinek' as 'one of the greatest men of the century', and should confess that in the last few days, since being asked to speak at the memorial service, he had been 'chuckling with Ian Fraser' and imagining him laughing at himself and saying, 'Well, that damned Progressive has had the last word after all!' And how right that other recent tribute from South Africa: an Honorary Doctorate from the University of Stellenbosch – the one Afrikaner University now distinguished by a growing liberal spirit.

Five hundred years ago it was said of another great man, Sir Thomas More, what I say of Ian Fraser today: 'As time requireth, a man of marvellous mirth and pastimes, and sometimes of a sad gravity.' The gravity – the deadly seriousness – was there when-

181

ever it was needed, and that was most of the twenty-four hours. Of course it was St Dunstan's and servicemen from all over the Commonwealth that got top priority. For Ian they were of a quite different order of importance from his business or political interests (and perhaps that was why he never became a Cabinet Minister).

He was never content with an achievement. 'Lead, kindly Light'; yes, but 'one step' was not enough for Ian: he *did* ask to see the distant scene. No one knew better than Ian the importance of the next step, but *one* step was never enough for him. His imagination was always peering ahead, and his realism kept him constantly aware that new challenges would come – economic depression, mass unemployment, even another world war – so that money-raising and good husbandry for St Dunstan's and the Royal British Legion must go on ceaselessly.

Yes, his gravity brings us back to the Samson of Milton's imagination: or, still further back, to the Homeric hero (and Homer, you know, is supposed to have been blind too). The dignity of those formidable good looks that wounds only made unforgettable. The gravity of the hero with responsibility for leadership. Brave, yes, and pretty tough, with no reluctance for a fight. But also forethoughtful, using the wiles of Odysseus – to get out of tight corners and round awkward ones – and his ingenuity too, to find new ways of helping the handicapped. Ian's flair for engineering and design drove him (as long ago as 1919) to drive the gramophone companies for fifteen years until 'talking books' became available for the blind (and incidentally the first long-play records for all of us). 'Sonic spectacles' came next, and the 'Optacon', a device that turns ordinary print into a form that can be read by touch.

'I will lift up mine eyes unto the hills.' So indeed we should, if we have eyes to lift. But the achievement of Ian Fraser's life can be summed up like this: *he* lifted up the *loss* of his eyes, in bounden duty and service, day by day for nearly sixty of his seventy-seven years of life. That living sacrifice was accepted and made creative of great good. It has put new heart into tens of thousands of the sightless (and the sighted) who came within its influence, and nothing will stop the good work now. The world will never be quite the same as if Ian Fraser had not lived and learnt the mystery of the road of suffering.

'He that overcometh shall inherit all things.' I dare to say that Ian Fraser's inheritance is 'that house where there is no darkness or dazzling but one equal light.' Thanks be to God.

3. Arthur Lehman Goodhart Hon. K.B.E. (Master of University College, Oxford 1951–1963)

The University Church, Oxford, 7 December 1978

You remember what Winston Churchill said on 20 August 1940 in the House of Commons: 'The British Empire and the United States will have to be somewhat mixed up together in some of their affairs for mutual and general advantage. For my own part, looking out upon the future, I do not view the process with any misgivings.'

Nor did Arthur Lehman Goodhart. Indeed, Arthur's own part in that 'process' – his own extraordinary success in aiding and abetting it through all his length of days – is what I would give pride of place to, in the long roll-call of his achievements, and what Arthur, I think, would be proudest to hear recognized by us this afternoon.

He was born and bred a citizen of the United States, and he died one. In no sense did he become expatriate. For more than sixty years he made England his home, and he died the greatest Anglo-American of his generation. But his speech, his manners and his attitudes at eighty-seven were still those of the 1912 class of un-reconstructed Yale.

His distinguished New York family, Hotchkiss and Yale, certainly gave him the full treatment until he was twenty-one. And nothing pleased him more than to become scholar-in-residence of the New York City Bar Association when he was nearing eighty. He went on sharing his legal knowledge with Harvard, Princeton and countless hearers up and down North America – harvesting in the process an almost record crop of honorary degrees, as well as membership of the American Acedemy of Arts and Sciences.

But meanwhile he had grown daily more intimate with Britain. His father, Philip Goodhart, admired British bankers (for no known reason but most fortunately) and in 1912 he sent Arthur to study economics in Cambridge (England). No doubt Cambridge would have done Arthur proud whatever subject he had studied there, but it was lucky for us all, I dare to say, that law, not banking, was his own choice in 1912. By 1914, and for the rest of his life, he was hooked on law. By 1914 he was also hooked on England. In fact he tried to fight for her, but that he could not do till 1917 – when the United States entered the war.

What was to happen when the war was won? In 1919 Arthur was

twenty-eight, and since 1912 he had been more than somewhat 'mixed-up' in Anglo-American affairs. Would he now stay mixed-up, or would he revert to the American style of his first twenty-one years of life? Wise old Will Spens of Corpus Christi College played his crucial card – and Arthur was back at Cambridge as a law don. Oxford took up the running twelve years later: Arthur succeeded C. K. Allen in the professorship of Jurisprudence and the associated fellowship at University College (Univ. for short).

But in the meanwhile something of still more pith and moment had occurred. Arthur had obstinately courted, won, and married Cecily Carter. For more than fifty years he was to have, as counterpart, the perfect English wife – beautiful, Anglican, and equally beloved each side of the Atlantic – her sensibility to match his common sense. Their sons and grandchildren were to ensure, for at least two more generations, the enrichment of a well mixed-up inheritance: Britain and the United States, Cambridge and Oxford, family life and public service.

Sir Michael Sadler was Master of Univ. when Arthur joined our Senior Common Room in 1931. We were an elderly bunch, small but nicely mixed: G. D. H. Cole and three or four other socialists; Colonel Farquharson, A. B. Poynton and other natural Conservatives; and a Master who filled the Lodgings with modern French masterpieces and the garden with sculptures by Henry Moore. Arthur and Cecily never put a foot wrong but made the best of all of us. Only seven years later, when the Mastership was about to become vacant, they had become so much a part of Univ. that some Fellows asked Arthur whether he was prepared to fill the vacancy. He was astonished – delighted – but clear that Mastership was not for him. By 1951 he was equally clear, thank Heaven, that it was.

By that time he had become a world-class lawyer and one-man symbol of the 'special relationship' between the United States and Britain.

Throughout World War II, seven days a week, he had worked on tirelessly (writing, and by spoken or broadcast word of mouth) to expound Britain to America and the Americans to Britain. Before, as well as after, the United States had declared war, his gospel was 'Aid for Britain – short of nothing'. How right that this United States citizen should, almost uniquely, take silk and become King's Counsel in 1943 and, in 1948, join the small band of Honorary Knights Bachelor of the Most Excellent Order of the British Empire. How right that he should be the first American to become head of an Oxford or a Cambridge college, and in 1952 be made a Fellow of the British Academy.

I like to *think* that Arthur and Cecily were at their happiest during their thirteen years as Univ's Master and Mistress. I *know* the College was never happier than then. As well as dons, the wives of dons were cherished. Not only undergraduates but graduates got a new deal. First-rate Americans (without too much unfairness to the other nationals) knew they would be specially welcome members of the College, and helped to raise intellectual standards notably. New fellowships were created in so many disciplines that by 1963 the governing body was more than twice its pre-war size. The post-war problem of the disappearing landlady was boldly faced. The College campus was ingeniously extended: new buildings went up wherever there was room. Giles Alington's service as fellow and dean was immortalized, through Goodhart generosity, by a new common room, of unique value to both senior and junior members of the College.

The Goodhart quad replaced what previously had been the squalid hindquarters of the College. Helen's Court and, later, Cecily's Court were made, and named for Arthur's sister and wife – with overtones of Cambridge for the discerning ear. And Arthur not only gave: he was the cause of generosity in others, such as his brother-in-law Frank Altschul and the Wolfson Trust. Through these and other forms of *largitatio* Arthur himself becomes, by any reckoning, the greatest College benefactor in seven and a quarter centuries. But what I like most to remember here is the small sum he once asked me to pass on to an undergraduate in rather unusual circumstances.

Only death (following, mercifully soon, a stroke) could stop Arthur working. So-called retirement, of course, could not. Throughout the fifteen years after his Mastership, he went on commuting between Oxford and New York; lecturing up and down both continents; writing his puckish letters to *The Times* – besides more and more learned articles; still entertaining all college freshmen from America; missing no College Servants' Christmas party; always available when the new Master wanted advice (but never profferring it); furthering with generous imagination each development of College policy.

Nor was it only Univ. or Oxford that he loved and cherished, as honorary Fellow of Nuffield here and of three Cambridge colleges. With characteristic ingenuity he also endowed a new visiting law professorship at Cambridge – matching the help already given to the new Law Library at Oxford.

Throughout his life he went on working because he went on *wanting* to work. He never had to scourge himself. He enjoyed work, more than almost anything. This was the secret of his positively rapacious attitude to each hour of the twenty-four. It made time his slave, and explains the long tally of his 'manifold works'. No-one wasted less time on trivialities. No-one of his wealth ever worked harder.

This power of happy concentration flowed, I believe, from his innate simplicity. For all his distinction as an intellect, there was a kind of *sancta simplicitas* about Arthur's character – a singlemindedness, a unity of heart and head. This was what children spotted, and one reason why they loved him. Cecily and he fielded a great Bluebell Party at Whitebarn every year, and this became one of the events of the College year. The families of the whole staff flowed up to Boars Hill and, when it was wet, their entertainment taxed all the Goodhart ingenuity. It never had Arthur beaten. He devised a full 'tour of Whitebarn' – room by room – and this could take quite a time, with Arthur leading one crocodile of children after another round the house.

And I think Arthur's simplicity helps to explain something in a more serious field. It helps to explain his success in understanding *relationships* between things which are in fact different but have important consanguinities: the relationship between common law and jurisprudence, for example, or that between Britain and the United States. In each case Arthur could ignore all superficial contrasts and similarities, and dig down to the heart of the relationship.

'Jerusalem is built as a city that is at unity in itself.' And what the psalmist wrote (in the psalm we sang just now) was true of Arthur. *He* was at unity in himself.

Unlike great sons of America such as Henry James or T. S. Eliot who came to Europe and became Europeans, Arthur remained American, however much he came to know and love England. Here was no double vision. Here was the focussing on Anglo-American relationships of a single-hearted, single-minded *American*. Here too was Cecily, the totally English counterpart. The team too was at unity in itself – and who could resist it?

Two strands were at unity in Arthur: respect for tradition, and reforming zeal. It was their combination within his simplicity that made both effective. Much more important to Univ. than Arthur's munificence was the College's immense good fortune of a Master who let young Fellows have their head. Occasionally of course they struck a vein of Herculean obstinacy – and that was that. But once you had his confidence, it knew no bounds and he would back you, sometimes on matters of great moment, within ten seconds. He was instinctively attracted by new proposals from someone he trusted, and so in the 'fifties he made change possible just when it was needed. But never for the *sake* of change. One

186

small example: Univ. continued throughout Arthur's time one of the few Colleges where antiphonal Latin grace is said by Master and scholar each evening before dinner in Hall.

In much of his service to the state, too, Arthur was a conservationist-reformer. Most clearly in trying to bring English law up to date – and here (through his own writings and almost interminable editorship of the *Law Quarterly Review*) he had some success, simply because he was savagely impatient of anomalies and at the same time ruthlessly pragmatic.

But he was much more than a law reformer – and at his most endearing when an advocate of some untrendy cause. As President for years of the Pedestrian Association, he wrote and spoke like an Old Testament prophet in his denunciation of the motorists (though, at the driving seat himself, he was *not* invulnerable). Long before most of us, he was a passionate conserver of the countryside. And when a Royal Commissioner on the Police (one of his many 'firsts' for an American citizen), for once he ignored current practicalities and wrote a flaming one-man memorandum of dissent, in favour of nationalizing all local police forces.

Arthur was a man who 'laboured night and day', but he was also a man who 'feared not what men say'. He gave light and leading to our times. He took the talents and the riches that parents and race and nation gave him, enriched that whole inheritance, and lavished it on us and those that will succeed him in his pilgrimage.

We give thanks for that long pilgrimage of Arthur's and for the companionship he had for fifty years of it. We remember his teasing wit, the pan face and the timing which made any speech of Arthur's memorable. And, most of all, we bless the memory of his kindliness and friendship.

4. Sir Seretse Khama, G.C.B., K.B.E. (President of Botswana, 1966–1980)

Westminster Abbey, 7 August 1980

Sir Seretse Khama, Knight Grand Cross of the most honourable Order of the Bath (King Henry VII's chapel in this Abbey is the

Chapel of that Order), Knight Commander of the most excellent Order of the British Empire, President of Botswana for the first fourteen years of the Republic's life, was born in 1921. In that year Khama the Third, his grandfather, was still chief of the Bamangwato, the largest of the eight principal tribes of Botswana (which was then the British Protectorate of Bechuanaland), and had ruled the tribe since 1875. Four years later the great Khama died and Seretse's father (who succeeded to the chieftaincy) was dead too. Seretse therefore, with his uncle Tshekedi Khama as regent, became Chief-Designate of the Bamangwato, at the age of four. No-one, I swear, could then have foreseen how great a Khama this infant four-year-old Chief-Designate would prove to be. In fact it was not till 1956, when Seretse was thirty-five, that he came back from exile to live in Bechuanaland – and, even then, as a private citizen who had renounced all claim to the chieftaincy.

What had been happening to the four-year-old Chief-Designate during this interval of thirty-one years? He had been educated, at schools and the university of Fort Hare in South Africa, at Balliol College, Oxford (he played rugby football for Balliol and later became an Honorary Fellow) and at the Inner Temple here in London (where the City University made him, during his State visit in 1978, an Honorary Doctor of Laws, as Princeton University in the United States had already done). Still more important, he and an English girl, Ruth Williams, daughter of a retired army officer and a person of the same heroic metal as himself, had fallen in love (in love of the Shakespearean kind: 'That looks on tempests and is never shaken'). In 1948 they fearlessly married, and for the next thirty-two years it was a marriage of true minds, unshaken by the tempests of controversy that at once broke out in Bechuanaland, South Africa and Britain.

My wife and I first met them in 1959 when I became the British High Commissioner for Bechuanaland, and we have been friends ever since. Here was a man of magnanimity and invincible good humour. With no sign of resentment against the British for their past mistakes (if people spoke of them, his eye would twinkle and a joke would follow), he gave his confidence to Sir Peter Fawcus (who became British Resident Commissioner in 1959), and he worked with tireless energy to help forge the new constitution which was the forerunner of full Independence. His wife not only cared successfully for his health and the happiness of a united family of four children, but from her early days in Botswana devoted great energy and talent to community development and welfare, founding the Botswana Council of Women and becoming President of the Botswana Red Cross and Chief Commissioner of the Girl Guides.

When my wife and I came back as private citizens in 1972, the President and Lady Khama were our generous hosts in State House, Gaberone. It was nine years after my job as High Commissioner had finished, and I saw for myself the elected Botswana Parliament in action. That in itself confirmed my hopes for the future of African democracy; for here was an Opposition party that could question the Government, here was free speech and open disagreement, here was a Government party (founded by Seretse in 1962 and successful in every general election since Independence) dedicated to individual liberty and the rule of law (there are no political prisoners in Botswana), and determined to make the country a united nation out of its many tribes and races.

Here too were exciting signs of social and economic development. While I was High Commissioner, Bechuanaland despite all our efforts remained one of the poorest countries in the world, with great distances and drought and cattle-disease to conquer, and at Independence nearly one half of Botswana's annual budget had to be met by subsidy from Britain. Since then Seretse's wisdom, trustworthiness and determination have been blessed: Botswana's economic growth each year has been one of the best and most consistent in Africa, and marvellous discoveries of copper, nickel and diamonds give promise of a quite new future for the nation. His great hope was that the new-found mineral wealth could be used to improve life in the rural areas, and in particular the cattle industry and agriculture.

But don't let us forget that an Act of the British Parliament in 1909 (which created the Union of South Africa) envisaged the eventual transfer of Bechuanaland from Britain to South Africa, and in 1956 when Seretse returned from banishment the Nationalist Government of South Africa was still pressing for this transfer to take place. And ten years later? Bechuanaland had become the independent nation state of Botswana – a full sovereign member of the Commonwealth and the United Nations – with Sir Seretse Khama her founding father and first President; South Africa had left the Commonwealth and become a Republic; and the storm had broken in Rhodesia/Zimbabwe.

Nothing in Seretse's life gives me more hope for the future than his success in handling Botswana's relations with all her neighbouring states throughout the fourteen years of his Presidency. He kept faith with his own conscience. He hated the cruelty and injustice of *apartheid*; so Botswana could have no truck with racialism or the South African Government's policy of Bantustans. This he made plain at the outset of his Presidency. But he also declared that

Botswana's policy was to maintain friendly relations with all neighbouring states, and here too he has kept his word. He was a realist who set out on no course of action that he did not believe he could carry through. So in the counsels of the Front Line States about Zimbabwe his quiet, persuasive, realistic comments had great influence, backed as they were by the example of Botswana's own government. No-one worked harder for peace in Zimbabwe, despite appalling provocation. No-one could have proved himself a better friend of Britain or of the Commonwealth.

I think the first secret of his success was his consistent calmness. Through all the ups and downs of his career, he stayed the same dignified, relaxed, delightful person, with the same fundamental modesty, the same lack of personal vanity or touchiness, the same sense of humour and the same charm. For instance, when he laid aside a prepared speech and spoke to his people in their own language, there were gales of laughter. In those who worked for him, whether black or white, he inspired the same loyalty and affection. And when he spoke round the conference table he was listened to, because he was clearly a good listener and believed that debate could be creative. He knew from experience that men could be sensible and change their minds (yes, even the British Government). And so he really believed that Parliamentary democracy could work (yes, and negotiation with international investors).

But his second secret was the strength of his convictions. He passionately believed in justice and in the need and possibility of peaceful change.

And thirdly there was his and his wife's courage: physical courage in the face of blood pressure, diabetes and other evil things; and moral courage, from first to last.

His death at fifty-nine is a sickening blow to all of us; but we can rejoice in a great life and the enduring hope it offers Africa. Thanks be to God – for Seretse Khama and the heritage he has bequeathed to future generations of his people.

190

Index

Horsburgh, Dame Florence, 2
Hot Springs Conference (1943), 42–3,
    64; J. R.-M. chairs a commission,
    137–8
Hudson, Robert (Viscount Hudson),
    40
Huijsman, N. B. J., 116
Hunter, T. S. G., 123
Hurley, Jim, 89
Hutton, Sir Maurice, 33
Hutton, Sir Noel, 26
Huxley, Sir Julian, 63, 65, 139, 155

Ibberson, Mary, 59
India, 23–4; and Unesco, 139–40
Irwin, Lord, *see* Halifax, Earl of

Jackson, Professor Pete, 33
James, M. R., 11, 150–1
Jellicoe, Earl, 129
Joad, Cyril, 33
Johannesburg: golden jubilee, 3, 116,
    156; J. R.-M's study of local
    government, 116–19; new form of
    local government, 117–19; and the
    Transvaal Government, 118, 119;
    finances, 119
Johnson-Marshall, Sir Stirrat, 54
Johnston, Sir John, 76 and n.
Jonathan, Chief Leabua, 83, 84
Jones, Aubrey, 69
Joseph, H. W. B., 22, 135

Keir, Sir David Lindsay, 21, 25
Ker, Alan, 18, 100
Keynes, Maynard (Lord Keynes), 61,
    62, 161
Kgosana, Philip, 89
Khama, Sir Seretse, 80–1, 84, 86;
    marriage to Ruth Williams, 80,
    81; return to Bechuanaland from
    exile, 80; first President of
    Botswana, 81, 84; J. R.-M's
    address at his memorial service,
    81n., 153n., 188–90
Knight, Jasper, 34
Knox, Monsignor Ronald, 165
Kremer, Guidon, 109
Kruger, Paul, 117, 118
Kybald Twitchen, 26

Laski, Harold, 24, 48
Laski, Marghanita, 157

Latimer, Robin (Sir Robert), 75
Law Quarterly Review, 187
Law, Richard (Lord Coleraine), 42
Layfield report, 117n.
League of Nations, 28; Committee for
    Intellectual Co-operation, 63
Leathers, Lord, 67, 68
Lehmann, Lotte, 63
Leigh, Roland, 18
Lennox-Boyd, Alan (Viscount Boyd
    of Merton), 38, 39, 76
Lesotho, 84
Leys, Kenneth, 136
Liesching, Sir Percivale, 75, 92
Lindemann, Professor F. A., 30; and
    the Ministry of Food, 35–6
    see also Cherwell, Viscount
Lindsay Sandy (Lord Lindsay of
    Birker), 28–30
Llewellin, Jay, (Lord Llewellin) 44–5;
    Minister of Food, 41–2, 45, 46
Lloyd, Geoffrey (Lord
    Geoffrey-Lloyd), 67
Lloyd, Selwyn (Lord Selwyn-Lloyd),
    88
Lloyd, Ted, 33
Local government, 22, 116–34,
    J. R.-M's book, 23, 24, 116 and
    n., in Johannesburg, 116–19
    in Britain, 120–34; national
    structure, 120–1; five types of
    councils, 121; attempts at reform,
    121–2; 1929 Act, 143; Local
    Government Management
    Committee, 122–4, 143–4; Royal
    Commission under J. R.-M's
    chairmanship, (1966–9), 124–7,
    137, 143, 144; Seebohm
    Committee, 126, 127; Royal
    Commission's recommendations,
    128, 133; reception of the report,
    128–9; Labour White Paper
    (1970), 129–30; Conservative
    White Paper (1971), 130; Local
    Government Act (1972), 118n.,
    131–2; the new authorities, 131–2;
    Callaghan Government's
    proposals, 132 and n.
London School of Economics, 112,
    113; Stevenson Lecture, 156
Longford, Earl of, 4
    see also Pakenham, Frank
Louw, Eric, 93–4

194

196

197

198